Evenings with the Bible

OLD TESTAMENT STUDIES

Volume Two

BY

ISAAC ERRETT

Annotations and Editing by Bradley S. Cobb

Charleston, AR:

COBB PUBLISHING

2017

Published in the United States of America by:
Cobb Publishing
704 E. Main St.
Charleston, AR 72933
www.CobbPublishing.com
CobbPublishing@gmail.com
(479) 747-8372

ISBN-13: 978-1540847560
ISBN-10: 154084756X

Cobb Publishing produces a large line of books: Commentaries, Sermons, Debates, Restoration Movement Biographies, Devotional Books, and much more. Contact us if you are interested in having *your* writings published.

Table of Contents

Editor's Preface

This work has been out of print for several decades, which is quite a shame. The vast amount of biblical knowledge, interpretation, and application found in these pages makes this book valuable to all true Bible students who want to deepen their faith and their moral character.

In preparing these volumes for publication, extreme care has been taken to give you, the reader, the best possible product. We have meticulously read the text, correcting any errors, updating all the verse references (for example, "xxviii. 3" is now 28:3), and adding explanatory footnotes throughout the book for any archaic or rarely-used words. In a very few instances, we have updated the spelling of a word ("especial" is now "special") or replaced an archaic word with a modern synonym ("hied him" to "hurried himself"). In a few instances, we split an extremely long paragraph into two or three smaller ones.

We pray that this book will be beneficial to you as you study deeper the lessons from the people and events revealed in the Old Testament.

Bradley S. Cobb,
Editor

Introductory Note

The first volume of "Evenings with the Bible" having met with unexpected favor from the press and the public, the author has felt emboldened to prepare a second volume, to complete the series of Studies in the Old Testament. The larger part of the Studies that compose this volume were first printed in a monthly magazine entitled "The Disciple of Christ," that they might be subjected to criticism, and that, after the excitement of composition had died out, they might be carefully revised before appearing in more permanent form. Several, however, of the later Studies have never before seen the light.

In preparing this second volume and placing it in the printer's hands, we had a feeling which we hardly knew how to express until we met with the following sentences in the preface to the first volume of Professor Benjamin Silliman's "Elements of Chemistry":

> *"If it does not excuse, it may account for, some inadvertencies, when it is known that an arduous and responsible work was written and printed under the unremitting pressure of absorbing and often conflicting duties. Life is flying fast away, while in the hope of discharging more perfectly our duties to our fellow-men, we wait in vain for continued seasons of leisure and repose, in which we may refresh and brighten our faculties and perfect our knowledge. But after we are once engaged in the full career of duty, such seasons never come. Our powers and our time are placed in incessant requisition; there is no discharge in our warfare; we must fight our battles, not in the circumstances and position we would have chosen, but in those that are forced upon us by imperious necessity."*

We postponed for years the preparation of these volumes, wishing for, and dreaming of, a time of release from absorbing employments, when we should be able to bestow on this work our undivided attention, and give it a finish that might perchance render it somewhat worthy of public acceptance. But we waited in vain. With increasing years came increasing duties, until we saw that if these volumes were ever prepared, it must be amidst the heat and flurry of our daily activities, the absorbing cares and anxieties that inevitably attend the life of an editor. These studies have, therefore, all been written under the pressure of our daily toils, in such hours as we could occasionally snatch from the inexorable demands of our editorial and other duties. While we have bestowed conscientious care on the revision, we could not, without entirely recasting the studies, make them what we would like them to be.

But let not the reader think that we presume to offer this consideration as an excuse for crudeness of thought or unsoundness of teaching. There can be no apology for such defects. While we coveted more leisure with a view to a better literary finish, the substance of what we have written is the result of a life-long study of the Scriptures, and presents our ripest judgment on the scope of Old Testament teaching. If the reader detects any crudeness or unsoundness here, we do not seek to hide from censure behind the plea of a hurried performance of our task — a plea that might justify silence, but could not justify us in thrusting unripe convictions or vague conceptions upon the public.

These volumes have a field of their own. They are not meant to take the place of such works as Stanley's "History of the Jewish Church," or Geikie's "Hours with the Bible." They are meant for a large class of readers to whom a briefer and simpler treatment of Old Testament facts and themes will prove more acceptable, and which, written in popular style, and with a stamp of originality in their method of handling Biblical subjects, will, we venture to hope, prove to the mass of readers less tedious than a detailed history, and more attractive than voluminous dissertations on ancient institutions, manners, customs, etc. We deal largely with the various phases of humanity presented in the Jewish Scriptures, and this affords ever fresh interest, delight, and profit. The great variety of life-pictures of men and women — kings, queens, military chieftains, priests, prophets, masters, servants, nobles, peasants, wives, mothers, fathers, sons, daughters — the good and bad, the rich and poor, the high and low — breaks up all tendency to monotony, and opens the way to teach valuable practical lessons that touch us at every point of public and private life. The Bible becomes a book of living interest, challenging attention and respect.

Beyond, this, we have had an eye to some popular tendencies

to cast aside the Old Testament as a collection of antiquated documents, saturated with ancient superstitions and thaumaturgical curiosities,[1] unworthy of the respect of this enlightened age. If we have not dealt directly with rationalistic interpretations, or given large space to the pretentious efforts of the New School of Criticism to cast doubt on the inspiration of the Old Scriptures and sap the foundation of faith in the supernatural, it is not because we have failed to pay attention to the best they have to offer in support of their theories. But we prefer to reach the popular mind — which knows little beyond mere scraps picked up in newspapers and pamphlets concerning these modern rationalistic teachings — in a more effective way. Our aim is to show, without entering into controversy, that there is a *unity of design* in the various and progressive revelations of these ancient Scriptures — one *great purpose* to be kept ever in view in their study; that, thus viewed, they command rational assent; that, studied in this light, the objections generally urged against them disappear as worthless; and that no other rational conclusion can be reached than that these Scriptures were "given by inspiration of God."

To have made our work complete, especially in showing God's design in electing and preserving the Jews as his own peculiar people, we must have given the history of that nation from Malachi to John the Baptist; but as these are "Studies in the Old Testament," it would have transcended our limits had we gone into that historical field, important as it is. We must therefore refer the reader to Prideaux's Connexion, and kindred works, for information concerning that period of Jewish history.

If life is spared, and we can secure some portion of that leisure for which we have not even yet ceased to hope, we purpose to complete this series in two volumes of New Testament Studies.[2] Meanwhile, we invoke the divine blessing on these studies in the Old Testament, that they may inspire a love of these holy writings in many hearts, and guide them to a better understanding of the

---

[1] Acts of a supposed magician.

[2] Isaac Errett was unable to accomplish his goal before he died. One volume of New Testament studies (*Evenings with the Bible, Volume Three*) was published after his death. It is now available from Cobb Publishing (see contact information on the copyright page).

great purpose of God that stretched over the ages and controlled the affairs of time for four thousand years — the "purpose of the ages" — the redemption of our race through the promised Messiah.

ISAAC ERRETT.
CINCINNATI, December 15, 1886.

Nathan the Prophet

There is one name conspicuous in the reigns of David and Solomon that ought not to pass unnoticed.

David, from his early association with the prophet Samuel, and from his acquaintance with the "school of the prophets" at Naioth, in Ramah (1 Sam. 19:18-20), was led, through all his public life, to pay special attention to prophetic counsel. Even when surrounded with a motley crowd of unfortunate and desperate followers in the wilderness, he had the companionship of the prophet Gad (1 Sam. 22:5), and we know not to what extent he was indebted to this companionship for the wisdom of his conduct under very trying circumstances. Gad was afterward known as "the king's seer" (1 Chron. 29:29; 2 Chron. 29:25; 2 Sam. 24:11), a phrase describing his relation to the throne, and intimating the importance attached by the king to the functions of the prophet. That Gad continued in this office until late in the life of David, is evident from his appearance at the time of the numbering of the people (2 Sam. 24:11-14). In view of the rebuke then administered to the king, it is plain that David did not support the prophet thus near to his throne for the sake of receiving flattery from hypocritical lips, but rather to be pointed in the way of truth and righteousness, even though it involved him in keen rebuke and threatenings of the wrath of God. To Gad was added Nathan at a later date, who, being known not merely as "the king's seer," as were Samuel and Gad, but distinctively as "the prophet" (1 Chron. 29:29), seems to have risen above them in dignity, and to have embodied that larger idea of the prophetic office which is suggested in 1 Sam. 9:9. There is nothing more worthy of study in David's character than this voluntary appointment of bold, faithful prophets as his counselors, and his reverential submission to their fearless and sometimes terrible rebukes.

The priesthood David ever held in strict subjection, as did Solomon after him. The priests had no controlling influence. But the prophets swayed an authority to which even the royal scepter was submissive, and the fortunes of the kingdom were largely controlled by their counsels.

This leads us to say that the dignity and grandeur of the Prophetical office rise far above those of the Priestly in the Old Testament. While it was true that the priests stood in a sacred position, as divinely appointed to draw near to God in behalf of the people, and while they were, in a certain way, the instructors of the people, so that it was said "the priest's lips should keep knowledge," it was also true that, in point of fact, their office was largely that of offering sacrifices, which called for physical strength and perfection rather than for high intellect or sanctified heart. The Levites were not allowed to enter on the service of the sanctuary until they were thirty years old (Num. 4:3, 23, 30, 35, 39, 43, 47), a limit afterward extended to twenty-five (Num. 8:24), and to twenty when the labor was lighter (1 Chron. 23:27), or to continue in it beyond fifty. The reason undoubtedly was that the heavy exactions of physical labor could only be met in the maturity of manhood. Although the priests are not separately mentioned, the presumption is that they were included, as Levites, in this regulation. At any rate we know that full *physical perfection* rather than *moral excellence* was required of them (Lev. 21:17-23), an intimation that their priestly duties called for physical vigor and wholeness as the supreme qualification. But the prophet must be a man of nerve and brain, of heart and conscience, of bravery and moral heroism — ahead of his age and above the people in personal righteousness, keen intellect, and sturdy virtue. It was his to arraign the people, and also their rulers, at the bar of divine justice, and in the majesty of his office, as the messenger of Jehovah, to cause them to tremble at the word of the Lord. He was, therefore, sovereign of sovereigns, proclaiming even to kings life and death, peace and war, the rise and fall of dynasties. One such prophet could make the whole land tremble, and shake the throne with terror. How mean and pusillanimous[1] was Ahab in the presence of the rough, hairy prophet of Gilead! How stricken and dependent was even David under the rebukes of Nathan! Let it also be remembered that the honors of the priesthood were hereditary. Priests shone in the light of the virtues of their ancestors — a borrowed light. But the prophet rose into dignity on the strength of his own personal character, or by virtue of a call from God, based on that personal character. He might have been a herdsman, like Amos, and a dresser of sycamore trees (Amos

---

[1] Timid and cowardly.

7:14); or, like Elijah, might have come forth from the wilderness, hitherto unheard of and unknown; and yet, by virtue of moral heroism and heavenly inspiration, cause kings to bow before him, and the nation to be swayed by his voice. Real manhood is found among the prophets rather than among the priests.

We know not the early history of Nathan. He first appears to view in connection with David at the time the king purposed to build a temple to the Lord (2 Sam. 7:2-3, 17). He must have occupied his station as the king's prophet some time before this, as he appears to view here as one already well-established in his office. Although, if he were exercising his own judgment, his counsel favored the king's purpose, the voice of God bade him overturn the royal intention — which he at once did. To come in direct conflict with a pet design of royalty is always perilous, but the readiness with which the powerful monarch yielded to Nathan's counsel is as remarkable as the frankness and boldness with which the counsel was given. It is refreshing to behold two such manly and pious men — the one holding all fear and all earthly interests in abeyance[1] that he may be true to God, and the other reverentially prostrating the power and majesty of the kingdom before the message from God which Nathan brought.

Nathan next appears to view in that memorable interview with the king concerning his sin against Uriah the Hittite (2 Sam. 12:1-12). There had been a black chapter of crime. The guilty king, in his pride of heart, had sought to silence his thundering conscience and hide his shame. His inward terrors made him gloomy and irritable, and while the demons of remorse and pride were struggling in him, there was extreme peril in approaching him on this question. But Nathan, brave and true, undertook to face him at the command of Jehovah. The skill and courage with which his dangerous task was performed give us a high idea alike of his ability and his faithfulness. The parable of the ewe lamb is skillfully constructed: its design being artfully covered under a pathetic narration of wrong-doing such as would stir any heart, not dead to all humane impulses, to hot indignation. Then the pointing of the finger at the king, who had already pronounced judgment, and the bold utterance of the words, more terrific than a thunder-crash to

---

[1] A state of suspension, or to treat something as though it is of no importance.

the ears of the guilty monarch, *"Thou art the man,"* came like a resistless avalanche upon the heart of the self-condemned monarch, and crushed it under their appalling weight. He was so cunningly captured and so terribly rebuked that he was helpless at the feet of the brave prophet.

That Nathan still held his place with undiminished influence, is in the highest degree creditable to the king. David knew how to appreciate at their real value men of truth and honesty. Their rebukes were as "excellent oil." Nathan evidently continued in high favor at court, for the education of the heir to the throne seems to have been entrusted to him, and he figures largely in securing the throne to Solomon, and in establishing his reign. He wrote two books: a life of David (1 Chron. 19:29), and a life of Solomon (2 Chron. 9:29). The language of this last quotation, "Now, the rest of the acts of Solomon, *first and last,* are they not written in the book of Nathan the prophet, and in the prophecy of Abijah the Shilonite, and in the visions of Iddo, the seer?" can hardly be taken to mean that Nathan recorded Solomon's acts from first to last, but rather that which was begun by him was completed by others; for it is quite improbable that Nathan outlived Solomon. It is much more probable that he died during Solomon's reign — perhaps in the early part of it, as he does not appear to view after his efforts to secure the throne to Solomon and to start his pupil prosperously in his royal career. We read, indeed, of two sons of Nathan (1 Kings 4:4), who occupied responsible positions near the throne, and this much would be freely accorded to the children of Solomon's beloved instructor and friend; but of Nathan himself we discover no further trace. Is it not extremely probable that, as David's reign was vigilantly and faithfully guarded from follies and sins by the dominant influence of Gad and Nathan, so the follies and crimes of Solomon's reign grew up after his noble counselors had passed away, and there was no longer a prophet of the Lord to stand between the throne and the throngs of corrupt men and corrupting influences that besieged it? We think so. Solomon's disregard of prophetic warnings (1 Kings 11:11-13), and his attempt to thwart the prediction of Ahijah (1 Kings 11:29-40), are intimations of the disfavor into which the prophetic office had fallen after Nathan's death. Who can estimate the value to a country or an age of even one man in high place who dares to be true to truth, "unawed by influence, and unbribed by gain"?

It is only glimpses we get of Nathan's life and character and public services, but they are such as to excite a desire to know much more of him. His books have perished, or we might have had an insight into the two remarkable reigns of David and Solomon and the life of Nathan, of rare interest.

It is always interesting and invigorating to study the life of a true man. Even these glimpses of the life and character of Nathan bring us into lively sympathy with his incorrupt integrity and rare manliness, and inspire the heart with courage to stand for truth and right, and with disdain for the base and truckling hypocrisy that so often paves the way to honor and profit in the courts of kings.

Grant, O Lord, that we may be so inspired by this noble example that, under all circumstances and in all presences, we shall be true to truth, and set our faces like a flint against all unrighteousness. Above all other endowments we desire that of true manliness.

Rending of the Kingdom

In view of the promises concerning the permanency and glory of the kingdom of David (2 Sam. 7:10-16), the history of that kingdom is disappointing, unless we look beyond material solidity and prosperity to that which alone is permanent and glorious — the "kingdom of heaven," whose sovereign is the Son of David, and whose spiritual realities were but dimly foreshadowed in the widest dominion and brightest glory of the reigns of David and Solomon. Taking in the three reigns of Saul, David, and Solomon, the kingdom of the twelve tribes lasted but a hundred and twenty years. But taking the period of Saul's reign as transitional, as merely preparing the way for the kingdom of David — then that kingdom, as embracing the twelve tribes, lasted but seventy-three years. David spent a large part of his reign in subduing his enemies, conquering the rightful territory of the kingdom, and preparing an inheritance of wealth and power for his son Solomon, who managed, within forty years, to so misuse and squander it that his successor had to be content to rule over the diminutive territory of Judah and Benjamin — about three thousand six hundred English square miles! It is the ever old and ever new story, which everybody knows, and which nobody believes. David, born in poverty, reared in the school of adversity, trained by hard necessity to self-denial and self-reliance, wins his way from the sheep-cote to the throne, and from a feeble and precarious sovereignty to an enviable dominion among the nations. Solomon, born in wealth, reared in self-indulgence, and succeeding to a dominion which cost him nothing, although, by inheritance and special endowment gifted with wisdom above all his fellows, within two-score years brings his kingdom to the brink of ruin, sinks himself in the depths of folly and wickedness, and, at less than threescore, — when he ought to have been in a glorious prime, happy in the loving homage of his subjects, and in the respect and admiration of other nations, — is a weary, cheerless old man, a sated and disgusted sensualist, a base idolater, with shattered nerves, and clouded spirit, and wrecked faith, sinking into a hopeless grave. And yet, we are never done mourning over the ills of poverty — never done sighing after wealth and luxury! What short-sighted, unreasoning children we are!

The three royal indulgences against which the law gave such emphatic warning were just those to which Solomon abandoned himself without license. "But he [the king] shall not multiply horses to himself, nor cause the people to return to Egypt, to the end that he should multiply horses; ... neither shall he multiply wives to himself, that his heart turn not away; neither shall he multiply to himself silver and gold" (Deut. 17:16-17). Solomon never rested until "he exceeded all the kings of the earth for riches," and "made silver to be in Jerusalem as stones." He "had horses brought out of Egypt," and he had "a thousand and four hundred chariots, and twelve thousand horsemen, whom he bestowed in the cities for chariots, and with the king at Jerusalem." And he "loved many strange women... and he had seven hundred wives and three hundred concubines" (1 Kings 10:14 — 11:4).

Do you ask why one so gifted, and so well-taught in the law of God, should thus set that law at defiance, and trample it under his feet? The answer is: Because he was possessed of irresponsible power, the most perilous of possessions. There is nothing that rises higher in the morally sublime than the spectacle of the tempted Jesus (Matt. 4), plied[1] by Satan with every art to win or drive Him to the performance of acts *which he had full power to perform*, yet holding that power in abeyance for duty's sake. That is the ruggedest and sublimest height of human virtue. How few, alas, ever reach it. Solomon, reputed the wisest of men, failed at this point. We fret and chafe over the limitations imposed on us by poverty, or sickness, or unhappy environment, when, to be entirely free from them would probably be our ruin. In the light of such examples as that of Solomon, we may learn to estimate the wisdom of that prayer, "Bring us not into temptation, but deliver us from evil."

No prosperity is real that is not based on right. Hence, while Solomon's reign seemed to be one of unparalleled prosperity, it was such only in appearance; in reality, it carried within it the seeds of destruction. True, he adorned the land and strengthened his kingdom by magnificent buildings, strong fortresses, aqueducts, highways, and other costly works of art for the public good

---

[1] Worked at.

or for the gratification of his own love of splendor; he also engaged in commercial adventures which brought much wealth into his kingdom, caused an influx of population from neighboring nations, and made the people familiar with luxuries and pomps to which they had hitherto been strangers; and his luxurious and splendid court and extensive harem made Jerusalem famous among the seats of royalty. But all this was at a cost beyond the capacity of the realm to sustain. In addition to the regular income for religious and civil uses, and the great riches flowing into the kingdom from commerce with other countries, and all the gifts that came from other courts, and the tribute from subjugated provinces, it was found necessary to resort to extra taxation, and to enforced labor on the public works, which, though at first required only of subjugated peoples, was at last exacted of the Israelites also. When we read (1 Kings 11:28) that Jeroboam is "in charge over all the labor of the house of Joseph" to exact money and labor from Ephraim and Manasseh for the public works, we may well understand that Ephraim, so long accustomed to rule, and so restive under the transfer of royal authority to Judah, will not patiently endure the infliction of such burdens as are now imposed for the maintenance of the royal dignity of Solomon. It needs only the tact and skill of a Jeroboam to bring to a head the long-suppressed discontent of this powerful tribe, and, through it, of the inferior and more remote tribes.

While the influx of population from heathen kingdoms carried with it an air of national prosperity, it was really subversive of the best interests of the Jewish nation as God's peculiar people. Geikie speaks forcibly on this point:

> *The friendly relations with heathen countries around; their adsorption into the empire; the influence of their populations, to whom the land was now open; the temptation to follow, in religion and morals, communities so much more advanced in arts and culture; and, withal, the natural tendency of national wealth to luxury and its vices, had further excited profound dissatisfaction in the best and most solid portion of the community, and also in the prophets — the representatives of ancient simplicity and obedience to the law of God, as the true King of Israel.*

Things had, indeed, completely changed since the Syrian conquests of David. Instead of a secluded nation of shepherds and farmers, Israel had become the center of a wide and restless commercial activity, which brought its people into contact with all the world. Almost the whole trade of the earth, as it then was, passed through the territories of Solomon. Nothing could reach Tyre from Asia or Arabia, except over Hebrew soil; nothing be exported to either except across it. The entrance to Egypt and the routes from it were through Palestine. Phoenicians, Arabs, Babylonians, Egyptians, caravan drivers and attendants, with a stream of foreign travelers and visitors, must have been continually passing through the country. Strings of camels and dromedaries from Midian and Ephah, Sheba and Seba; vast flocks from Kedar and Nebaioth, for the temple sacrifices; traders to the fairs of Palestine, with yarn and linen from Egypt; cloths and foreign goods, trinkets and jewelry from Tyre, were everyday sights. Every village and hamlet was now familiar with the traveling "merchant," the peddler of those days. But foreign intercourse brought foreign morals. The "strange," or foreign, "woman," followed the "strange man," and spread immorality to such an extent through the land as to occasion the constant warnings of the prophets. It was clear to all thoughtful minds that mere external glory had not fulfilled the ideal of Israel.[1]

While the costly harem of Solomon — scarcely equaled in size and splendor at the most powerful courts of Asia or Africa — was evidently regarded as an evidence of the wealth and greatness of his kingdom, it was in a reality a fruitful source of the calamities that so soon befell it.

"For it came to pass when Solomon was old [think of a man being old, faded, jaded, worn out, and losing his wits at fifty! It is an awful commentary on the murderousness of self-indulgence], *that his wives turned away his heart after other gods...for Solomon went after Ashtoreth, the goddess of the Zidonians, and after Milcom, the abomina-*

---

[1] *Hours with the Bible*, Vol. 3: pp 451-452.

tion of the Ammonites... Then did Solomon build a high place for Chemosh, the abomination of Moab, in the hill that is before Jerusalem; and for Molech, the abomination of the children of Ammon. And likewise did he for all his strange wives, which burnt incense and sacrificed unto their gods. And the Lord was angry with Solomon, because his heart was turned from the Lord God of Israel, which had appeared unto him twice, and had commanded him concerning this thing, that he should not go after other gods: but he kept not that which the Lord commanded. Wherefore the Lord said unto Solomon, Forasmuch as this is done of thee... I will surely rend the kingdom from thee, and will give it to thy servant" (1 Kings 11:1-11).

Whatever other causes were at work (humanly speaking) to bring about this result, the *divine* reason for spoiling Solomon's kingdom of its glory was this hideous prostration of the king at the idolatrous shrines which he had caused to be erected on Mount Olivet — hard by Jerusalem, and in sight of the temple of Jehovah. The idol-worship mentioned in the quotation above embraced in it everything of licentiousness and cruel superstition that it is possible to imagine, and more than can be described. That Solomon the Wise, whose royal career opened with heavenly visions, should be found, before he was sixty, prematurely old and dotish[1] — a jaded sensualist, following like a spaniel at the heels of paramours to the licentious, cruel, and blasphemous rites of heathen shrines, and prostituting the majesty of Israel in traitorous devotion to those foreign idols, is simply one among ten thousand evidences that human nature is not to be trusted away from God. Its only safety is in guarding against the first steps of departure from the law of God. It is safe when walking in the light of God. It is safe under no other circumstances. Every step away from God's commandments is a step towards ruin. "There is no wisdom, nor understanding, nor counsel, against the Lord."

O Lord, teach us to know how frail we are; what treacheries lurk in our hearts; how subtle and corrupting are the influences of unbroken prosperity. Teach us to work out our own salvation with

---

[1] Foolish, weak.

fear and trembling; and do work in us to desire and to work, according to Thy good pleasure.

Rending of the Kingdom (Part Two)

It is worthy of note that the *divine* reason for rending the kingdom of David is very different from the *human* reason by which the ten tribes justified themselves in their revolt. The divine reason was the encouragement given by Solomon to idolatry (1 Ki. 11:9-11). The continued union of the tribes in one kingdom, and their continued prosperity, would simply have been an abandonment of the nation, with all its wealth and power, to idolatry. In union there is strength; but it may be strength for evil. When the whole world was of one speech, and that one speech, together with the memory of their common origin, was likely to be a bond of union to hold the race together in rebellion and idolatry, it became evident that the union would be a great curse; therefore the one language was supplanted by a confusion of tongues, that this oneness in rebellion might be destroyed (Gen. 11:1-9). And so, in the present instance, when the continued union of the twelve tribes must necessarily result in the surrender of the kingdom to the pollutions and iniquities of idol-worship, thus subverting the very purpose for which these tribes were chosen to be Jehovah's peculiar people, division became preferable to union, because the strength arising from union would be strength for evil. This was the reason underlying the *divine* proceeding that caused the rupture in the united and powerful kingdom of Solomon. It is expressly said that "the cause was from the Lord" (1 Ki. 12:15, 24).

But the *human* reason for this rupture was very different. When the tribes made known their grievances to Rehoboam, and asked that they be redressed,[1] there was not even a hint of displeasure or disaffection on account of the prevalent idolatry. To this treasonable departure from the law of God they seem to have had no objection. They complained merely of oppressive exactions of service and money. "Thy father made our yoke grievous; now, therefore, ease thou somewhat the grievous servitude of thy father, and his heavy yoke that he put upon us, and we will serve thee" (2 Chron. 10:4). This was not the whole reason of their discontent, as we shall find in the sequel; but whatever causes of dissatisfaction were

---

[1] Righted, corrected.

at work, they were all so far removed from the cause of divine displeasure that there is not even the most distant allusion to it on the
people's part, from first to last.

We pause to say that we have here an illustration of the entire
freedom of man's action, even when accomplishing God's preor-
dinations. How often we hear it said that if God has foreordained
that certain things shall be done, those who fulfill his purposes
have no responsibility for their actions — they are merely accomplishing God's will. But look at this case. It was Jehovah's purpose
to rend the kingdom. And the people accomplished it. But in accomplishing it they acted with perfect freedom. They had no reference to the will of God in what they did, nor did they pause to inquire whether their conduct was pleasing in His sight. No divine
restraint was put upon their proceedings. They consulted their own
interests; yielded to the play of their own prejudices, passions, and
selfish interests; freely decided on their own course of action. The
only intervention of divine power in the case is the prophetic announcement to Jeroboam that ten of the tribes would be given to
him (1 Ki. 11:29-38); but it does not appear that this was generally
known, nor is it urged as a reason for, or justification of, the revolt
in which these tribes engaged. It seems to us impossible to read the
history of this rebellion without a conviction that it was the free act
of those who engaged in it, and that for it they were willing to be
held responsible. It does not appear that God was in their thoughts
at any stage of the proceeding. If it be asked, 'How could they be
guilty in doing that which God had determined should be done?'
we answer: In determining on the quality of an action, or the merits
of a course of conduct, we must never lose sight of the *motive* that
prompts it. God's motive was to arrest the progress of idolatry, and
make certain the fulfillment of His purpose concerning the Messiah, by preserving Judah for His own service; whereas, if the kingdom was not divided, Judah, with all the rest of the tribes, would
be lost to His service. The motive was righteous and benevolent,
and the deed was wise and good. But, on the part of the people,
there was no such motive. They were impelled by considerations
merely selfish; they sought only their own advantage, and this motive decides the moral quality of their conduct. They were under no
compulsion to act as they did. It was voluntary. Had they seen
proper to remain under the authority of Rehoboam, God could

have adopted other means to effect His purpose. He chose this method because the instruments were ready to His hand, and the end could be reached through them without the least interference with their liberty of action.

This suggests another passage of Scripture which has been a puzzle to many: "For of a truth in this city against thy holy Servant Jesus, whom thou didst anoint, both Herod and Pontius Pilate, with the Gentiles and the people of Israel, were gathered together, to do whatsoever thy hand and thy counsel foreordained to come to pass" (Acts 4:27-28). How, it is asked, could it be a crime to do that which God had foreordained should come to pass? Here, again, we must consider what was done, in the light of the motive that prompted it. On God's part, it was *love* that ordained the death of His Son for the salvation of the world. "God so loved the world, that he gave his only begotten Son," etc. But men so *hated* Jesus, that they put him to death to gratify their own unholy passions. They did not crucify him with a view to accomplish what God's hand and counsel had foreordained, but to accomplish their own unrighteous and malignant purposes. So that, while they did really carry out God's purpose, they did it *unintentionally;* they had no such purpose. It was their own free act, springing from the wickedest of motives. They were not *compelled* to do this deed. On the contrary, every dissuasion that could be urged was brought to bear to turn them from their purpose. They acted in spite of every influence, short of absolute compulsion, that could be brought to bear on their understanding, their sense of justice, and their compassion. While God used their murderous rage for highest and holiest purposes, on *their* part there was not only no sympathy with the divine purposes, and no intention of fulfilling them, but an utter absence of all benevolent, or merciful, or just intention, and a deliberate and persistent determination to gratify their causeless hate.

We have made this the one thought of this essay, because it is of itself a sufficient lesson for one sitting, and deserves to be deeply pondered. We are apt to take credit to ourselves, many times, and to indulge in a self-complacent view of our actions, when there is no just warrant for it. Incidentally or accidentally, or by some providential overruling, beneficent results have flowed from our doings, and we point to these as the blessed consequences of our deeds, when, in fact, a close inspection of our motives should cause us to blush at the falseness of our boast; for, in those motives, such results were never for a moment thought of or purposed! Think of Joseph's brethren pointing to the grand results of his official career in Egypt, and boasting that if they had not sold him into slavery, a nation would have perished of starvation! As if any such *motive* entered into their envious and cruel hearts when they sold him! No, no: they were unnatural and brutal — as clearly and fully so as if Joseph had pined in slavery, and performed only menial tasks, and suffered under hard taskmasters all his life. It does not change the wickedness and cruelty of their conduct, that God overruled it for beneficent ends. It is just as Joseph told his brethren: *they* meant it for evil, but God meant it for good. We can glorify God for the happy outcome of their evil deed; but we must ever abhor their conduct, because its *motive* was base and malignant. There was no salvation for Egypt in their purpose. That God brought good out of it does not in the slightest degree relieve the blackness of their crime.

And thus a preacher may win many souls to Christ, and help many forward in their spiritual life, and shed a wholesome moral and religious influence over a large community, and flatter himself that he is doing a noble work, when, if his motives were laid bare, it might be found that no love of souls, no sympathy with a pure spiritual life, no desire for the moral welfare of the community, has any place there; he is prompted merely by a selfish ambition to shine as an orator, or by a selfish purpose to win a living in the way most pleasing to him. He is a mere slave to his selfish interests. Can any of these souls shine as stars in his crown of rejoicing? The benefactions of a man of wealth bring blessings, it may be, to thousands; and he says, "See! those orphans owe their bread and shelter to me; that orator on whose words of wisdom and eloquence the multitude hang in breathless admiration, was educated at the college that I founded; that artist of world-wide fame pursued his studies in the school of art that I endowed: ought I not to be happy in the consciousness of the good I have done?" And yet, if his heart were laid bare, it is not impossible that the one ruling motive in the bestowal of what was much less than a tithe of his possessions, might be found written in these words: "*To be seen of men.*" The few dollars handed over, rather unceremoniously, to a solicitor, may save a deserving but unfortunate family from starvation; and the giver says, with great self-complacency, "Well, there is one good deed to go to my credit, anyway!" Yet the motive of his heart in giving was the cheapest way to get rid of an annoyance! He had no *intention* to relieve a starving family, but merely to banish a nuisance, in the shape of a persistent beggar, from his office! Will the blessing of him that was ready to perish come upon him? History reveals many beneficent results to nations and ages flowing from long and bloody wars. God overruled them for worthy ends. But those who kindled the bloody strifes, and they who perpetuated them, meant nothing of the kind. Aggrandizement, revenge, lust of power, were the inspiring motives in their hearts. Are they to be counted among the benefactors of our race?

On the other hand, where the motives of the heart are at once enlightened and pure, one is not to be held responsible for the apparent evils that may incidentally or providentially result from his truth-prompted and love-inspired actions. How many times the noblest impulses are smothered by a fear of the consequences of obeying them! Had Jesus yielded to such pressure as this, the world would have never been redeemed. He came, not to send peace, but a sword — to kindle a fire in the earth. That is, such results would necessarily flow from His teachings and actions, although these teachings and actions sprung from the most peaceable and loving of hearts. Must He quench the inspiration of truth and love, for fear of results that enter not into His heart, and that form no part of His cherished purpose? If, incidentally, or through the perversion, by others, of His teaching and His acts, He is brought into conflict with opposing powers and must fight His way through these to the accomplishment of His beneficent purposes, or fail in His mission—must He, on this account allow truth to perish, and abandon the world to endless ruin? Yet, how many noble and holy inspirations are allowed to die in men's hearts, through a fear of giving offense, or of arousing opposition! It is not possible, in a world like this, where error, falsehood, and iniquity so abound, to be true to high and holy motives without incurring dislike, and even hate, from some quarter. Even the honest and the good, through prejudice or misinformation, or from a narrow or shallow view of the interests at stake, may misinterpret one's motives, and misjudge his conduct. But every true man will be true to himself — true to the purest instincts, most enlightened judgment, and holiest inspirations of his own soul. Of infinitely more worth to him is the consciousness of worthy motives, and honest convictions, and perfect integrity of purpose, even if the world and the church both frown on him, than the approbation of his fellows, — the momentary breath of human applause, — which cannot silence the thunders of self-condemnation. Nor will the righteous judge hold him responsible for consequences that did not enter into his motives, and that spring not legitimately, but only incidentally, from an enlightened and conscientious course of conduct.

We cannot be too careful as to the motives that underlie our actions. Not what we may seem to others to be, but what we *are*, must decide our standing before God, and our destiny. No accidental or providential results of one's actions, however beneficent, can give to him the stamp of a righteous character, when in his heart there was no righteous purpose. No results of one's actions that others may deem unfortunate or mischievous, can stamp his character with unrighteousness, or shut him out from the favor of God, when his course of life has been inspired and guided by a spirit of courage, of love, and of a sound mind.

O Thou, who searchest the hearts and triest the reins of the children of men, search me, and know my heart; try me, and know my thoughts; and see if there be any wicked way in me; and lead me in the way everlasting.

Rending of the Kingdom (Part Three)

The tribe of Ephraim was powerful and ambitious. Descended from Joseph, of illustrious memory; receiving the special blessing of the dying Jacob (Gen. 48:13-20); proud in the mighty exploits of Joshua, who, next to Moses, was revered as the leader of Israel — holding within its borders Shechem, with Ebal and Gerizim, and Shiloh, so long the home of the tabernacle, and the center of ecclesiastical power; and possessing the fairest and most secure portion of the land in Central Palestine, free from the incursions to which other tribes were exposed, and crossed by highways from all parts of the land, giving easy access to the other tribes to the sacred spots to which they were all attached, thus affording to Ephraim free and constant intercourse with all Israel — it is not surprising that this tribe held a leading influence in the control of national affairs, and looked with jealousy upon the rising power of any other tribe. See judges 8:1; 12:1. The first king belonged, indeed, to the tribe of Benjamin; but Benjamin had become so closely related to Ephraim by marriage (Judges 21:16-23) that next to the choice of a king from their own tribe, a selection from the tribe of Benjamin was pleasing to them, and favorable to their supremacy. After Saul's death, they readily accepted his son Ishbosheth as their sovereign (2 Sam. 1:8-9). But when David ascended the throne, and the glories of Shechem and Shiloh paled before the rising glory of Jerusalem as the center of both political and ecclesiastical power, the supremacy of Ephraim passed over to Judah. Of this, David speaks (1 Chron. 28:4; Ps. 78:67-68) in terms which must have been somewhat galling to the pride of the Ephraimites. But the magnificent triumphs of David's reign and the glamour of wealth and prosperity thrown over the reign of Solomon prevented any public exhibition of discontent. That there was, all the while, an under-current of hostility to Judah, and especially during the reign of Solomon, when taxes and draughts on the service of the people became very oppressive, is presumable from the complaints made immediately after Solomon's death, and from the rebellion that followed on the refusal to listen to these complaints.

The selection of Jeroboam, of the tribe of Ephraim, to lead the rebellion, is significant. He was a man of courage and enterprise.

Because of his tact and skill and courage, Solomon appointed him over his own tribe to superintend the exaction of labor from the Ephraimites; he "made him ruler over all the charge of the house of Joseph." That he managed to please Solomon without losing the esteem of his tribe in the performance of so unpleasant a task, indicates great tact and ability (comp. 1 Ki. 9:15 with 11:26-28). That Jeroboam had any other thought than that of loyalty to Solomon, we have no reason to assert. But when the prophet Ahijah announced to him the purpose of Jehovah to rend the kingdom, and to make him king of the ten tribes (1 Ki. 11:29-39), it kindled new ambitions in his soul, and he must have seen at a glance how readily he could wake the slumbering discontent of Ephraim and rekindle the ambition of that powerful tribe to assert its former supremacy, and rally the other tribes in opposition to Judah. Solomon himself saw all this, and the only remedy against the approaching catastrophe to his kingdom was to kill Jeroboam (1 Ki. 11:40); but his purpose was defeated by Jeroboam's flight into Egypt.

The secession of the ten tribes was managed by a master hand. There was no rash outbreak. The people were held in quietness until the time came for Rehoboam to meet them at Shechem, that they might confirm him in his kingdom. Then they came forward with Jeroboam at their head, not to threaten a rebellion, but to offer a respectful and reasonable petition, and to assure the king of their loyal submission, if their petition was granted. They asked only relief from "the grievous service" which Solomon exacted. They did not even ask entire release from that service, but that it should be made lighter. The king took three days to consider. He consulted the aged men who were familiar with the affairs of the kingdom, and understood the people. They earnestly advised a favorable answer to the petition. Then he sought the counsel of the hot-headed youths who had been brought up with him; and they advised a scornful rejection of the people's prayer. He evidently sought this counsel because he was displeased with the advice of the old men. Proud, impetuous, overbearing, unused to restraint, and inflated with the conceit that is born of ignorance, he listened to the advice that gratified his own bad passions and harmonized with his own haughty ambition to rule with undisputed sway. "All's brave that youth mounts and folly guides." He therefore "answered the people roughly; and forsook the old men's counsel that they gave him, and spake to them after the counsel of the young men, saying, My father made your yoke heavy, and I will add to your yoke; my father chastised you with whips, but I will chastise you with scorpions" (1 Ki. 12:1-14). It is scarcely possible to imagine a greater folly than this. It amounts to infatuation; but it is an infatuation which readily springs from the pride of arbitrary power and intense selfishness, blended with the conceit and rashness and untamed passions of inexperienced youth. "Pride goeth before destruction, and a haughty spirit before a fall." The response of the scorned multitude was: "What portion have we in David? Neither have we inheritance in the son of Jesse: to your tents, O Israel; now see to thine own house, David." And ten of the tribes turned to Jeroboam, and made him their king. Thus, a few rash, scornful words from a hot-headed, presumptuous youth drove a large portion of the kingdom into rebellion. Kind words might have averted the calamity, and preserved the glory of Solomon's reign, at least for a time.

There is a great lesson here for the young, especially in this country, where youthful energy is so self-asserting. "Young men for war," but "old men for counsel." The strength of youth is a great treasure, but it needs to be wisely directed. It ought not to require profound reasoning to satisfy us that knowledge gathered in the school of experience has solid value, and that the wisdom of age is indispensable as an endowment to the inexperience of youth. To despise the counsels of age is at once a folly and an iniquity. It is to close our eyes to the lessons of experience, and to make the young life a blind and reckless venture, such as can only be prompted by a preposterous self-sufficiency, as odious as it is baseless. Lives thus scornful of the lessons of age and experience are sure to prove either ridiculous or infamous. In the Family, the Church, the State, the conservative power is found in the wisdom of the aged; and when reverence for age is lost, danger is at hand, and destruction is not far off. When children cease to revere the counsels of their parents; when the younger portion of church members grow impatient of the rule and rebel against the counsels of the seniors; when "Young America" rushes headlong into political measures, regardless of the lessons of the past, and the warnings of men of larger experience, broader horizon, and life-long patriotism; it requires not a prophet to declare the approach of mischief and calamity. Let youth reverence age and gladly appropriate its treasures of wisdom, and the Home, the Church and the State will prosper.

There is some question as to the extent of the disaster to Solomon's kingdom. We read (1 Ki. 12:20) that "there was none that followed the house of David but the tribe of Judah only." Yet the next verse mentions the tribe of Benjamin along with the tribe of Judah. It is true that, formerly, the tribe of Benjamin had close affinity with Ephraim. The long strife between the house of Saul and the house of David, and the murder of Abner by Joab, and the passing over of royalty from Benjamin to Judah, were all calculated to estrange the former more and more from the latter. Even as late in David's reign as the death of Absalom, the revolt of Sheba, a Benjamite (1 Sam. 20:1-2), indicates the continued hostility of Benjamin to Judah. But time had wrought a great change. Jerusalem was on the border line of the two tribes, and occupied, in part, the territory of Benjamin. Many of the Benjamites became inhabitants of the holy city, and most of the tribe, having easy access to the city and temple, came to be one with Judah in interest and sentiment. Then, the tribe of Levi remained loyal to Rehoboam. And many from other tribes refused to be separated from the altar and temple of Jehovah. See 2 Chron. 11:12-17; 15:9; 30:11-18. Oehler, in his "Old Testament Theology," has investigated this question minutely, and the following extract, from page 485, will be of interest to Bible students:

> *The question, how the ten tribes which composed the northern kingdom are to be reckoned, is so difficult to answer, that many, with Keil, have endeavored to regard the number ten as merely symbolical; which view the expression "we have taken ten parts in the king" (2 Sam. 19:43), may perhaps be considered to corroborate. The tribe of Levi not being reckoned in the political division of the nation, and Benjamin belonging, according to 1 Ki. 12:21; I Chron. 11:3; 10:23; 14:7, to the kingdom of Judah, it would seem that the number ten must refer to the remaining tribes, Manasseh and Ephraim making two. But the tribe of Simeon cannot possibly be set down to the northern kingdom, although 1 Chron. 15:9 assumes that Sime-*

onites belonged to it. The lot of this tribe lay, according to Josh. 19:1-9, within the realm of Judah, in the southwest, toward Philistia and Idumaea. It seems not to have formed a compact province, but to have consisted of several single towns and districts. The Simeonite town Beer-sheba is, in 1 Ki. 19:3, expressly said to have belonged to Judah. On the other band, Bethel, Gilgal, and Jericho, chief places in the tribe of Benjamin, appear as towns of the northern kingdom; and the Benjamite town of Ramah, only nine miles north of Jerusalem, belonged, at least under Baasha, to the same, according to 15:17, 21. The tribe of Benjamin, too, in virtue of ancient kinship, had always adhered to the house of Joseph, and during the march through the wilderness bad been combined into a triad with Ephraim and Manasseh (Num. 2:17 seq.; 10:21-24). . . .The actual state of things was that the tribe of Benjamin was divided between the two kingdoms. The greater part of the country belonged to the northern kingdom, while the certainly more populous part, in which the northern part of Jerusalem and its neighborhood were situated, was united to the kingdom of Judah. Thus it was true both that the house of David, strictly speaking, possessed but one (entire) tribe, as it is expressed 1 Ki. 11:13, 32-36, and that numerous members of the tribe of Benjamin belonged to Judah. That portion, too, of the tribe of Dan which dwelt in their original lot (Josh. 19:40 seq.) between Benjamin. Judah, and Ephraim, belonged to Judah. A few Danite cities are mentioned (2 Chron. 11:10; 28:18) as pertaining to the kingdom of Judah; but since this tribe dwelt partly in the north, it may nevertheless be reckoned among the ten. Thus Rehoboam's army may correctly be spoken of (1 Ki. 12:23) as "all the house of Judah, and Benjamin, and the rest of the people." Among the children of Israel who dwelt in the cities of Judah, mentioned [in] ver. 17 as Rehoboam's subjects, were probably included members of other tribes also. And when to these are added the numerous emigrations from the northern kingdom into that of Judah in succeeding centuries (comp. 1 Chron. 15:9), it may be said that among the Jews, which name now arose in the southern kingdom, all Israel was represented.

If we have lingered long over what appears to be a not very attractive subject — the rending of the kingdom of Israel — it has been for the sake of valuable practical lessons. Having pointed out these lessons as we proceeded with our investigation, we do not need to repeat them now. It is sufficient to say, in conclusion, that the security of society and the permanent prosperity of nations are not to be found in mere worldly wisdom, nor in riches, nor in pomp and show. "The fear of the Lord is the beginning of wisdom," and where this is not, there is sure to be failure and disaster. "Thus saith the Lord: Let not the wise glory in his wisdom, neither let the mighty glory in his might, neither let the rich glory in his riches. But let him that glorieth glory in this, that he understandeth and knoweth me, that I am the Lord, who exercise loving kindness, judgment, and righteousness in the earth: for in these things I delight, saith the Lord" (Jer. 9:23-24).

Jeroboam

(Read 1 Ki. 11:26-40; chapters 12-14)

We have already spoken of the circumstances under which Jeroboam came into public notice, and of the rivalry — suppressed but not extinguished by David and Solomon — between Ephraim and Judah, which, after the death of Solomon, again asserted itself and led to the revolt of the ten tribes from Rehoboam, Solomon's son.

The Septuagint version differs materially from the original Hebrew in the history of Jeroboam; but, as critical investigation is not our object; as the lessons which we aim to teach are not affected by these differences; and as the account given in the Hebrew is that which is in possession of our readers in the English version commonly used, we shall not vary from this version, nor pause to consider the merits of the narrative in the Septuagint.

That Jeroboam was a man of decided ability and energy, and possessed many of the qualities of a successful ruler of men, is apparent from 1 Ki. 11:28, in which he is described as a "a mighty man of valor," or a man of strength and activity; as "industrious;" and as elevated by Solomon to a place not only of great trust, but calling for particular tact and skill — superintendent of all the forced labor exacted from the house of Joseph in building Millo and fortifying Jerusalem. Having fled to Egypt from the wrath of Solomon, he returned after Solomon's death, and was unanimously chosen by the ten tribes as their king. The way had been prepared for this by (1) Jeroboam's attempt at rebellion against Solomon, for we read that he "lifted up his hand against the king" (1 Ki. 11:26) — an act that commended him especially to the powerful tribe of Ephraim; (2) by the prophecy of Ahijah (1 Ki. 11:30-39), a prediction that could not be kept entirely secret; and (3) by the part which Jeroboam acted as leader of the discontented tribes in demanding of Rehoboam a lightening of the burdens of labor and taxation (1 Ki. 12:2). This last transaction exhibits admirable tact and skillful policy on the part of Jeroboam. He appears not as the rival or enemy of Rehoboam, but as the representative of an oppressed people. The fact that he had been a representative of royalty in practicing the oppressions of which the people complained, and was therefore familiar with the wrongs inflicted on them, gives peculiar emphasis to the request made through him as their mouthpiece. Moreover, he does not even hint at rebellion. On the contrary, after making a respectful and reasonable presentation of the people's wishes, he pledges them to serve Rehoboam if their righteous request is granted (1 Ki. 12:4). He thus cunningly forced on Rehoboam the responsibility of winning the people to his throne or of driving them to despair; and, while cunningly plotting the division of the kingdom, placed himself in the attitude of a defender of the rights of the people, and as driven by the cruel tyranny of Rehoboam to assume sovereignty over the ten tribes, to protect them from an unscrupulous and heartless oppressor. This was a masterstroke of policy.

There seems to have been no religious element in Jeroboam's character. He is a bold schemer, possessed of remarkable political sagacity, and boundless energy to carry out his schemes, with supreme confidence in his own power to rule, and a selfish ambition to magnify his own name. The prophet Ahijah had pointed out to him the way to success in his reign, in a message from Jehovah: "And it shalt be, if thou wilt hearken to all that I command thee, and wilt walk in my ways, and do what is right in my sight, to keep my statutes and my commandments, as David my servant did, that I will be with thee, and build thee a sure house, as I built for David, and will give Israel unto thee." This was a very plain road to permanent success. It left no room for doubt. The fulfillment of the first part of Ahijah's prediction, in Jeroboam's elevation to royal authority over the ten tribes, should have been to him a perfect assurance of the fulfillment of that which related to the future of his kingdom, on the condition mentioned. But Jeroboam is not alone in forgetting the Hand that blessed him. It is alike surprising and humiliating to learn, in our own experiences, the baseness and ingratitude of the human heart in forgetting God, and the insane self-reliance which so readily and recklessly substitutes human policy for divine counsel. "And Jeroboam said in his heart, Now shall the kingdom return to the house of David: if this people go up to do sacrifice in the house of Jehovah at Jerusalem, then shall the heart of this people turn again unto their lord, even unto Rehoboam, king of Judah, and they shall kill me, and go again to Rehoboam, king of Judah" (1 Ki. 12:27). Reasoning from a merely human standpoint, he was right. The rallying of all the tribes to Jerusalem as their *religious* center would powerfully tend to their reunification politically. So deep-seated is the power of religious faith — especially a faith sustained by such a wealth and glory of national tradition as that which had its center at Jerusalem — that political pressure is generally feeble against it; and even when political unity is destroyed by extraordinary pressure, the rupture is apt to prove but temporary if religious unity is not broken. To make political alienation complete and permanent, there must be religious alienation also. *Faith,* however, would have suggested to Jeroboam that as he had but fulfilled the will of Jehovah in accepting sovereignty over the ten tribes; and as the prophet had assured him that the ten tribes should be permanently his if he would but walk in God's counsel; his safety was to walk in this counsel, leaving it to Him who had given the kingdom to preserve it unto him in His own way. But Jeroboam was not a man of faith; he was a man of self-will and of policy. The divine presence was entirely overshadowed by his own importance. He "took counsel," indeed, but not of Jehovah. He sought such counsel as pleased him — just as *we* are apt to do, when we are stubbornly bent on a predetermined course: we profess to seek the advice of others, but are careful to seek it where we are pretty sure it will coincide with our own previous determinations! Without waiting to learn the *divine* way out of his difficulty, he proceeded to establish two places of worship, one at Beth-el and one at Dan, placing in each a golden calf, probably a golden figure of Mnevis, the sacred calf of Heliopolis, whose worship he had witnessed in Egypt. The tribe of Levi remaining loyal to the throne of David (2 Chron. 11:13-14), Jeroboam made priests of any that would serve in that capacity from any of the tribes (1 Ki. 12:31-32; 13:33), they being consecrated to the office by the sacrifice of a young bullock and seven rams (2 Chron. 13:9). He ordained also a national feast on the fifteenth day of the eighth month, — a time which the historian significantly says "he had devised of his own heart." Then he said to the people, "It is too much for you to go up to Jerusalem: behold thy gods, O Israel, which brought thee up out of the land of Egypt!" He showed sagacity in the selection of these centers of worship. Beth-el — the house of God — was already hallowed by many sacred associations, from the time that God there appeared to Jacob (Gen. 28:11-19, 35:9-

15), on to the repose of the ark there under the guardianship of Phinehas (Judg. 20:26, 28), and to the solemn assemblies held there by Samuel (1 Sam. 7:16). Even Dan was not without sacred associations (see Judg. 18:30-31), though they were of a more doubtful character; and its situation in northern Palestine made it a convenient place of gathering for some of the tribes, and a bulwark against the invasions of heathen religions.

There is this much to be said in apology for Jeroboam: He was not as bad as Solomon had been in the introduction of idol-worship (1 Ki. 11:1-8), nor as Rehoboam proved to be (1 Ki. 14:22-24). There was nothing shocking to the public conscience in the setting up of molten images. It does not appear to have been with a design to promote idolatry that the king of Israel established these shrines of worship, but simply to keep his subjects away from Jerusalem — where, indeed, if on one hand they might have found a purer national worship, they would, on the other hand, have been exposed to more alluring and corrupting forms of idol-worship.

Yet his was a daring and inexcusable sin. If any excuse could be found for him in ignorance, or in the plea of a necessary policy, even that was taken away when the prophet of Jehovah met him at the altar at Beth-el and rebuked his wickedness (1 Ki. 13:1-6). Maddened at the message brought to him, he stretched forth his hand against the messenger; but his hand was withered, and only at the intercession of the prophet was it restored. But "Jeroboam returned not from his evil way." Another warning was added. Jeroboam had a son whom he called Abijah — meaning "Jehovah is my desire." Such a name would hardly have been given, if it had been the purpose of the king to disown Jehovah. He evidently did not regard his own inventions as a denial of Jehovah, but rather as adapting His worship to the necessities of the times. Abijah was a child of much promise, religious (1 Ki. 14:13), and perhaps heir to the throne. In his deep anxiety for the child, the king sent the queen in disguise, with a present indicating poverty in the visitor, to the prophet Ahijah, at Shiloh. The prophet, divinely warned of her approach, told her who she was, predicted the child's death, and announced the terrible woes to come on the home of Jeroboam for his great wickedness (1 Ki. 14:1-18). Even this produced no reformation. In the rare and forcible language of the prophet, he had "cast God behind his back," and continued in his perversions to the end. He had no settled peace during his reign. He and Rehoboam were engaged in almost constant predatory warfare. Abijah, successor to Rehoboam, came against him with a powerful army, made a great slaughter, and captured the cities of Beth-el, Jeshanah and Ephrain, so disabling him that he never recovered from the disastrous blow (2 Chron. 13:20). His reign lasted but twenty-two troubled years, and the sad testimony of the close is, "The Lord struck him and he died" (2 Chron. 13:20). He was succeeded by his son Nadab, who reigned only two years, when Baasha killed him. This regicide also "smote all the house of Jeroboam; he left not to Jeroboam any that breathed, until he had destroyed him, according unto the saying of the Lord, which he spake by his servant Ahijah the Shilonite: because of the sins of Jeroboam which he sinned, and which he made Israel sin, by his provocation wherewith he provoked the Lord God of Israel to anger" (1 Ki. 15:25-30). Thus, for less than a quarter of a century of uncertain power and false glory to him and his house, and these mingled with much trouble, anxiety, domestic grief, and public disaster, Jeroboam had bartered his honor and dishonored his God. How contemptible, in the distance, as we look back to them, appear these shadowy pomps of royalty, these "triumphs of an hour." Yet perhaps, while we are condemning Jeroboam, and lamenting over his folly and wickedness, we are feverishly struggling for the possession of toys more trifling, and casting the Lord behind our back, that we may be free to walk in our own ways!

Two lessons are suggested by this narrative, which we shall do well to heed.

1. Seldom, if ever, can a more plausible apology be found for departure from the counsel of God, than in the case of Jeroboam. The difficulty which he was compelled to face was formidable. His reasoning on it, regarding it merely as a problem for human solution, was plausible and forcible. As a question of policy, politicians would say his treatment of it was judicious and statesmanlike. But the *moral* element was eliminated from the problem. He "cast God behind his back," and reasoned from a purely human stand-point, treating that as a question of mere *policy*, which ought to have been to him a question of *righteousness* and of *piety*. The disastrous result admonishes us that "there is no wisdom, nor counsel, nor understanding, against Jehovah." Unless legislators and sover-

eigns learn this lesson, they will be sure to fail. Unless, in every individual life, it is learned, destruction is sure. It is alike alarming and disgusting to see how, in our own land, in State and National politics, the gravest and most pressing questions of humanity and righteousness are coolly ignored, or shamefully trifled with, from pitiful considerations of policy; and that, too, in the face of all the warnings sounded in the inevitable disasters that have always followed a time-serving policy. Nor is it less disgusting to witness the extent to which individual lives are shaped and controlled by the wretched sophistries of a utilitarian morality, while the eternal and immutable verities of truth and justice are treated as if they were but shadows. Shall we ever learn that truth is truth, and right is right, and God is God, for ever and ever?

2. It should give us pause when we are in danger of a false step, to reflect that such a step may bear injury with it to others as well as to ourselves. This is especially true concerning those who are in public life, but it is true also of every life, however obscure. "None of us liveth to himself." We cannot if we would. It is not in our power to isolate ourselves from our fellows to such an extent as to cut them off from our influence; for the isolation itself sways a power over them for evil or for good. It is said of Jeroboam not only that he sinned, but that "he made Israel sin" (1 Ki. 14:16). Not only did he lead those of his own generation to sin, but his evil deeds lived on into future generations. Nadab, his son, "walked in the way of his father, and in his sin wherewith he made Israel to sin." Baasha, although he overthrew the house of Jeroboam, "walked in the way of Jeroboam, and in his sin wherewith he made Israel to sin." So of Zimri (1 Ki. 16:19); Omri (verse 26); Ahab, who improved on his model (verse 31); Jehoram (2 Ki. 3:3); Jehu (2 Ki. 10:31); Joash (2 Ki. 13:2); Jehoahaz (verse 11); Jeroboam II (2 Ki. 14:24); Zachariah (2 Ki. 15:9); Menahem (verse 18); and so on from generation to generation. What a fearful immortality of wickedness is this! How it must augment, in the judgment-day, the terrors of evil doers, to see the far-reaching results of their ungodly deeds unrolled before them! What were the short-lived honors and pleasures of Jeroboam, as an offset to the ever-living and ever-accumulating wrongs and miseries springing from his never-dying sin? To be the author of a wrong that haunts the ages with a perpetual power to curse and blight, is dreadful beyond expression. Be

careful, then, dear reader, how you put forth your hand to sin; for one sin may crush not only your own soul, but the souls of many more, under its ever-multiplying power to curse, — a power which not even your repentance can arrest. There is no aspect of sin that is not terrible.

Merciful Father! Keep us from following the devices of our own hearts. Teach us to tremble at Thy word. More and more may we learn to dread every sin, not only that we may be ourselves saved from an inevitable curse, but that we may be saved from the awful guilt of corrupting others by our evil example.

Rehoboam

(Read 2 Chron. 11-12)

The terrible disaster to Rehoboam's kingdom in the revolt of the ten tribes — a disaster, which though it might sooner or later have been inevitable from the irrepressible rivalries of the two powerful tribes of Ephraim and Judah, was hurried by his own folly and arrogance — seems to have so far sickened him with the rashness and recklessness of his young associates, and to have impressed him with the wisdom and discretion of the aged counselors who had adorned his father's reign, that for a few years his conduct was marked by prudence and piety. "For three years," we are told, the people "walked in the way of David and Solomon" (2 Chron. 11:17). Forbidden to make war on Jeroboam, although he had gathered an army of one hundred and eighty thousand men for that purpose, he employed his resources in building "cities for defense in Judah." Then was need for this. He was in danger from Jeroboam on the north, and from Shishak, king of Egypt, on the south. The Egyptian monarch with whom Solomon stood in close relations, had passed away, and his dynasty died with him. Shishak was the first king of a new dynasty, and his name connects, in the testimonies of the Egyptian monuments, the history of Egypt with that of Judah. If we accept the narrative concerning Jeroboam in the Septuagint, this Shishak was the friend, and probably the ally of Jeroboam; so that Rehoboam was placed between two great dangers, which might break upon him in unison. He therefore formed a girdle of fenced cities around Jerusalem. But he was stronger in the favor of Jehovah than in the strength of his fortified cities. As long as he walked in the law of the Lord, he was safe, and his kingdom prospered. In addition to the tribes of Judah and Benjamin, "the priests and the Levites that were in all Israel resorted to him out of their coasts;" and "out of all the tribes of Israel, such as set their hearts to seek the Lord God of Israel, came to Jerusalem to sacrifice unto the Lord God of their fathers," and "strengthened the kingdom of Judah." In spite of Jeroboam's rival seats of worship, the temple service had superior attractions, and the most pious and worthy in all the tribes cast in their lot with Judah because of their attachment to the temple and the law of Jehovah. Rehoboam's strength was thus found to be in his faithfulness to Jehovah. But his piety had not taken deep root. After three years, when he thought he had sufficiently strengthened his kingdom and was secure both north and south, against attack, "he forsook the law of Jehovah, and all Israel with him." The regular temple service was maintained, but the idolatries which had disgraced the close of Solomon's reign were again tolerated and encouraged. "Judah did evil in the sight of the Lord, and they provoked him to jealousy with their sins which they had committed, above all that their fathers had done. For they also built them high places, and images, and groves, on every high hill and under every green tree. And there were also Sodomites in the land: and they did according to all the abominations of the nations which the Lord cast out before the children of Israel" (1 Ki. 14:22-24).

We are not informed as to the motive of Shishak in declaring war against Rehoboam. Probably Jeroboam enticed him into it, with a promise of assistance and of great spoil. But, whatever the motive, it was but two years after Rehoboam had forsaken the law of Jehovah when Shishak came up against Jerusalem "with one thousand two hundred chariots, and sixty thousand horsemen, and people without number — the Lubim, the Sukkiim, and the Ethiopians" (2 Chron. 12:2-3), and took the fenced cities, and captured Jerusalem, and "took away the treasures of the house of the Lord, and the treasures of the king's house . . . . and the shields of gold which Solomon had made," two hundred of the large, and three hundred of the smaller size (1 Ki. 10:16-17). The value of the gold in these shields alone, would be, in our money, probably $1,500,000, but with a vastly larger purchasing power than is now expressed by that sum. The king of Egypt obtained great spoils and reduced Rehoboam to a sort of vassalage. It is not surprising that among the conquests he recorded in sculptures on the outside of the great temple at Karnak, should be found *Melchi Judah — the kingdom* of Judah.[1] Whatever may have been *his* motives in making war on Judah, the Scriptures represent it as divinely permitted because of the transgression of Rehoboam and his people. "Ye have forsaken me, and therefore have I also left you in the hands of Shishak" (2 Chron. 12:5). What were the "fenced cities" worth

---

[1] See Smith's Dict. of the Bible, Art. "Rehoboam."

now? As long as Jehovah was his defense, Rehoboam was safe. As soon as he forsook the law of Jehovah, his fenced cities were worthless to protect him from overwhelming disaster. There was no excuse for Rehoboam. He was now forty-six years of age — in his prime. His first experience had taught him the value of wise and pious counsel, and of his safety when he walked in the ways of the Lord. His straying now, and his toleration of abominable idolatries that turned the nation away from God, indicated base ingratitude as well as daring impiety, and justly called down on him severe judgments. The one honorable thing connected with it is, that "the princes of Israel and the king humbled themselves; and they said, Jehovah is righteous" (2 Chron. 12:6). "There was yet good in Judah;" or as we read in our Common Version, "In Judah things went well" (2 Chron. 12:12). All was not corrupt; and, upon the general relenting, Jehovah stayed the hand of judgment, having taught them by adversity what they would not learn through prosperity.

Just here, it may be well to note an objection sometimes raised in view of the frequent lapses of Israel and Judah into apostasy. "God chose them to be a peculiar people, and to show forth his praise to the nations; but surely, in view of their disgraceful apostasies, the choice is shown to have been unwise." The answer is: (1) The result would have been about the same had any other people been chosen. God must work, if he works at all, with such material as human nature affords. (2) There is no failure. God made the punishment of their iniquities teach lessons as valuable as the reward of their obedience. In both cases, sin was rebuked and righteousness approved. And these ends were sometimes more effectively served by the punishment of their sins than by the reward of their faithfulness. The impression made on them and on the surrounding nations was deeper and more abiding. Thus the world was educated in righteousness through this people, whether they obeyed or disobeyed. In the weakness and distresses of their captivities, as well as in their highest national prosperities, they served the divine purpose to make the nations acquainted with the one living and true God.

Poor Rehoboam! We cannot suppress a smile when we look at him; for he cuts a sorry figure, even at his best. He evidently repented, and publicly testified his repentance and his desire to undo the mischief of his former bad example, by proceeding in a public way — in a solemn and imposing procession — to the temple services. This was well; and the king evidently designed to make it as public and as imposing as possible, to attract the attention of the people. He attended in state, preceded by his body-guard, bearing shields. But as Shishak had robbed him of all the gold shields of Solomon, and he was unable to replace them, he substituted shields of *brass;* determined to *make believe* that he was still a powerful monarch! There is a ridiculous vanity in this that provokes a smile at his weakness; and yet, the smile might well spend itself nearer home! How many there are who once went with joyful step to the house of God, their golden shield of a pure faith shining in the light of heaven with a genuine glory, who have been stripped by some Shishak of worldly ambition, or pride, or selfishness, of their golden treasure, and who still come, poverty-stricken in faith, but with unabated show of piety, bearing only a shield of brass! Indeed, it requires a large amount of brass to enable one who is bankrupt in faith and piety to keep up an unembarrassed show of religion. It were better to be true to one's self — to approach the altar with bared head, confessing one's bankruptcy, and imploring heaven for another gold shield. There is too much ridiculous pretension in brass. Let us be honest enough to appear as we really are, and not attempt to deceive others and minister to our wretched vanity by mere appearances. Shams are odious.

Little more is told of Rehoboam, except that, during the last year of his reign, "he strengthened himself in Jerusalem" (2 Chron. 12:13). He had learned enough to stay at home and mind his own business, and put his trust in God. He had eighteen wives and sixty concubines, twenty-eight sons and sixty daughters. His greatest success seems to have been in his harem, and his greatest ability was in the management of his children. In place of keeping them in Jerusalem to cause trouble and make conspiracies, as did the children of David, "he dispersed them through all the countries of Judah and Benjamin, unto every fenced city" (2 Chron. 11:23); thus giving them employment, bestowing on them such honors as they deserved, and guarding them from the temptation to conspire against Abijah, the son of the beloved Maachah, and heir to the throne. Had he ruled his kingdom as wisely as he ruled his family, he would have stood in the first rank of Judah's monarchs.

His reign lasted seventeen years. In that time he managed to drive nine of the twelve tribes into revolt, and to bring what remained of his kingdom to the brink of ruin by provoking the wrath or the avarice of the king of Egypt. With all the prestige of the son and heir of Solomon, with all the advantage growing out of the possession of the throne of David and the City and House of God, with the possibility of preserving the unity of the kingdom, and with the certainty of enjoying great prosperity from the hand of God, even in his reduced territory, he sinned away all his opportunities and left his kingdom impoverished and in great peril. Only the divine purpose to keep a light burning for David in Jerusalem prevented its utter destruction.

Rehoboam was not one of the worst of men. He was not cruel or treacherous; but he was vain, arrogant, weak, and foolish, yet subject to good impulses, and not beyond the reach of repentance when he had gone astray. Had he been trained religiously, and put to work in his boyhood, compelled to win his way by personal merit to the throne, be might have come into possession of practical wisdom, and his moral nature might have reached a vigor and a sensitiveness that would, at forty years of age, have preserved him from wrong and fitted him to rule in righteousness. But, brought up in a corrupt court, with royal honors unearned awaiting him, and with every indulgence that wealth could purchase at his command, it is to his credit that he did not become more thoroughly spoiled. We have to say of him what Lord Macaulay said of James 1 — though there is no parallel in the characters of the two kings — that "fortune placed him in a situation in which his weakness covered him with disgrace, and in which his accomplishments brought him no honor."

Were human lives studied aright, it would be found that there is much in wealth and luxury to be dreaded, and that the stern discipline of poverty and toil — of which we so much complain — if not absolutely essential to true manhood, is at least the fruitful source of strength, virtue, courage, and of most of the elements of true greatness.

We pray, O God, that we may not forget the Hand that blesses us, and ungratefully turn away from Thee. Yet, if we be tempted into such forgetfulness and apostasy, and Thy hand of chastening is laid upon us, grant that we may be led to repentance and return to Thee, adoring the mercy that saves us, even through severe judgments, from our foolish and wicked wanderings.

Conflicting Voices

(Read 1 Kings 13; 2 Kings 23:15-20.)

We have already referred to the startling incident that marred the pomp and pageantry of inauguration-day at Beth-el — the sudden intrusion of a Judaean prophet upon the spectacular ritualism of the newly invented worship, in which Jeroboam himself, blending the splendors of royalty with the solemnities of priesthood, united the crown and the miter, the throne and the altar, and with his own sovereign hands swung the censer of burning incense. Suddenly and defiantly the man of God, in rough garb and with austere mien,[1] rushed in and broke the unhallowed enchantment by the utterance of a direful prophecy. He would not recognize the presence of a majesty already forfeited by Jeroboam's impiety. He did not even look upon the king, who had "cast Jehovah behind his back," and made other gods and molten images, and established ordinances of his own. With his eye upon the altar, he sent forth a curse that must have thrilled with horror the king and his courtiers, the priests and the apostate throngs that participated in the false worship. "O altar, altar, thus saith the Lord: Behold a child shall be born unto the house of David, Josiah by name, and upon thee shall he offer the priests of the high places that burn incense upon thee, and men's bones shall be burnt upon thee." He accompanied this prediction with a sign — a present judgment to confirm the prediction of coming judgments: "This is the sign which Jehovah hath spoken: Behold, the altar shall be rent, and the ashes that are upon it shall be poured out." This, from a hated Judaean, was more than could be borne. The imposing worship was interrupted. The enraged king stretched forth his hand, crying, "Lay hold of him." "And his hand which he put forth against him died up, so that he could not pull it in again to him. The altar also was rent, and the ashes poured out from the altar, according to the sign which the man of God had given by the word of Jehovah." There he stood, beside the riven and fireless altar, his royal right arm, outstretched to curse, withered and impotent! No army had come against him. No unsheathed sword of foe glittered in the sunlight. No vengeful

---

[1] Unsmiling attitude.

forces of nature gathered in storm-clouds or swept in hurricane over the impious scene. A solitary man — a penniless and sword-less footman — in rude garments, stood there against all the force of the kingdom, and at his word a thunderbolt descended on the altar and the king! It was an unmistakable visitation of the wrath of Jehovah — a terrific rebuke, in the very hour of inauguration of this new-fangled religion, this daring usurpation of divine authori-ty. Yet, terrible as was this monition[1] of coming judgments, it was beautifully blended with a display of gentleness and mercy which, more eloquent than speech, gave assurance to the king and the people that, if they would repent, these judgments would be avert-ed. "And the king answered and said unto the man of God, Entreat now the face of Jehovah thy God, and pray for me, that my hand may be restored me again" (1 Ki. 13:6). He acknowledges the hand of God in this affliction, and throws himself on His mercy. "And the man of God besought Jehovah, and the king's hand was re-stored him again, and became as it was before." Mercy rejoices against judgment. The revelation was complete: calamity and ruin, if Jehovah's law is despised; healing and prosperity, if transgres-sors will repent and return to God. But there is no hearty repent-ance. "And the king said unto the man of God, Come home with me, and refresh thyself, and I will give thee a reward." A banquet and a present — this is the upshot of Jeroboam's repentance! No confession of sin — no surrender of his rebellious purpose. "After this thing Jeroboam returned not from his evil way." How gladly would we atone for our darling sins by a little extra devotion to some virtue to which we are readily inclined, and make a costless offering to God!

But the stern prophet was not to be lured by such royal com-plaisance. "If thou wilt give me half thine house, I will not go in with thee, neither will I eat bread, nor drink water in this place: for so it was charged me by the word of Jehovah, saying, Eat no bread, nor drink water, nor turn again by the same way that thou camest." He was probably in need alike of food and of money. He had trav-eled some twelve miles, and was dependent on the good will of the people for support — a good will that he could not expect to find among a hostile and apostate people; a support which he was for-

---

[1] Telling, revealing.

bidden to receive from them. There was great power, then, in the temptation which the king spread before him — not only a feast to a hungry man, and a present to a child of poverty — but these from a royal hand! But he triumphed bravely over this, and "went another way, and returned not by the way that he came to Beth-el." In all this we discover only the utmost fidelity and courage.

We can readily understand why he was forbidden to eat and drink with the Israelites. They were apostates; he went to testify against them; it was proper that he should testify in deed as well as in word, and show in every action that he had no fellowship with them. Least of all could he have fellowship with the king — the head and front of this apostasy. Why he was forbidden to return by the same route to Jerusalem is not so apparent. Probably it was with a view to guard against attracting attention to him and his mission. At any rate, he was under this prohibition, and it was enough that God had said so, whether the reason for the prohibition was understood or not. It was his to obey, not to inquire into the reasons for the inhibition.

We are now brought to a deeply interesting portion of this narrative. "An old prophet in Beth-el" now comes upon the scene, who, learning of the proceedings of this Judaean prophet, goes in search of him, persuades him to disregard the divine interdict under which he was placed, and thus brings upon him swift destruction.

The character and proceedings of this old prophet have an air of mystery about them which has given rise to a variety of opinions among commentators. By some he is regarded as a false prophet — an impostor; by others as a man of strangely mixed character, like Balaam, who, notwithstanding his obliquities, possessed and exercised the prophetic gift. Josephus[1] regards him as (1) jealous of the influence of the new prophet over the king, lest it should displace his own; (2) as scheming, therefore, to get him out of the way; and (3) as going to the king, after the new prophet's death, to persuade him that this strange prophet was an impostor — that the trouble in the king's hand "was that it was enfeebled by the labor it had undergone in supporting the sacrifices; and that as to the altar, it was but new, and had borne abundance of sacrifices, and those large

---

[1] *Antiquities of the Jews*, book 8, chapter 9.

ones, too, and was accordingly broken to pieces and fallen down by the weight of what had been laid upon it." If there be any truth in this, modern Rationalists have little to boast of. Here is a rationalistic effort to dispose of the supernatural, with a skill that would not dishonor Kuenen, or Oort, or Hooykaas.

We are led, from all the hints furnished in the sacred narrative, to form an estimate of the old prophet's character somewhat different from any we have met with.

1. That he had been a genuine prophet of Jehovah. He is styled a prophet, without the slightest intimation of any lack of genuineness in his prophetic gifts.

2. That he had been bereft of his inspiration through his base compliance with prevailing corruptions. We learn (2 Chron. 11:16) that when Jeroboam set up his own inventions, and drew the people away from the true worship, not only the Levites left their suburbs and their possessions and went to Jerusalem, but "out of all the tribes of Israel, such as set their hearts to seek Jehovah, God of Israel, came to Jerusalem" and "strengthened the kingdom of Judah." There were prophets, like Ahijah, that feared Jehovah, who yet remained in the territory of Jeroboam, but they faithfully testified against the sins of kings and people, and were thorns in the sides of the apostate sovereigns of the ten tribes (see 1 Kings 14:6-16). But this old prophet neither went with Judah nor testified against the sins of Israel. He dwelt at Beth-el — where Satan's seat was — yet his voice was never heard in rebuke of the great sin of Jeroboam, wherewith he made Israel to sin. That he was in friendly relations with this wicked king, and quietly acquiesced in his wickedness, if he did not actually forward it, is evident from his sons being present among the worshipers at the formal inauguration of the new system of worship. He was a timeserver. He floated with the current. He lacked the courage to stand up against the multitude for the truth. He had smothered the divine inspirations that came upon him, and God had departed from him. There came to him no dream, or vision, or voice from God, anymore. It was this prophetic barrenness, we take it, that caused such eagerness to see and commune with the strange prophet. He would seek, through him, the revelations that were no longer granted to himself. If calamities were coming, he wanted to know it, that he might flee; for the same mean selfishness that had led him to for-

sake God and cling to Jeroboam, would now impel him to forsake Jeroboam in a time of peril. He therefore sped to the Judaean prophet, to learn of the fortunes of the new kingdom. It need not be surprising that he resorted to falsehood to gain his end, for he who could be false to Jehovah to advance his own interests, could readily prove false to a fellow-being for the same reason.

Now comes the "conflict of voices." The Judaean prophet was sitting under the spreading limbs of a terebinth tree; weary, hungry, weak, perhaps meditating on the stern interdiction which had shut him out from the king's hospitality and bounty. Much depends on the mood we are in when a message comes to us. The old prophet approached him kindly, and offered hospitality. *He wanted to accept it*, being restrained only by the divine inhibition. He was ready to yield, if only he could be released from that. He was holding on to duty, but with no firm grasp. The old prophet assured him that he had just received a divine message, countermanding the previous order. Here, now, was a conflict of voices: "Thou shalt eat no bread nor drink water here." "Bring him back with thee into thine house, that he may eat bread and drink water." Which shall he believe? Reason and conscience said, "Hold on to what you *know* to be true." Appetite said, "Believe that which you *want* to be true." And appetite carried the day. He eagerly seized that which he *desired to be true*, that he might escape from hunger and lonesomeness — shielding himself behind a mere pretense of revelation which he had no just reason to regard as worthy of acceptance.

To many, it seems unjust and cruel that he should have been condemned for a *mistake,* being imposed on by the falsehood of a fellow-prophet. As we are all likely, in the course of our Christian experience, to be troubled with conflicting voices, it may be well to pause and consider this case. Was the way of duty really obscured by this second revelation? Was it a mere mistake that he accepted it? Was he a helpless victim of falsehood?

(1). The original prohibition was made known *directly to himself.* He *knew* it came from God. And it had been confirmed to him as divine by the seal placed on his mission in the miracles wrought at the altar. There could be no mistake about this.

The second revelation came to him through another — an entire stranger — unaccompanied by any evidence of a divine origin. There could be, and there was likely to be, mistake in accrediting a message thus received, especially when it directly contradicted the word which he knew he had received from the Lord. To put the best face on it, he was abandoning a certainty for an uncertainty.

(2). He had a right to presume that if Jehovah meant to countermand the original order, He would make the new revelation as unmistakable as the former — communicating it in the same way. There was no need for the intervention of another prophet, and he was under no obligation to accept what was communicated through a doubtful channel.

(3). The presumptions were all against the truth of this new message. The old prophet's voluntary residence at Beth-el, the center of apostasy; his faithlessness amidst the prevailing corruptions; the identification of his family, without protest on his part, with the apostate people against whom the Judaean prophet was sent; the absence of any intimation from Jehovah that He had a prophet at Beth-el to whom He wished him to show respect: all these were strong presumptions against the genuineness of a message which rested for authority on *the unsupported word of the messenger.*

There ought to have been no perplexity here. There would have been none, but for the pleadings of hunger. The prophet had just passed through an exciting scene, in which his strength and heroism had been taxed to the utmost. A reaction had set in. In this perilous moment the temptation came, and in his weakness he yielded. It is to be considered, likewise, that the temptation came in a form that did not arouse suspicion. Jeroboam he had resisted bravely, for he was an undisguised foe; but now the temptation comes in friendly guise. We may resist evil in one approach, and yet be captured by it when it approaches in some other form.

His sudden and violent death added to the impressiveness of the divine warning to Jeroboam and his people. They would learn that God is no respecter of persons — that disregard of His law would be punished, whether the transgressor belonged to Judah or to Israel; and that if those whom He specially acknowledged as His own were not spared when they transgressed, surely such apostates as Jeroboam and his subjects need not expect to escape the just judgments of God.

As to the "old prophet," his meanness and cowardice are conspicuous to the last. He was willing to atone for his great and unprovoked wrong to the Judaean prophet by giving him decent burial after he had caused his death; for he could thus, under pretense of mourning, cover his own iniquity. And in this, he exposed himself to no peril; for it was safe to show honor to a man whom the king had invited to his own table. How hideous is the hypocrisy of one who seeks to honor a man dead, whom, while living, he had foully wronged! The request of the old decayed prophet, that after his death he should be laid by the side of the true prophet, has nothing in it but mean selfishness. He would borrow a post-mortem reputation for prophetical dignity by this association! Moreover, he was willing to be known as the companion of this faithful rebuker of sin — as siding with him in his denunciations of Israel's apostasies — *when such* a *testimony could cost him nothing,* when he could not be persecuted for it! Thus, even in the grave, men seek to deck themselves in borrowed plumes, and to wear a reputation that does not belong to them! It is possible, moreover, that the old man had, in common with his people, a pious horror of the disturbance of his bones; and that he thought to insure his mortal remains against desecration by thus associating himself in death with one whose grave would be safe from violence when the day of vengeance came. In this he showed wise judgment (see 1 Kings 23:15-18), but also supreme selfishness. He plans only for himself

Two lessons of grave import come to us from this curious chapter of history.

1. If the view we have taken of the old prophet's character be correct, there is here an impressive warning to those who have been richly gifted of God. How often those who were mighty as men of God, dwindle into weakness and sink into insignificance! They attribute their decay of power to the caprices of the people, when, perhaps, it is due to their own unfaithfulness. They failed to be true to the truth committed to them. They shrank from duty in the day of peril. They chose Beth-el before Jerusalem, and kept silence in the day when stern rebuke was demanded of them. They went with the multitude, forsaking the faithful few who stood for truth in the evil and dark day. Doubtless they have plausible apologies for their weakness and treachery. So, doubtless, had the old prophet in Beth-el. But nonetheless their power is blighted, and their glory departed. They laid their heads in the lap of some Delilah of ease, or pride, or fortune, or fame, and they rose up shorn of

their strength, blind and fettered, to grind like slaves at the mill of their captors. We have watched the course of several who, once grand and mighty, in an evil day surrendered the truth that had made them great, and basely bowed the knee to popular idols. Where are they now? Their scepter is broken, and they have faded out of sight. They live in obscurity, grinding as slaves at some sectarian mill, or they have died "unwept, unhonored, and unsung." The glory has departed from them. Men who are true to their convictions, and nobly use the gift that is in them, grow in power as they grow in years; but men who "hold the truth in unrighteousness" will, like the old prophet in Beth-el, wither into feebleness, and sink into obscurity. And if, in death, they are not utterly forgotten, it will be because they had been associated with others better than themselves, whose virtues entitle them to grateful remembrance.

2. The conflict of voices is heard in every life. There are times when the certainty of our faith and the integrity of our life come into question. The voice of Christ is contested by the voice of rationalism; the voice of self-denial is opposed by the voice of pleasure; the voice of duty is overpowered by the clamors of self-interest; the voice of conscience is likely to be hushed by the pleadings of passion. And these false voices are apt to be the voices of sirens. The suggestions of falsehood come to us in the counterfeited voice of truth; temptations to evil approach in the guise of holiness. It is bewildering. The sophistries that would lure us from safe ways are subtle and plausible, and it is difficult to escape from their meshes. Is there no safety? Must we be ever subject to bewilderment? Can we not *know* that we are going right? If you have an honest heart, YOU May find safe ground. If your heart is dishonest, you will be sure to go wrong. It rests mainly with yourself. We cannot here go largely into a discussion of these questions; but, in concluding a paper already too long, we will take space enough to offer three suggestions, which may serve to guard the tempted soul from needless bewilderment, and place it on safe ground.

(1). *Beware of the Voice of Passion.* — Passion is blind. Its pleadings, however cunning, are insane. When you find yourself inclined to listen to these, stop your ears, and be sure to go another way. You are safe always in rejecting that for which passion pleads against the voice of conscience.

(2.) *Never be deaf to the Voice of Conscience.* — It is better to be true to the voice of conscience, even if wrong, than to be accidentally right against the pleadings of Conscience. For that spirit of fidelity to your truest convictions, even should those convictions be erroneous, is your best guarantee that you shall be led into more truth. He who is false to his conscience is hopelessly false.

(3.) When, in the border-land of truth and error, you are at a loss to trace the dividing line, *be sure to stop far enough within the territory of ascertained truth to know that your ground is undisputed.* Thus, if you are tempted to doubt the divine mission of Christ, reflect that if there is no safety in Christ, there is no safety anywhere. *There is everything to lose and nothing to gain by surrendering Christ.* It is safe, then, to abide in Christ. Reflect, too, that the evidences of Christ's divine mission are and ever must be superior to any evidence in opposition to it.

"If weak thy faith, why choose the harder side?"

If you are likely to be lured into any doubtful act or habit or association, remember that there is a *safety* in resisting that there never can be in yielding. If any pleasure or indulgence seems inviting, recollect that the motives to virtue are always superior to the motives of vice, and you are *safe* in abstaining, while there is always peril in yielding to such allurements. There is nothing on earth that *can* be firmer and safer than the word of God as revealed in Jesus Christ. He who walks in this light walks securely; he who departs from it is sure to wreck his loftiest hopes, his purest joys, his noblest inspirations, and that without compensation. It is all loss, without gain. All reason and all experience declare that Jesus is the Way, the Truth, the Life. Blessed are all they that put their trust in Him.

O Thou who art Truth itself, may we ever listen to Thy voice. However tempting the false voices that so often speak to us, may we ever hear the voice of the Good Shepherd, and follow Him, and be deaf to the voice of strangers. May we take heed what we hear, that no siren voices may lure us to destruction. Amid the thousand voices of error, of vain speculation, of blatant skepticism, of sectarian controversy, of worldly allurement, that are heard on every hand, may we ever have an ear to what Thy Spirit saith, that we may be saved from delusion, and be led in the paths of peace.

Ahab and Jezebel

(1 Kings 16-22)

The government of the ten tribes was a military monarchy. Although Jeroboam seems to have been the choice of the people at large, it was not so with his successors. The war that was kept up against Judah for nearly half a century required a large military force, and the soldiery assumed the right of making and unmaking kings, according to their own caprice, or under the promptings of ambitious aspirants among their own leaders. Thus Nadab, Jeroboam's son and successor, after a reign of only two years, was slain by Baasha, one of his military officers, during the siege of Gibbethon (1 Kings 15:25-28), and the house of Jeroboam was utterly overthrown. Baasha reigned twenty-four years, and was succeeded by his son Elah, a mere debauchee.[1] After two years, "his servant Zimri, captain of half his chariots, conspired against him as he was in Tirzah, drinking himself drunk in the house of Arza, steward of his house in Tirzah" (1 Kings 16:9). Zimri also "slew all the house of Baasha." But Zimri reigned only seven days. He had acted on his own responsibility, without consulting the army, which at this time was engaged in besieging Gibbethon, a town then in possession of the Philistines. As soon as this unauthorized usurpation was known in the camp, the army elected Omri, captain of the host, to be king, and the siege of Gibbethon was raised, that the whole military force might proceed to Tirzah to place Omri on the throne. A considerable part of the *people* desired to have a certain Tibni for king, and raised a standard in his behalf; but Omri, having the support of the army, was successful. Tirzah, the capital, having been greatly damaged in the siege, and Zimri having "burnt the king's house over him with fire," Omri showed his good judgment in purchasing the hill of Shemer for the site of a new royal city, calling it after the name of Sheme, the former owner; Samaria, or Shomeron.

> *As Constantine's sagacity is fixed by his choice of Constantinople, so is that of Omri by his choice of Samar-*

---

[1] An immoral, unrestrained, and self-indulgent person.

56

ia. Six miles from Shechem, in the same well-watered val-
ley, here opening into a wide basin, rises an oblong hill,
with steep yet accessible sides, and a long level top. This
was the mountain of Samaria, or, as it is called in the
original, Shomeron, so named after its owner Shemer, who
there lived in state, and who sold it to the king for the
great sum of two talents of silver. It combined in a union
not elsewhere found in Palestine, strength, beauty, and
fertility. It commanded a full view of the sea and plain of
Sharon on one hand, and of the [valley] of Shechem on the
other. The town sloped down from the summit of the hill; a
broad wall with a terraced top ran round it. . . . The infe-
rior houses were built of white brick, with rafters of syca-
more; the grander of hewn stone and cedar. It stood
amidst a circle of hills, commanding a view of its streets
and slopes, itself the crown and glory of the whole scene
(Isa. 28:1). . . . It was the only great city of Palestine cre-
ated by the sovereigns. All the others had been already
consecrated by patriarchal tradition or previous posses-
sion. But Samaria was the choice of Omri alone. He in-
deed gave to the city which he had built the name of its
former owner, but its special connection with himself as its
founder is proved by the designation which, it seems, Sa-
maria bears in Assyrian inscriptions — Beth Khumri,
"The House, or Palace, of Omri."[1]

Samaria soon became not only a stronghold of royal power, but
a seat of wealth, luxury, vice, and oppression, as may be learned
from various allusions in the prophets, and especially in the book
of Amos. In all that related to material prosperity, Omri appears to
have been a wise ruler. He put an end to the bloody and ruinous
strifes in which, for nearly half a century, Israel and Judah had
been engaged. He also entered into intimate relations with the
Phoenician power of Tyre, the great seat of commerce and of
wealth.[2] Tyre, too, had been subject to political convulsions and
revolutions. One king after another had been dethroned, until Eth-

---

[1] Stanley's *History of the Jewish Church*, Lecture 30.

[2] For a vivid picture of the commerce, wealth, learning and material strength
of Tyre, see Ezek. chaps. 26-28.

baal, a priest of Astarte, mounted the throne, having murdered his predecessor — his brother Phelles. Previous commotions had necessarily impaired the strength of the State; many wealthy and powerful families had emigrated to Northern Africa to plant new colonies; the powerful king of Damascus was threatening Phoenicia with invasion: it became the interest of Phoenicia as well as of Israel to form a close alliance for mutual protection — and to cement this alliance, Jezebel, the daughter of Ethbaal, was given in marriage to Ahab, son of Omri, and heir to the throne of Israel. While it is true that previous Jewish monarchs had taken wives of the old Canaanite races — David having married a daughter of the chief of Geshur (1 Chron. 3:2), and Solomon taking Zidonian women to wife (1 Kings 11:1) — this was the first instance in which the *chief* wife — the queen — of an Israelite king was taken from that accursed race. While Omri was prudent and skillful in promoting the peace and material prosperity of his kingdom, he was reckless as to the religious character of the people and the high religious mission of the nation. With him, heathenism was as good as the religion taught by Jehovah, if only it would advance the prosperity and security of his kingdom. He looked on religion with the eye of a politician, valuing it according to its power to serve the royal welfare. His alliance with Tyre opened the way for the return of the corrupt and licentious worship of Astarte, and even the calf-worship at Beth-el and Dan, established by Jeroboam, seems no longer to have been favored at court. That worship was the worship of Jehovah under sacred symbols; but now the worship of Jehovah was to be entirely supplanted by the worship of Baal. We read, therefore, that "Omri wrought evil in the eyes of the Lord, and did worse than all that were before him" (1 Kings 16:25); and the bitter memory of "the statutes of Omri" in favor of idolatry still lingered in the hearts of the pious two centuries later (Mic. 6:16). In the next reign the poisonous fruit of this treachery to Jehovah comes to ripeness.

After a reign of twelve years, Omri dies, and Ahab succeeds him. Ahab was not thoroughly bad. He exhibits, now and then, excellent qualities, and his reign, on the whole, was prosperous. The fact that a marriage was consummated between Jehoram, son of Jehoshaphat, and Athaliah, daughter of Ahab and Jezebel (2 Kings 8:18), and that so eminently pious a monarch as Jehoshaphat paid a visit to Ahab, and made a military alliance with him (1 Kings

22:2), indicates that Ahab was not entirely abandoned to evil. His reign of twenty-two years was one of peace, and, apart from the years of terrible drought, of general prosperity. He seems to have had a strong hold on the affections of his people, and the peaceful policy initiated by his father gave an opportunity for the cultivation of the arts of peace. But though personally brave when forced into action, he was sadly lacking in *decision of character.* He was weak in will, and therefore easily impressed by others, especially by those of strong will, like Elijah and Jezebel.

Had his wife been a devout worshiper of Jehovah, and had his court been made up of men of true faith, his reign might have been the most illustrious in the history of the kingdom; for his pliable nature would readily have taken the impression of their faith and piety, and his delight in the arts of peace — especially in architecture (1 Kings 22:39) — would have filled the land with the blessings of a righteous prosperity and with monuments of his beneficent power and elegant taste. But, unfortunately, his wife was a fanatical idolater, and a woman of imperious will. Though in later times her name has found a welcome under the form *Isabella,* in its ancient form of *Jezebel* it is covered with infamy. Possessed of a fierce energy and an indomitable will, vindictive, fanatical in her devotion to the idol-worship of Phoenicia, unscrupulous as to the measures she adopted, and licentious as she must have been in her supreme devotion to a licentious worship, she was in fact the sovereign, and Ahab her pliant slave. An immense temple to Baal was built in Samaria (1 Kings 16:32; 2 Kings 10:21), adorned with idolatrous images, with a figure of Baal on a stone pillar in front of the imposing structure (2 Kings 10:26, 27). Here Ahab himself attended the worship in state (1 Kings 16:31). At Jezreel, where Ahab had built a royal palace, Jezebel built a temple to Asherah, the Canaanite Venus, and four hundred priests ministered in its courts, while four hundred and fifty were employed in the temple at Samaria (1 Kings 18:19). An exterminating war was waged against the prophets of Jehovah. (See 1 Kings 18:4, 13, 22; 19:10, 14; 2 Kings 9:7.) These men of God were far more numerous in Israel than in Judah, and they had been thorns in the sides of her unfaithful rulers. They were more dreaded than armies by the guilty monarchs against whom they launched their thunderous rebukes and threatenings of the wrath of Jehovah. Their influence with the people was strong — sometimes resistless; hence many of them were preserved through this fierce persecution; and after Jezebel had spent her wrath, they were still found in considerable numbers at Beth-el, Gilgal, and Jericho (2 Kings 1:2-7, 15-22, 4:38, 6:17). We have but brief hints of the terrors of this persecution. That these prophets were hunted from place to place, and put to the sword wherever they were found, is evident. (See Heb. 11:36-38, which clearly refers to this as well as other persecutions.) Obadiah, Ahab's chief minister, "the Sebastian of this Jewish Diocletian," hid a hundred of them in caves and secretly supplied them with bread and water (1 Kings 18:13).

It has been well remarked that this is the first great persecution for conscience' sake of which we have any record. "The extermination of the Canaanite," says Dean Stanley, "however bloody, and unlike the spirit of Christian times, had yet been in the heat of war and victory. Those who remained in the land were unmolested in their religious worship, as they were in their tenure of property and of office. It was reserved for the heathen Jezebel to exemplify the principle of persecution in its most direct form. To her, and not to Moses or Joshua, the bitter intolerance of modern times must look back as its legitimate ancestress."[1] When we pause to think of the long and cruel reign of intolerance, and reflect that, even in Protestant countries, the doctrine of toleration, so called — in reality simply the doctrine of *justice* — was, until recently, a hideous heresy, we may well wonder at the deep-rooted tyranny, so infamous in its origin, which, in spite of all the light of New Testament teaching, so long crushed the souls of men, and filled the earth with tears and blood, with cruelty and slaughter.

We sometimes hear it argued in favor of woman suffrage, that if women were allowed to vote, there would soon be an end to drunkenness, disorder, corruption, and fraud, and the beginning of a reign of order and virtue such as heaven has not yet looked on. It may be that woman ought, in this country, to be invested with the full rights of citizenship. Concerning that, we say nothing here. But, so far as this argument is concerned we have to say that we have no confidence in it. In regard to the use and abuse of political power, so far as history testifies, we see no great difference be-

---

[1] *History of the Jewish Church*, Lecture 30.

tween men and women. There is nothing generous, good, and pure of which women have not proved themselves capable; and there is nothing unjust, false, corrupt, or cruel, of which they are not shown to be equally capable. Think of Delilah, Jael, Jezebel, Athaliah, Herodias, Cleopatra, Amestris, Statira, Lucrezia Borgia, Catharine de Medici, Faustina, the Catharines I and II of Russia, not to speak of those of greatly mixed character, like Maria Theresa, Marie Antoinette, Mary Queen of Scots, and the Empress Eugenie. Then think of Deborah, Jehosheba, Esther, Semiramis, Zenobia, Margaret Queen of Denmark, Margaret of Valois, Josephine, Elizabeth and Victoria; and say if, in all the varieties of good and evil, of gentleness and cruelty, of truth and falsehood, of righteousness and unrighteousness, of purity and impurity, of all that exalts and ennobles human nature, and of all that debases and degrades it, there are not as complete illustrations in the public and private lives of these women as of the same number of men in public positions and with similar surroundings. We have no reason to believe that, if women were invested with all the powers and privileges of citizenship in this country, they would be any better or worse, as politicians, than men. No more desperate fight against unrighteousness, cruelty, and outrage do we care to read of than that of Elijah against Jezebel.

Just when this haughty and cruel queen was in the full tide of success in the extirpation[1] of the prophets and the subjugation of the people to the dominion of the priests of Baal, a rough, rude Gileadite, tall, gaunt, hairy, swift of foot, clothed in a simple tunic and a mantle of sheepskin, with his unshorn hair hanging down his back, appears suddenly on the scene, to do battle for Jehovah and His law — "the grandest and most romantic character that Israel ever produced." His name is Elijah.

O Lord, teach us to guard against evil associations, lest we be entangled in the follies and vices and crimes of wicked companions. And grant us such strength of will that when we are endangered by evil surroundings we may be able to resist, and stand firm for truth and righteousness. And when we see into what excesses of wrong and cruelty even woman's gentle spirit may be tempted, may we learn to beware of even the slightest uprising of a spirit of

---

[1] The removal by force of something undesired.

disobedience, under whose accursed power everything gentle and womanly, as well as everything brave and manly, is blighted.

Elijah

(1 Kings 17-19)

There is something weird and startling in the suddenness of the appearance of this child of nature — this half-wild Gileadite — in the presence of royalty. Alone, unheralded, in coarse garb, and of uncourtly mien,[1] with his long shaggy hair flowing down his back, this hirsute[2] child of the mountains springs noiselessly from the forests of Gilead and bursts unceremoniously, like an apparition, into the presence of the proud monarch of Israel, utters his woeful message, and in a moment is invisible! His dress, his look, his manners, his words—all peculiar. Who is he? Whence came he? His previous history is shrouded in mystery. Like Melchizedek, he is "without father, without mother, without genealogy, without beginning of days or end of life." He stands before us for what he is worth in his own personality, shining in no borrowed luster save that which he derives from heaven, sustained by no family or tribal prestige; in a very peculiar sense a "man of God." How often does Jehovah, in selecting His men, pour contempt on the pride of ancestry and on all the fictitious sources of human greatness! All that we know of Elijah's antecedents is found in a single sentence: "Elijah the Tishbite, of the inhabitants of Gilead," — and as if even this were too much to be known, the term "Tishbite" is of doubtful meaning, and if there was such a place as Tishbi or Thisbe, its locality is unknown.[3] There may be a glimmer of light in his name. Elijah means "Jehovah is my God." It is possible that we trace here the loyalty to Jehovah of his parents in a time of widespread idolatry, or a prophetic announcement of that championship of Jehovah to which he was destined from his birth. This would involve a careful religious training in the knowledge and worship of Jeho-

---

[1] Attitude.

[2] Extremely hairy.

[3] The Speaker's Commentary says on Kings 17:1: "The two words rendered 'Tishbite' and 'inhabitants,' are in the original (setting aside the vowel points), exactly alike, and it is scarcely conceivable that the writer could intend by them two entirely distinct things. The meaning consequently must either be 'Elijah the stranger, of the strangers of Gilead,' or (more probable) 'Elijah the Tishbite, of Tishbi of Gilead.'"

vah.

That he belonged to Gilead is unquestionable. Gilead was a mountainous region east of the Jordan, extending from nearly the south end of the Sea of Galilee to the north end of the Dead Sea — about sixty miles, with an average breadth of about twenty. It will be better known to the reader as Peraea. This portion of the Israelitish trans-Jordanic territory was largely broken into mountains and ravines, and was chiefly valuable for pasturage (Num. 32:1). Yet it was not destitute of attractiveness.

> *"In passing through the country,"* says Mr. Porter, *"one can hardly get over the impression that he is roaming through an English park. The graceful hills, the rich vales, the luxuriant herbage, the bright wild flowers, the plantations of evergreen oak, pine, arbutus; now a tangled thicket, and now a grove scattered over the gentle slope, as if intended to reveal its beauty; the little rivulets, fringed with oleanders, at one place running lazily between alluvial[1] banks, at another dashing madly down rocky ravines — such are the features of the mountains of Gilead."*
>
> *"Gilead,"* says Geikie, *"was a land of chase and pasture, of tent-villages and mountain castles; with a population of wandering, half-civilized, fierce shepherds, ready at all times to repel the attacks of the desert tribes, or to go out on a foray against them."* See 1 Chron. 5:10, 19-22.

They were in many respects like the Bedouin Arabs who inhabit that region at the present time. Gideon (Judges 6-7) and Jephthah (Judges 11) were typical men of that region. To Gilead, Abner conveyed Ishbosheth, the son of Saul, when the throne of Israel was in dispute, relying on the valor and integrity of its people (2 Sam. 1 8-9); and thither David fled in the day of his calamity (2 Sam. 17:22-24), counting on a refuge among its uncorrupted and brave inhabitants from the treachery and cruelty of his own son. It was in these wild scenes of nature, and among these hardy, brave, simple-minded people that Elijah was reared — far from the corruptions of camps and courts, a free child of the deserts and the

---

[1] Formed by sediment deposited by flowing water.

mountains, living on simple fare, accustomed to exposures, trained to physical hardihood, and holding unembarrassed communication with Jehovah in Nature's pure and quiet temples.

There is an expression in Elijah's first speech to Ahab which lets in a little more light on his previous life. "As Jehovah God of Israel liveth, *before whom I stand.*" As the slave stood in the presence of his master awaiting his command, Elijah announces himself as the bond-servant of Jehovah, doing His bidding. This was his calling. In this service he had spent his past life. It is not unlikely that among the prophets — at that time numerous in Israel, for Obadiah, Ahab's minister, had hidden away one hundred of them (1 Kings 18:13), and Jezebel had proclaimed a war of extermination against them, as the power she most dreaded — he was well known and recognized as a leader, as farther along he is recognized by the sons of the prophets as having preeminence (2 Kings 2). It is evident that though, to us, he bursts suddenly on the scene of action, he had been well prepared for his peculiar mission. When all the prophets had been slaughtered or driven to the dens and caves of the earth, this tall, gaunt, hairy Gileadite, unarmed, unfriended, penniless, stands forth the one champion of Jehovah — one loyal man against an apostate nation — one man of God against the power of the throne and the dread dominion of the priests of Baal. He flings defiance in the face of Ahab, and the war begins. It looks like a hopeless contest on the part of Elijah, but Jehovah and he are a majority.

"As Jehovah, God of Israel, liveth, before whom I stand," said Elijah to Ahab, "there shall not be dew nor rain these years, but according to my word;" and instantly he vanishes. This first thrust was terrible. Ahab, with all his royal power; Jezebel, with all her fierce energy; Baal, with all his dread forces of superstition, god of nature and of power as he assumed to be, could not lock or unlock the stores of Jehovah's power. With the heavens over them as brass and the earth under them as iron, in a land where water and life were almost equivalent terms, throne and temple, king and priest, treasury and army, were but mockeries. It was only a question of time as to their surrender. They braved it long, these stubborn devotees of superstition. For three years and a half they stood out against this awful sovereignty of Jehovah (James 5:17), and Elijah meanwhile is hidden away from their persecuting rage (1 Kings

18:10). At first he is directed to a hiding-place in the Wady Cherith. Its location is not known. It may have been in his own country, in the green thickets of some deep ravine, where the torrents rushed in the rainy season; where water and moisture and vegetation, yet untouched by drought, under the shade of forests would continue long after exposed surfaces were parched, and to which the birds would naturally flock from the desolate regions around. Here, hiding in the thickets that hung over the still unexhausted stream, "the ravens brought him bread and flesh in the morning, and bread and flesh in the evening; and he drank of the brook."[1] We presume to say that not Ahab and Jezebel, at the royal table, had healthier fare, or enjoyed more delicious repasts.[2] But, as the drought progressed, the waters of Cherith were exhausted, the prophet's leafy covert no longer served as a hiding place, the birds came no longer thither for shelter and refreshment. Then "the word of Jehovah came to him, saying, Arise, get thee to Zarephath, which belongeth to Zidon" This was a heathen village, about ten miles south of Sidon, on the shore of the Mediterranean; and although the heights of Lebanon must have supplied Phoenicia with water long after it had become scarce in Israel, it seems that Phoenicia too was suffering severely from drought. Meander, as quoted by Josephus, mentions this drought, and states that it lasted one year. Why Elijah should have been sent into a heathen country, and almost to the gates of the city where Baal, against whom he was fighting, had his seat of power, we do not know. The most reasonable suggestion is that he would be safer from Jezebel's spies there than in Israel as no one would think of seeing him in so unlikely a place. Even the woman to whom he was directed seems to have been a heathen, for she says, "*Thy* God," not *my* God (1 Kings 17:12). It would never occur to Jezebel that this dread foe of Baal would be sheltered by one of Baal's own devotees — and that, too, almost under the shadow of Baal's image. The history of this transfer from Cherith to Zarephath is brief but interesting, and is best told in the language of the sacred narrator:

---

[1] The attempt to change Orebim, ravens, into Arbim, Arabs, so as to make Arabians feed Elijah, has not generally been approved. It is unsustained by any of the Hebrew MSS.

[2] Meals.

So he arose and went to Zarephath. And when he came to the gate of the city, behold the widow woman was there gathering sticks: and he called to her, and said, "Fetch me, I pray thee, a little water in a vessel, that I may drink." And as she was going to fetch it, he called to her, and said, "Bring me, I pray thee, a morsel of bread in thine hand." And she said, "As the Lord thy God liveth, I have not a cake, but a handful of meal in the barrel and a little oil in the cruse[1]: and, behold, I am gathering two sticks, that I may go in and dress it for me and my son, that we may eat it and die." And Elijah said unto her, "Fear not; go and do as thou hast said: but make me thereof a little cake first, and bring it unto me, and after make for thee and thy son. For thus saith Jehovah, God of Israel: The barrel of meal shall not waste, neither shall the cruse of oil fail, until the day that Jehovah sendeth rain upon the earth." And she went, and did according to the saying of Elijah; and she, and he, and her house, did eat many days. And the barrel of meal wasted not, neither did the cruse of oil fail, according to the word of Jehovah, which he spake by Elijah.

A simple, but touching narrative. Elijah, worn with travel, and hungry and thirsty with fasting during his journey through a land of drought, petitions a poor heathen woman for bread and water. A desolate and poor widow, with the wolf at her door, gathering sticks to cook the last meal for herself and her son, expecting then to die of starvation, hears a cry of distress from a stranger and a Jew, and she forgets her own sorrows in her sympathy with another in his needs. God bless thee, heathen as thou art; for His own spirit of goodness glows within thee. Thou art not more desolate-hearted than generous-hearted, who, on the edge of starvation thyself, canst seek cheerfully to relieve the wants of a stranger. She will give what she can command — a cup of cold water. If her own heart is breaking, why should she leave another to suffer, stranger and enemy though he be? Was it with his eye on this beautiful incident that Jesus said, "Whosoever shall give to drink unto one of these

---

[1] A pouch or bottle used to store liquids.

little ones a cup of cold water only, in the name of a disciple, verily I say unto you, he shall in no wise lose his reward"? But when the hungry man speaks of *bread,* it gives her pause. Phoenicia was dependent on Palestine for supplies of grain, and hence, in this long drought, bread was scarce, and beyond the power of the poor to purchase. She does not refuse, but she lays her case before him, and leaves him to decide. There is just enough meal and oil left for one meal for her and her son. After that, there is nothing but death. What shall she do? Noble, generous woman! Who would not rather be this poor, desolate, starving, but great-hearted woman, than selfish, cruel Jezebel, in her royal pomp, with murder in her heart and blood on her hands? "Fear not," said Elijah, "for I bear a message to thee from Jehovah, God of Israel: the barrel of meal and cruse of oil shall not fail until rain come." Something in the bearing of the prophet gave her hope, perhaps, that it might be even so; but she had, as yet, such slender grounds of confidence, that we must attribute her resolution more to her goodness of heart than her faith in this message. If death had to come, it might as well come at once, and her life might better close crowned with a generous deed than dishonored by an act of selfishness. So the cake for the prophet was first baked out of the handful of meal yet remaining.

And is such goodness ever in vain? Never. For, (1) the soul is nobler for it, and the purest happiness the soul ever knows — that of doing good — is worth all it costs. (2) In the righteous workings of God's providence, this supreme devotion to goodness is never left unrewarded. O, if niggardly[1] souls could but know what an inevitable curse attends their selfishness in withering the best sympathies and smothering the noblest impulses of their own souls; if they could but see from what a world of beautiful and blessed compensations they have barred themselves out; they would loathe and curse the meanness of their selfish inspirations, and joyfully give up all the wealth so meanly earned for the ineffable peace and joy that filled the heart of the poor widow of Zarephath.

Yet it seemed, for a time, as if even such supreme goodness as hers would be crowned with calamity. True, the barrel of meal and the cruse of oil did not fail; but her son was smitten with death — and what value had the meal and the oil when this only light of her

---

[1] Stingy, miserly, ungenerous.

eyes was quenched? Ah! It is this dreary and apparently interminable succession of calamities that sorely tries even the best of souls. They bear one or two heavy strokes of adversity with becoming submission, and even rise to greater goodness and nobility of spirit, surely believing that their obedient response to the rod of chastisement will secure them against additional suffering. But when, in the face of their supremest efforts at submission and pious trust, the rod continues to fall with heavy stroke, it is too much for them, and they are apt to cry out despairingly, "Who is the Almighty, that we should serve him? And what profit shall we have if we pray unto him?" Even Job became confounded at the terrible succession of calamities, and the darkness about him became so dense that he could not look through it to "the *end* of the Lord," and realize that in and through all his troubles, "He was very pitiful and of tender mercy." And this terrible bereavement wrung from the poor mother's heart as she sat with her dead boy in her arms, a piteous cry: "What have I to do with thee, thou man of God? Art thou come to me to call my sin to remembrance, and to slay my son?" What a dreadful thing sin is! Away back in her life somewhere, some hideous sin had stained her soul. It had evidently wrenched her spirit terribly, and had darkened her life. But she had turned away from it, and risen above it, and almost forgotten it, Perhaps her occasional bitter remembrance of it and the humiliation of soul growing out of it had prompted her to extraordinary efforts to be good, and urged her to just such self-sacrificing virtue as we have witnessed in her conduct towards Elijah; and, as she felt that she had conquered, the bitter memory faded out, and it seemed as if the hideous sin were dead and buried forever. But here, in this awful hour, she feels herself in the clutch of the Nemesis — her sin rises up before her in all its old-time ugliness and enormity, till it wrenches from her this bitter cry. There is no escape from sin but in the covenant grace of Him who hath said, "Your sins and your iniquities will I remember no more," and who hath sealed the promise with the broad red seal of a Savior's blood. Even then, though God remember it not, the sinner, pardoned though he be, will sometimes remember it, and perhaps go mourning all his days.

Elijah took the dead lad from the frantic mother's bosom, and bore him to the upper chamber, where he dwelt. There he cried to Jehovah for the mother's sake: "O Jehovah, my God, I pray thee let this child's soul come into him again."

> *And Jehovah heard the voice of Elijah, and the soul of the child came into him again, and he revived. And Elijah took the child, and brought him down out of the chamber into the house, and delivered him unto his mother: and Elijah said, "See, thy son liveth!" And the woman said, "Now by this I know that thou art a man of God, and that the word of Jehovah in thy mouth is truth."*

Until now, her heathen superstitions and prejudices had refused to give way. But in the presence of this stupendous miracle — and as merciful as it was stupendous — she accepted Elijah as a prophet of the true God, and turned her back to Baal and all false gods. How could she doubt that only an omnipotent Hand could thus bind up her broken heart, and only a divine Heart thus provide "beauty for ashes, the oil of joy for mourning, and the garment of praise for the spirit of heaviness"? In all this there is rich compensation for her own noble self-sacrifice. "There was," as Dean Stanley says, "a rebound of unexpected benefits such as sometimes, even in the prose of common life, equals the poetic justice of an ideal world."

The Jews have a tradition that this lad afterwards waited on Elijah in his journeys, and finally became the first prophet to the heathen world — Jonah, the son of Amittai — the messenger of God to guilty Nineveh.

After more than two years spent in this humble home, during which the purposes of Jehovah had been ripening, Elijah returns to the scene of conflict.

May it ever be ours, O Lord, to catch the inspirations of a true life, like that of thy servant Elijah. Whether we are battling for the truth against mighty odds, or gently ministering to the poor and needy, fill us with lofty faith and courage for the conflict, and with benevolence and compassion for the ministries of mercy. And when we learn of the kindness of a poor heathen woman, forgetting her own distresses in the distress of a stranger, may we learn how noble an act may be the giving of a cup of cold water to the thirsty, and be taught not to scorn even the slightest deed of kindness. Though we may be poor, may our scant means be employed in doing good to others — in humble trust that our barrel of meal and our cruse of oil, though well-nigh exhausted, shall not fail.

Ahab, Jezebel, and Elijah

(1 Kings 18)

More than three years of drought had come and gone, until all the horrors of famine were felt in Ahab's dominions. Baal had brought no relief. Its terrors were felt even in the royal palace. It was in the last extremity that the king and his chief minister, Obadiah, divided the land between them, and went forth in a search for grass "to save the horses and mules alive." While Obadiah is on this search, Elijah suddenly appears to him. For two years and more they had scoured the land in search of this Gileadite prophet, and explored adjoining territories in vain; but now he voluntarily appears, and bids Obadiah to bear word to the king of his presence. It is due to Obadiah to say that, though standing so near the throne, he had been, through all temptations, true to Jehovah, and, during these terrible years, had silently supplied bread and water to a hundred of His prophets. He must have been a man of rare qualities to hold his place without compromising his faith — perhaps a man of great influence with the people, whom it was necessary to honor, in order to bind the people to the house of Omri. And it does not speak ill for Ahab — though it may do no more than indicate his indifference to a controversy that Jezebel waged so furiously — that he placed his trust in one who he must have known had no sympathy with the religion of the court. The bearing of Elijah is still stern and lofty, worthy of the representative of the Divine Majesty. He is gentle and kind with Obadiah, but to Ahab there is no complaisance. "Go, tell thy lord, Behold, Elijah is here," is all the word he has for the king. He sends no obsequious[1] message of submission; he does not even ask the privilege of appearing in the royal presence. He is here, and the king may come and see him if he will — that is all. Nor was this unseemly. He represented a King infinitely greater than Ahab, and Ahab knew it; for had not the word which Elijah had spoken been fulfilled? He held in his hand the key of power to unlock the treasures of rain, while helpless Ahab was searching every nook to obtain grass to keep his horses and mules from starvation. Ahab could not, therefore, stand

---

[1] Eagerly submissive.

on his dignity. He assumes, indeed, something of royal bluster in his harsh greeting of Elijah: "Art thou he that troubleth Israel?" But he becomes meek and submissive under Elijah's firm and bold reply: "I have not troubled Israel; but thou and thy father's house, in that ye have forsaken the commandments of Jehovah, and thou hast followed Baalim." Ahab was silent, because he knew this to be true, and he cowered before the strong, bold prophet, whose superiority he felt, and, for the time, admired. Ahab does not appear to have been a man of bad intention; but he was weak, and submissive to stronger natures. Elijah was strong, and could control Ahab when he was present with him; Jezebel was strong, and controlled him when he was under the spell of her imperious will and fiery enthusiasm. And as most of his life was spent in association with her, his conduct was largely shaped by her. Yet he no sooner comes into the presence of Elijah than Jezebel's influence wanes, and he meekly does the bidding of this "man of God." Elijah now demands that the people shall be summoned to meet him on Mount Carmel, along with the four hundred and fifty prophets or priests of Baal at Samaria, and the four hundred priests of Astarte at Jezreel. Ahab instantly complies. The people are summoned to meet the prophet of Jehovah, and the priests of Baal and Astarte are likewise summoned. The great controversy between Jehovah and Baal is to be settled. The people come, and also the four hundred and fifty priests from the temple of Baal at Samaria; but the priests of Astarte in Jezreel fail to obey the summons — probably because they are directly under Jezebel's control, and she will not expose them to danger.

Mount Carmel has many sacred associations. Its position, its beauty, the ruggedness and sublimity of its scenery, the excellence of its forests, the richness and variety of its vegetation, the salubrity[1] of its climate, and the opportunities for retirement which it afforded, made it a favorite religious resort. It is not unlikely that even in patriarchal times, or in the early history of the nation of Israel, before Jerusalem became the permanent capital, and when the worship of Jehovah on "high places" had some justification, the "altar of Jehovah" which Elijah repaired (1 Kings 18:30) had been a religious center for patriarchs or Jews — though it is possi-

---

[1] Favorable for health.

ble that it was erected by pious Jews after the worship of Baal was established in Samaria. It seems to have been a place of resort on new moons and Sabbaths (2 Kings 4:23). Elijah seems to have made it a favorite haunt, and Elisha had his abode there for a time. Pythagoras is said to have visited it; Vespasian offered sacrifices there; and to this day it is held sacred by Jews, Christians, and Moslems alike. "The excellency of Carmel" is celebrated by the prophets (Isa. 35:2, 33:9; Mic. 7:14), probably with reference to its fertility and beauty.

> *Rocky dells[1] with deep jungles of copse,[2] shrubberies thicker than any others in Central Palestine, open glades, and slopes bright with hollyhocks, jasmine, flowery creepers, and a world of blossoms, shrubs, and fragrant herbs, still delight the eye. In comparison even with the hills of Samaria, the sides of which alone were fruitful, Carmel, crowned as well as clothed with verdure,[3] was the paradise of the land.[4]*

The historical interest that gathered about it is also worthy of mention.

> *At its base was the great battle-field of sacred history — the plain of Megiddo or Jezreel; with the torrent Kishon, passing, as its name implies, in countless windings through the level valley — that 'ancient stream' on whose banks had perished the host of Sisera, and the host of Midian, before the army of Deborah and Barak, before the sword of the Lord and of Gideon.[5]*

Carmel is a mountain range running from the south end of the Bay of Acre inland in a southeast direction. It separates the plain of Esdraelon from the great southern plain along the Mediterranean. At the northwestern end it terminates in a bluff about 600 feet high, and at the southeastern end in a bluff about 1,600 feet high — the distance between these being over twelve miles. The highest

---

[1] Small valleys.
[2] Trees.
[3] Vivid green vegetation.
[4] Geikie's Hours with the Bible, Vol. 4: pp. 67-8.
[5] Stanley's *History of the Jewish Church*, Lecture 30.

point is some four miles from the east end, 1,728 feet above the sea. The place of assembly in the famous controversy between Jehovah and Baal was at the southeast end of the ridge, where a shapeless ruin, composed of great hewn stones and standing amid thick bushes of dwarf-oak in the near vicinity of a perennial spring, is known to the Arabs as El-Maharrakah, "the burning," or "the sacrifice."

> *All the circumstances of the locality adapt it for the scene of the contest. It is the part of the mountain nearest to Jezreel, which is in full sight. It is easily accessible from that place. It commands a glorious prospect over a great portion of the country of Israel. It possesses the necessary adjuncts of wood and water, and from a point near it is seen the blue water of the Mediterranean. There is every reason, therefore, to believe that tradition has for once been faithful, and that El-Maharrakah or its immediate vicinity was the site of Elijah's altar. The multitude would have found abundant room on a wide upland sweep immediately below the ruins, under the shade of ancient olives, and in the vicinity of the precious spring.*[1]

While Jezreel, at that time the royal residence, was in full view, Carmel was sufficiently distant from both Jezreel and Samaria to make it a safe place for Elijah's purpose.

There, early in the morning, the multitudes assembled at the hour when Baal was worshiped as the rising sun. There stood Ahab, in his royal dignity, with the four hundred and fifty prophets of Baal in their white, priestly robes, and the vast throngs of the apostate people of Israel. Over against these stood Elijah, arrayed in his simple tunic bound with a leather girdle, with a mantle of sheepskin over his shoulders, and his unshorn hair hanging down his back, or floating in the mountain breeze — alone, save the one servant that waited on him. It had been three years and a half since he initiated this public controversy with the corrupt and apostate court and people of Israel, and his argument had been a blaze of heat, without a cloud, under which every green thing had withered and famine had spread its terrors over all the land; and Baal had

---

[1] *Speaker's Commentary*, note on 1 Kings 18:20.

proved impotent to stay the curse. It is time that answer was made by the suffering people. Elijah, therefore, demands a decisive answer. He cries aloud to the people: "How long halt ye between two opinions?" Rather, "How long will ye limp and totter, now on one foot and then on the other?" — with sarcastic allusion to the tottering dances around the pagan altar, first on one foot and then on the other. "If Jehovah be your God, walk straight after Him; if Baal, walk straight after him."[1] "And the people answered him not a word."

Determined to force the issue, Elijah submitted this proposition: "I, even I only, remain a prophet of Jehovah [that is, he alone appeared in public in the character of a prophet], but Baal's prophets are four hundred and fifty men. Let them, therefore give us two bullocks; and let them choose one bullock for themselves, and cut it in pieces, and lay on wood, and put no fire under, and I will dress the other bullock, and lay it on wood, and put no fire under. And call ye on the name of your gods, and I will call on the name of Jehovah; and the God that answereth by fire, let him be God." This was a fair test. If Baal, the sun-God, could do anything, surely he could answer by fire at such a time as this. "And all the people answered and said, It is well spoken." So the prophets of Baal prepared their sacrifice, and cried from morning till noon, "O Baal, hear us," at the same time leaping up and down, or dancing in their peculiar fashion around the altar. "But there was no voice, nor any that answered." Then Elijah mocked them: "Cry aloud — for he is a God; either he is talking, or he is pursuing, or he is in a journey, or he is sleeping and must be awaked!" Stung to madness by Elijah's raillery, they worked themselves into a frenzy of fanatical desperation. "They cried aloud, and cut themselves, after their manner, with knives and lancets, till the blood gushed out upon them."[2] But all in vain. "When midday was past, and they prophe-

---

[1] See Stanley's *History of the Jewish Church*, Lecture 30.

[2] Modern superstition is not less absurd. Geikie quotes from Orelli, *Durch's Hezlige Land,* the following description the dance of dervishes in Egypt:

"About thirty dervishes stood in a half-circle, bowing themselves backwards and forwards with great energy to the sound of kettle-drums and cymbals. Every time they rose upright, a frightful cry broke out from each, 'Allah is good.' These were howling dervishes; but there was also a dancing dervish present. Dressed in white, he stood in the middle of the half-circle, and turned round and

sied until the time of the offering of the evening sacrifice, there was neither voice, nor any to answer, nor any that regarded." The failure was complete. The whole force of Baal's official represent-atives in Samaria, backed by the favor of the throne, had been al-lowed full sway for many hours, even to the time of the evening sacrifice, and, knowing all that was at stake in this tremendous contest, had exhausted all their power and devices; but on the wild scene of fanatical tumult and superstitious frenzy settled down the darkness of despair.

Now comes the grand contrast: the quiet dignity of Truth against the bluster and glamour of Falsehood; the calm assurance of Faith against the noisy terror of Superstition. The lone champion of Jehovah stands forth in the presence of the king, the priests of Baal, and the gazing multitude. He rebuilds the altar of Jehovah that had been thrown down by fanatical idolaters. Despite the en-mities and rivalries of Israel and Judah, he places twelve stones in the altar — a quiet but impressive testimony that all the tribes still belong to Jehovah as His chosen people and elect witnesses against idolatry. "He built an altar in the name of Jehovah" — calling out the name of Jehovah as he reared it. He made a trench round about it. In the presence of all the people he laid the wood upon the altar, and the slain sacrifice on the wood. He then had four water jars filled with water, and poured it on the sacrifice. This was thrice repeated, until the altar was drenched, and the trench filled with water. All were made to see that by no human agency could the pile be set on fire. Then, calmly and reverently approaching the

---

moved with incredible speed, his arms stretched out to the full. The sheik acted as leader to the whole. The common dervishes seemed vulgar and poor, and were variously clad. The most zealous had long hair hanging loose, which fell over their faces as they bowed, reaching to their feet; then, as they rose, flying back far behind their heads. This lasted a quarter of an hour, the rate of bowing always growing faster, and the noise more and more terrible."

"The modern dervishes," says Van Lennep, "like Baal's priests, when in their highest excitement, often cut themselves with knives and swords till they faint with loss of blood. They also pierce their almost naked bodies with wooden or iron spikes, from which they hang mirrors framed in wood."

To the dishonor of Christianity it must be confessed that excesses scarcely less degrading have not unfrequently been committed at her altars, and have been confidently appealed to as evidences of the presence and power of the Spirit of God!

altar, the prophet uttered a brief prayer in the hearing of all the people:

> *Jehovah, the God of Abraham, Isaac, and Israel, let it be known this day that Thou art God in Israel, and I Thy servant, and that I have done all these things at Thy word. Hear me, O Jehovah, hear me, that this people may know that Thou, Jehovah, art God, and that Thou hast turned their hearts back again to Thyself.*

"Then the fire of Jehovah fell, and consumed the burnt sacrifice, and the wood, and the stones, and the dust, and licked up the water that was in the trench." The answer was immediate. The demonstration was complete. The verdict of the nation was promptly rendered. All the people fell on their faces and cried: "Jehovah, He is God! Jehovah, He is God!" The lone prophet of Jehovah becomes, for the moment, absolute sovereign of king, priests, and people. Ahab is utterly passive. The priests of Baal are paralyzed. The people at large flock to Jehovah's banner. "Take the prophets of Baal," commands Elijah, "let not one of them escape." Instantly these persecuting minions of Jezebel, who had slaughtered the prophets of Jehovah, are seized and hurried down the mountain slopes to the gorge of the Kishon, where, either by Elijah's own hand, or by his authority, they are slain, and their bodies tumbled into the channel of the Kishon, to be carried out to the sea by the torrents which the approaching storm will soon create. Returning to the mountain summit, Elijah spreads the feast which properly follows a sacrifice; and Ahab, awed into submission, sits down meekly among the participants. But Elijah did not pause to eat and drink. Ascending still farther towards the loftiest summit of Carmel, with his servant, he "cast himself down to the earth" on the slope of the hill, "and put his face between his knees," in an intensity of prayer. Jehovah, who has already answered by fire, is now to answer by *water,* and thus double the demonstration that He is indeed the living God, commanding all the forces of nature. When Israel turned away from Jehovah, the treasures of rain were locked up, and for three years and a half the land had been burned and blasted with drought. Now that the people have turned back to Jehovah, the treasures of rain are to be unlocked, that all the land may know that it is He who answers by fire and by rain. "Go up now, look toward the sea," said Elijah to his servant. The servant ascended to the crest of the hill, and looked out on the sea. But, in the calm evening twilight, the sky was cloudless, and the sea unruffled. He returned and reported, "There is nothing." Seven times was this repeated. After the seventh outlook came the glad report, "Behold, there ariseth a little cloud out of the sea, like a man's hand" — the well-known token, in the Levant,[1] of an approaching storm. Ahab is promptly admonished to mount his chariot and hurry to Jezreel, while the prophet, snatching up his mantle, and girding him with his leather belt, with the fleetness he had learned in his native wilds, ran ahead of the royal chariot through the storm with which the night set in, to the entrance of Jezreel — a distance of some sixteen miles. He thus gave the king to understand that he would stand by him through darkness and storm, if he would but return to the ways of Jehovah. But he only went to "the entrance of Jezreel." He would not trust himself within its walls until he learned the effect of this day's mighty revolution on the purposes of Jezebel. So he vanished in the darkness at the gate of the city, to await tidings from the proud and vindictive queen — the *de facto* ruler of the kingdom — on whose idolatrous ambition the events of the day would come like an avalanche with crushing power. Exultant, yet anxious; grandly victorious, yet faint and weary; the glory of the day's triumphs somewhat overshadowed by fears of the furious Jezebel, Elijah sought a hiding-place, and waited for the dawning of a new day.

How glorious, O Lord, are the victories of thy truth! Deliver us from all cowardice, and increase our faith in Thy presence and Thy power to save them that trust in thee. Let us learn that in Thy blessed service one shall chase a thousand, and two put ten thousand to flight. Enable us not only to fight Thy battles courageously, but to persevere in prayer until, in Thine own time, Thou shalt answer us. Blessed are they that put their trust in Thee.

---

[1] The Eastern Mediterranean region.

Ahab, Jezebel, and Elijah (Part Two)

(1 Kings 19 — 2 Kings 2)

Perhaps the most emphatic testimony to the terror of Jezebel's name is found in the conduct of Elijah. The only timorousness this daring man ever exhibited was caused by this fierce tigress. Ahab he could awe into submission. Without a tremor he could stand alone against four hundred and fifty priests of Baal. He faced the representatives of the whole nation of Israel unblenched by fear. But Jezebel he uniformly shunned. He never came into her presence. Even after the overwhelming victory at Carmel, though Ahab was obsequious[1] to his every word, he feared to pass within the gates of Jezreel — for Jezebel was there; he waited outside the walls to learn whether at last her haughty and vindictive spirit would yield. And it must be confessed that there is a sublimity of courage in her wickedness. Baal dishonored, four hundred and fifty of his priests slain, Ahab subdued, the nation turned back to Jehovah, the living presence and power of Jehovah vindicated unmistakably by drought and famine, fire and flood, and the splendid fabric of idolatry which she had reared tottering to its foundations — she yet stands erect even when Ahab and Baal are prostrate, as fierce and relentless as ever, and promptly sends a defiant and murderous message to Elijah: "So let the gods do to me, and more also, if I make not *thy* life as the life of one of them tomorrow about this time." The tremendous battle between Jehovah and Baal is concentrated into a single-handed contest between the stern prophet of Gilead and the imperious daughter of Ethbaal — and Elijah runs for his life, leaving Jezebel mistress of the field! We do not suppose that she was sincere in her threat. Had she meant to murder him, she would not have announced to him her purpose; but she hoped to terrify him into flight, that the land might be rid of his tormenting presence — and she succeeded.

It may be strange, and even startling, that as fearless a man as Elijah should, in the very flush of victory, betake himself to ignominious[2] flight. But a careful consideration of all the circumstances

---

[1] Submissive.

[2] Shameful, a total loss of dignity and self-respect.

will remove much of the mystery.

(1) He had good reasons to fear the implacable vengeance of this haughty, cruel, and unscrupulous queen. She was the chief support of the idolatrous system he had so fiercely and triumphantly assailed. For years he had been hiding from her vengeance. He had just completed an overwhelming demonstration of the impotence of her gods — a demonstration that shook the very foundations of the great temple she had reared to Astarte, and made her throne to tremble. If this did not break her haughty spirit, his power was exhausted. He knew that "hell hath no fury like a woman scorned," and that the terrible defeat of Baal at Carmel did not cause her to relent, her revengefulness would be fiercer than ever.

(2) His nature was impetuous. His force was the force of a mountain torrent that spends itself, and ceases. Everything must be borne down before his impetuous charge, and yield to his fiery zeal. It seemed to him that after the mighty demonstration at Carmel, king, queen, court, and people should all have surrendered without farther opposition. He evidently dared to hope for this. He did not expect such a message, even from Jezebel; and he did expect that the people would flock around him and hold up his hands. But this bloody message came to him from Jezebel; and the people, although he had them under his spell at Carmel, showed no signs of rallying to his support. There were no symptoms of an uprising. His impetuous nature could not brook such treatment.

(3) It is important to note the great reaction in his own feelings. He had been wrought up to the highest pitch of excitement, and, tough as he was, his nervous system had been taxed to the utmost. He accordingly sank to a corresponding depth of weakness and discouragement when the reaction came. He was in no mood to reason. He was swayed by the emotions of the hour. *This sudden swing of the feelings from one extreme to another is always perilous.* Coming at such a time, the threat of Jezebel assumed, to him, the awfulest proportions and the most terrible aspect.

(4) Elijah had had little to do with courts or courtiers. All that he knew about them was bad. He feared and detested them. He was no diplomatist. He loved solitude and the scenes of nature, and more now than ever, since his mighty achievement had failed to accomplish its purpose.

(5) Elijah had his gift — but it was destructive, not construc-

tive. It did not belong to him to parley with kings, and circumvent the treacheries of queens, and plod patiently through years of apparently fruitless effort to recover the people from their errors. The fiery prophet had but one mission, and his greatness lay in one path of achievement.

He arose in haste and fled for his life, accompanied only by his faithful servant, a distance of some ninety miles, pausing not until he had reached the extreme southern border of Judah! Even here he did not tarry; for Jehoshaphat, king of Judah, was on terms of close alliance with Ahab (1 Ki. 22:14), and might deliver him up; so, dismissing his servant, he went yet a day's journey into the wilderness southward before he paused to rest. Here, utterly exhausted, he laid down under the shade of a broom-shrub,[1] and prayed that he might die! He fell asleep, and was awakened by the touch of a messenger — whether a human or celestial messenger does not concern us here — who pointed him to a cake and a cruse of water, and bade him arise and refresh himself. He ate and drank, and again sank into slumber, so very weary was he. Again the messenger roused him, and bade him eat a second time; and on the strength of that food he went forty days, until he came to Horeb, the mount of God. Horeb was only 170 miles distant, so that he did not make a straight journey to that point. He wandered about aimlessly, loving to be alone, fond of desert scenes, indulging his gloomy and discouraged spirit within these lonely surroundings. His wasted energies could best be recuperated by a return to his native habit of wandering alone in Nature's solitudes. "Grand, gloomy, and peculiar" in spirit and in character, he came at last in his wanderings to Horeb — to the sublime scenery in the midst of which Jehovah had pronounced that Law which he had sought in vain to restore; and, entering a cave, laid him down to rest. It is reasonable to suppose that his stern spirit reveled in the sublime memories of Horeb. The crashing thunders, "the sound of trumpet and voice of words" accompanying the delivery of the law — so

---

[1] It is agreed now on all hands that the tree here mentioned (the rothem) is not the juniper, but a species of broom (Genista monasperma); called retkem by the Arabs, which abounds in the Sinitic peninsula. It grows to such a size as to afford shade and protection, both in heat and storm, to travelers — *Speaker's Com.*

terrible that even Moses said, "I do exceedingly fear and quake" —
would be delightful music to Elijah's tempestuous soul; the terrific
lightnings would be hailed as the flashes of the all-seeing Eye;
while his restless spirit would heave with the earthquake that shook
the mountain, and exult in the overpowering terrors that accompanied the proclamation of the fiery law. Whether the vision that
came to him was in his waking or his sleeping hours, makes little
difference; the way was prepared for it by the gloomy perturba-
tions of his own mind, and the flashes of a disturbed conscience
that now and then broke in upon his fierce mental denunciations of
an apostate nation. His mind would naturally revert to the time
when Moses received the law, and to the history of this rebellious
people from that day to his own; to the faithfulness of Moses in
interceding for them; and to his own failure and flight — coming
to the Mount of God not like Moses, in discharge of a great duty,
but in flight from the field of duty and of danger. Falling asleep in
this gloomy and troubled mood, it would not be strange if, even
without the slightest touch of the supernatural, he should be confronted with such a dream.

A solemn voice breaks on the stillness of the night: "What
doest thou here, Elijah?" If it came in his sleep, it reveals a conscience ill at ease; if a revelation in his waking hours, it was designed to startle his conscience. The answer is somewhat circui-
tous. "I have been very jealous for Jehovah, God of hosts; for the
children of Israel have forsaken thy covenant, thrown down thine
altars, and slain thy prophets with the sword, and I, even I only, am
left, and they seek my life, to take it away." Instead of telling what
he is doing *there* — under what authority he had fled to that hiding
place — he proceeds with a sorrowful story of what *they* have
done. It is *they—they—they,* all the way through. Thus it is that,
when we are wrong ourselves, we try to hide our *own* faults behind
a bold array of the faults of *others.* He is invited forth to the mountain side; but while he stands at the mouth of the cave, the terrific
scenes at the giving of the law are reproduced . A fearful hurricane
came rushing through the gorges of the mountain, and tossed and
whirled the granite rocks like playthings in the air, and then sent
them crashing and thundering down the mountain side. The prophet looked and listened, but he saw no sign of that presence of Jehovah for which his spirit yearned, nor did he detect any voice such

as he longed to hear. His heart was untouched. *God was not in the tempest.* Then came the heavings of an earthquake, causing the mountain to nod and tremble, until it seemed as if the mighty granite masses would be broken and the lofty mountain peaks would topple over and go crashing down with thunderous power. But in all this wild scene of tumultuous upheaval, the prophet detected no sign of the Presence he so much needed. *God was not in the earthquake.* Then came the fearful peals of a thunderstorm, and vivid lightnings that played among the mountain crags and spread in broad sheets over the mountain side, until it seemed as if the whole mountain was on fire; but He who had answered by fire on Mount Carmel gave no token of His presence in the tremendous blaze. The heart of Elijah remained untouched. *God was not in the fire.* And then succeeded a great stillness, such as settles down on that peculiar region, broken by no sound of waterfall, or voice of bird, or low of cattle, or bleating of sheep, or human speech; and on that stillness there stole "a still small voice" — a whisper as gentle and tender as love itself — which caught the ear and penetrated the dark, cold heart of the prophet, and thrilled it with a power so sweet that he hailed it as indeed the voice of Jehovah; and, wrapping his face in his mantle in token of reverence and worship, he obeyed the summons to come forth and stand upon the mount before the Lord. *God was in the still small voice.*

What lessons are here! How far Elijah penetrated their meaning, we may not know. Perhaps he never fully comprehended their import until, standing on another mount with Moses and Jesus, he talked with them of the death that Jesus was to accomplish at Jerusalem, and the conquering might of the "still small voice" of redeeming love that should go forth from Calvary (Luke 9:30-31). But to us, standing in the full light of the gospel, there is immense significance in this scene at Horeb. Let us briefly suggest some of its lessons:

1. Consider it as a reproduction of the scene at the giving of the law. In this view, the lesson is, that *the law is not the most winning and effectual revelation of Jehovah;* that there were other and greater revelations of God to come, of which the law given at Sinai was but the precursor; and that even as Elijah had not bowed his heart or hid his face in the presence of the tempest, the earthquake, and the fire, as he did when he heard the "still small voice," so

human hearts everywhere would yet be won by sweeter revelations of love and mercy, though they had failed to yield to the thunders and the terrors of the "fiery law."

2. Elijah was himself, in his spirit and his work, the exponent of the law's majesty, sternness and terribleness. Because this did not succeed, he thought nothing would succeed. This scene taught him — taught him so that his own heart knew it — that Jehovah's resources were not exhausted; and that, after his stern and terrible mission had done its work, it would be succeeded by other missions of less phenomenal grandeur and awfulness, but really of greater power.

3. Perhaps the more immediate interpretation, for Elijah's own benefit, would be that suggested by Dean Stanley:

> *The queen with fire and sword, the splendid temples of Jezreel and Samaria, the whole nation gone astray after her, seemed to be on one side, and the solitary Prophet in the solitary wilderness, on the other side. So it seemed; but so it was not. Nor was He in the power and grandeur of the State or Church of Israel. Deep down in the heart of the nation, in the caves of Carmel, unknown to him, unknown to each other, are seven thousand who had not, by word or deed, acknowledged the power of Baal. In them God was still present.*
>
> *It is farther a revelation to Elijah, not only concerning himself and the world, but concerning God also. He himself had shared in the outward manifestations of divine favor which appear to mark the Old Dispensation — the fire on Carmel, the storm from the Mediterranean, the avenging sword on the banks of the Kishon. These signs had failed; and he was now told that in these signs, in the highest sense, God was not; not in these, but in the still, small, gentle whisper of conscience and solitude was the sweet token that God was near him. Nay, not in his own mission, grand and gigantic as it was, would after ages so clearly discern the divine inspiration, as in the still small voice of justice and truth that breathed through the writings of the later prophets, for whom he only prepared the way — Hosea, Amos, Micah, Isaiah, and Jeremiah. Not in*

the vengeance which through Hazael and Jehu was to sweep away the house of Omri, so much as in the discerning love which was to spare the seven thousand; not in the strong east wind that parted the Red Sea, or the fire that swept the top of Sinai, or the earthquake that shook down the walls of Jericho, would God be brought so near to man, as in the still small voice of the child at Bethlehem, as in the ministrations of Him whose cry was not heard in the streets, in the awful stillness of the cross, in the never-failing order of Providence, in the silent sensible influence of good deeds and good words of God and of man.[1]

The lessons suggested by this study can only be hinted at here.

1. *The danger of violent reaction.* — Let us be watchful in times of great excitement. The soul is peculiarly susceptible to temptation when reaction sets in. We may lose in an hour what we have struggled for years to gain.

2. *The might of gentleness* — the superiority of love over wrath.

3. *The preciousness of the still small voice of the gospel*, as compared with the tempest and thunder and earthquake of a fiery law.

4. The lesson everywhere taught in Nature and Society of the superior power of gentle, silent forces, such as air, light, gravitation, etc.

5. *The danger and sin of yielding to fear*, even in the darkest hours. How many, like Elijah, while contending for truth and right, have been left apparently alone — the battle gone against them, and the defeat apparently total — when, in fact, as the result proved, there were thousands that sympathized with them, and the enemy that appeared invincible finally melted away into weakness and nothingness.

Elijah went back to active life a humbler and a stronger man. He had learned that the case was by no means so desperate as he had supposed; that God could conquer through very feeble instrumentalities and that none has a right to give up the contest for truth and righteousness — for even the gentlest whisper of truth has

---

[1] *The History of the Jewish Church*, Lecture 30.

more might and endurance in it than all the might of material forces arrayed in behalf of error and wrong.

We beseech Thee, our Heavenly Father, to write upon our
hearts the lessons of Thy word. When the bold, brave Elijah gives
way in the hour of trial, may we watch and pray, that we enter not
into temptation. What weak creatures we are at best! We would
adore that mercy and compassion that bear with us in our weakness. Especially may we learn to confide more and more in the
might of gentleness, and to bless Thee for that still small voice of
Love that conquers when the tempest and the fire and the earthquake fail. Bring us, O Lord, under the dominion of Thy love.

Ahab, Jezebel, and Elijah (Part Three)

During the following years of Elijah's life, from the time he hid in the wilderness of Damascus (1 Ki. 19:15), he seldom appears to public view. It was a transition period from the sternness and terror of his ministry to the gentler and more patient ministry of Elisha. In his retirement he enjoyed the companionship of Elisha (1 Ki. 19:21), whose milder and more cheerful spirit doubtless asserted a soothing and cheering influence over his own imperious and gloomy nature. Elijah was a pessimist; Elisha, an optimist. While bound to each other by a common loyalty to Jehovah, each found in the other what was lacking in himself; so that their friendship was mutually helpful.

We cannot suppose that Elijah was idle or listless during these ten or twelve years. From hints scattered here and there in the narrative, we infer that he busied himself in reorganizing the schools of the prophets, which had existed from Samuel's time (1 Sam. 19:18-24), and which had been broken up by the persecutions of Jezebel. The existence of such schools at Gilgal, Beth-el, and Jericho (2 Ki. 2), and their recognition of the supreme authority of Elijah, as afterwards of that of Elisha (2 Ki. 2:15), sufficiently indicate the work in which he had been engaged during these years of obscurity. He doubtless perceived that the "still small voice" of truth, uttered from house to house, and at the religious retreats, such as that at Carmel (2 Ki. 4:22-25), and spoken now and then, in the ears of kings and courtiers (2 Ki. 3:12-14; 1 Ki. 22:1-28), was hereafter to be relied on as the power of God, rather than the fierce judgments on which he had hitherto depended; and he therefore busied himself in training a company of prophets, alike from Israel and Judah, who should, after his departure, teach the law of God to the people, and rebuke sin and wrong in high places. These disciples were trained to the same self-denial and asceticism of the Nazarites by which Elijah himself had been distinguished (Amos 1:11). It is even regarded as probable that it was through Elijah's influence that the Rechabites were placed under such strict regulations by their chief, Jehonadab (2 Ki. 10:15; Jer. 35:1-11). It is not improbable that everything in that corrupt age which bore the stamp of self-denial, righteousness, or piety, was encouraged and fostered, if not inspired, by this zealous prophet of Jehovah.

Twice, during this period, he flashes out upon us in the old spirit.

Ahab and Jezebel had, most unjustly and cruelly, extirpated[1] the family of Naboth, that they might seize his coveted property, adjoining the royal gardens in Jezreel (1 Ki. 21). It was an appalling outrage. When Elijah learned of it, his righteous spirit flamed with indignation, and he hastened to Jezreel, to face once more the guilty king. Ahab had hastened from Samaria, to take possession of the coveted vineyard; but the avenger was on his path — for Elijah hastened from Carmel, that he might meet the guilty monarch in the very act of taking possession of the territory purchased by falsehood, perjury, and murder — and suddenly wither his wicked joy by a blast of righteous indignation (1 Ki. 21:16-24). When Ahab arrived, Elijah was there, in the deserted vineyard of Naboth, ready to confront him, and blast his impious joy with words of fierce rebuke and predictions of an awful fate. The utter extirpation of his house, the king's own sad doom, and the awful fate of Jezebel, were predicted in words so burning and indignant, that Jehu and Bidkar, who attended the king, were evermore haunted by them, and, many years afterward, repeated them as familiar words, whose vividness was not lost, even amidst the furious excitements of the terrible hour of their repetition (2 Ki. 9:25-26). They were words that penetrated the hardened conscience of Ahab more effectively than any he had heard before — insomuch that he "rent his clothes, and put sackcloth on his flesh, and fasted, and lay in sackcloth, and went softly." As far as a nature so perverted was capable of repentance, this was evidently a sincere repentance; for the Lord said concerning it, "Seest thou how Ahab humbleth himself before me? Because he humbleth himself before me, I will not bring the evil in his days" (1 Ki. 31:27-29). It is refreshing to catch even this gleam of repentance — for it is but a gleam; his subsequent conduct shows that he soon relapsed into his evil ways, and illustrates the extreme difficulty of repentance after so long a life of opposition to the will of God.

Three or four years after this, when Ahab was dead, and his son Ahaziah was on the throne, Elijah made his last appearance to the

---

[1] Removed as undesireable.

house of Omri. Ahaziah had received an injury that threatened his life. With an insult to Jehovah more daring than any of which his father had been guilty, he ignored utterly the prophets of the Lord, and sent to Ekron to inquire of a heathen oracle as to his chances of recovery. Elijah, divinely forewarned, met the messengers on their way to Ekron — probably at Mt. Carmel — and turned them back toward Samaria, to tell the king that, because of this insult to Jehovah, he should surely die. But Jezebel was still living, and, with her manipulation, a message from the hated Elijah could only stir up wrath. It was known from the messenger's description of "the hairy man with a girdle of leather about his loins," that the message had come from Elijah the Tishbite, whose shadow still lay across the pathway of the guilty house of Omri. Unawed even by the terrible memories of the overthrow of Baal at Carmel, the king sent a troop to arrest Elijah; but Jehovah was still the God that answered by fire. The fire of God came down from heaven and consumed the captain and his fifty. A second captain with his troop met a similar fate. The third captain with his troop only escaped by persuading Elijah to go with him to Samaria. Approaching the royal presence, he only repeated the message he had previously sent. So overawed was the king by the fearless spirit and the stern message of the prophet, that Elijah went forth unharmed (2 Ki. 1). Perhaps no more striking exhibition of the contrast between the earthquake, fire, and tempest, and the still small voice — between the spirit of the law and the spirit of the Gospel — is to be found, than in the use made of this terrible incident by our Lord (Luke 9:51-56).

Only one other instance of Elijah's proceedings during the closing years of his ministry is preserved. Jehoram, sort of Jehoshaphat, married a daughter of Ahab and Jezebel, and as a result Jerusalem and Judah were overrun with the abominations of Baal worship. Elijah pursues this iniquity even to the court of Judah, sending a writing to the king to rebuke him for his treachery to Jehovah, and to warn him of his doom (2 Chron. 21:12-15).[1]

---

[1] This is a puzzle to many, since, according to the chronology in 1 Kings, Elisha was translated before Jehoram began to reign. But, either Jehoram was associated with his father on the throne for several years, according to 1 Ki. 8:16; or, the translation of Elijah is narrated out of its chronological order, and he lived

At length the toilsome and perilous mission of Elijah came to an end. The narrative of his departure is singular and thrilling. Aware that his end was near, though not, perhaps, aware of the way in which his mission was to close, he made a last visit to the various schools of the prophets, to give his last counsels to, and bestow his last benedictions upon, the disciples to whom he looked as a forlorn hope — the last reserved force for the recovery of apostate Israel and Judah. He had a longing to revisit the scenes of his youth, and to rove once more, *alone,* through the solitudes of Gilead, so dear to his heart, so sweetly contrasting, in their peace and beauty, with the turbulent and perilous scenes of his public life. But Elisha clung to him, crossed the Jordan with him, and followed him until the horses and chariot of fire appeared, and "Elijah went up by a whirlwind into heaven" — a fitting close to his tempestuous career. It had been fire and whirlwind all along his path. At his birth, the Jewish legends say "he was wrapped in swaddling bands of fire, and fed on flame." During the whole of his career, "he rose up as a fire, and his words blazed as a torch" (Ecclesiasticus 47:1).[1] "In fire and tempest, as the representative of the fiery Law," and the stern executor of its terrible judgments, he had exulted; and these lend their sublimities to his triumphal translation. Horses, and chariots of fire, and a whirlwind, are grand accompaniments of his departure (2 Ki. 2:1-15). We hear of him no more until, on another mountain, he appears in glory, to talk with Jesus of His coming death (Luke 9:28-35), and to learn, more fully than ever before, how the mission of redeeming love — the still small voice — excels in power and in glory the stern mission of Law, with its earthquake, fire, and tempest.

What remains to be said of Ahab must be said in few words. We have already referred to the infamy enacted at Jezreel. The situation of Jezreel gave it free play of the sea-breezes from the Mediterranean, which Samaria did not enjoy; hence the former city became the royal summer residence. Ahab, to enlarge the area of his gardens, desired to purchase the adjoining patrimony of Naboth;

---

longer than is generally supposed.

[1] Ecclesiasticus is a book contained in the Apocrypha, which are included in Catholic versions of the Bible.

and, failing to obtain it, pouted and sulked like a spoiled child. He had been pampered and indulged from infancy, and he lacked the strong will, even in full manhood, to practice the least self-denial. It is a humiliating spectacle — a man and a sovereign throwing himself petulantly on his couch, and turning his face to the wall, as if some great calamity had overtaken him, refusing to eat and becoming sick with disappointment, all because his neighbor refused to sell to him the inheritance of his fathers — just as a child might fret because it could not get some other child's ball, or top, or doll! And then, when Jezebel proposes to obtain, by fraud, perjury, and murder, the coveted vineyard, he meanly and basely consents, without one word of objection or protest, merely taking himself out of the way to Samaria, that he might not be personally implicated in the crime. And when the terrible outrage has been wrought — when the blameless Naboth has been fraudulently charged with crime, and worthless wretches have perjured themselves for hire, and the still more base officials have, in base subserviency, pronounced sentence against the innocent, and Naboth and his family have been cruelly murdered, and Jezebel sends word to her husband to come and possess the coveted land, Ahab, tickled and exultant as a child with the offer of a new toy, comes back from Samaria to enjoy the fruits of a crime he was too cowardly to commit. No words at our command are sufficient to express the detestation due to such a character. There may be some admiration of the fearlessness and energy of Jezebel, even in the commission of infamous crimes; but for this selfish weakling, sneaking into the possession of a prize won by violence and crime to which he consented, but which he lacked the courage to commit — there can be nothing but contempt and loathing. There are few more detestable instances of littleness, meanness and baseness on record.

There is some little relief to the blackness of this character in what remains to be told of Ahab. We have already referred to the gleam of repentance over these infamous crimes. Let the most charitable interpretation be put upon it — for the selfish, cowardly wretch needs the benefit of the largest charity. It may be that it was not all a selfish sorrow over the doom pronounced against him. Let us try to accept it as a gratifying evidence that conscience was not utterly deadened — that there was at least a spark of genuine contrition. In our ignorance of the human heart, it is better to judge charitably.

When he went forth to battle against Syria (1 Ki. 21), early in the fight Ahab received a mortal wound, but he would not let it be known. He bravely stayed himself up in his chariot until the evening. This indicates that he was not lacking in personal courage — that on this great occasion he could suppress his childish weakness and rise to the demands of the emergency. Yet it may be that, believing Elijah's prophecy to be true, "In the place where the dogs licked the blood of Naboth, shall dogs lick thy blood, even thine" (1 Ki. 21:19), he was convinced that he could not die at Ramoth-gilead; and that this was the secret of his manly bearing on this occasion. But let us give him credit for all the virtue that can possibly be claimed for him; for, after we have done all this, there is so much that is weak, little, selfish, odious, and contemptible in his character that we can look on it only with disgust and abhorrence. The curse pronounced on him by Elijah was withdrawn in view of his repentance (1 Ki. 21:29); yet, in view of his after wickedness in the treatment of Micaiah, and his stubborn rejection of divine counsel, the curse was essentially fulfilled at Samaria, if not at Jezreel. His life went out in darkness, in an hour of overwhelming defeat and disaster, and "the dogs licked up his blood."

The part taken by Jezebel in the Jezreel tragedy leaves her character without one redeeming trait, except that of decision and energy. Selfish, false, ambitious, idolatrous, cruel, murderous, deaf to every voice of innocence, humanity, truth and justice, she showed herself capable of any and every crime against God and man. She was a monster of iniquity, hideous in her inhumanities and impieties, but sublime in her unconquerable energy of will. Though she triumphed long in her iniquities, and the twenty-two years of Ahab's assumed reign were in fact all years of *her* reign of cruelty and treachery, the long-sleeping judgment of Jehovah awoke against her at last. That which Elijah was not allowed to perform, Jehu was anointed to accomplish — and he accomplished it with a vengeance inspired by his personal knowledge of the hideous iniquities of this fierce and unscrupulous idolatress. He was present when Ahab came to Jezreel to take possession of Naboth's vineyard, and knew the whole story of that terrible tragedy; and he had never forgotten it. Jehu, with his guard, came to Jezreel. Jehoram the king, son of Ahab, was slain "in the portion of Naboth the Jezreelite," and his body was then given to the vultures and the dogs; Ahaziah, king of Judah, son-in-law of Ahaz and Jezebel, received a mortal wound; and Jehu pushed on to the gates of Jezreel. Jezebel, learning of His approach, "painted her face, and tired her head, and looked out at a window" of the watch-tower. She who had been so accustomed to conquer, relied on her arts and wiles to conquer even now. Recalling the victory of Omri over the usurper Zimri (1 Ki. 16:8-20), she cried out "Had Zimri peace, who slew his master?" She sought to appall him by recalling the fate of the treacherous Zimri. But Jehu, commissioned of God, could only be enraged by this comparison of him to a treacherous wretch. He looked up, and said, "Who is on my side? Who?" Two or three eunuchs of the palace looked out in response to the inquiry. Not even within the royal household had this "cursed woman" a friend left.

"Throw her down," cried Jehu; and they hurled her from the high window of the tower. She fell between the palace and the chariot of Jehu, and her blood splashed upon the wall of the palace, and upon the horses as they advanced to crush her under their hoofs. Jehu and his company entered the palace, and gave themselves to feasting and merriment. When this was over, the conqueror bethought him of Jezebel's disgraceful exposure to vulgar gaze, and said, "Go: see now to this cursed woman, and bury her; for she is a king's daughter." "And they went to bury her; but they found no more of her than the skull, and the feet, and the palms of her hands" — the dogs had "eaten Jezebel in the portion of Jezreel," according to the word of Elijah (2 Ki. 9:30-37). Retribution, though slow, was sure.

> "Because sentence against an evil work is not executed speedily, therefore the heart of the sons of men is fully set in them to do evil. Though a sinner do evil a hundred times, and his days be prolonged, yet surely I know it shall be well with them that fear God; but it shall not be well with the wicked, neither shall he prolong his days, which are as a shadow; because he feareth not before God" (Eccles. 8:11-13).

Let it never be forgotten that God's judgments are sure.

If we have lingered long over this thrilling history of Elijah, Ahab, and Jezebel, it is because their lives belong to a tremendous crisis in the history of Israel — a crisis sure to bring out prominent actors in bold relief, and to furnish striking examples of righteousness and of iniquity, such as will give clear insight into the workings of human nature under the strongest impulses, whether for evil or for good. Not what we are, but what our nature is *capable of becoming,* in glory or in infamy, is the great lesson to be learned.

O, God of righteousness, may we so partake of Thy Spirit as to be ever indignant at wrong. When we see the dreadful end of the wicked, may we learn to abhor that which is evil; and when we behold the final triumph of the righteous, may we learn to cleave to that which is good. In the sublime victory granted to Elijah at the end of his toilsome and anxious but faithful life, and in the dreadful fall of Ahab and Jezebel, may we learn to adore that mercy which never fails to those that do Thy will, and that justice which is sure to be visited on those who despise Thy counsels.

A Great Woman

(Read 1 Kings 4:8-37, 8:1-6)

Having dwelt so long on the hideous character of Jezebel, it may be a relief, before we proceed to sketch the character of Elisha, to produce the portrait of another woman whose character stands in glorious contrast with that of the daughter of Ethbaal.

Her name is unknown. She is described simply as "the Shunammite," her home being in the humble village of Shunem, on the southern slope of Little Hermon, commanding a splendid view of the plain of Esdraelon, and Mount Carmel. It was a place so humble that all that is known of it can be expressed in a few brief sentences. It has a melancholy interest as the camping ground of the Philistines before the last great battle with Saul, so fatal to the king of Israel, his family and his throne. But it is indebted, for the immortality of its name, to this noble though nameless woman, whose virtues are embalmed in the sacred narrative.

She is called "a great woman." How much was intended to be expressed in that phrase, it is difficult to say. It is used to signify the possession of large wealth (1 Sam. 25:2; 2 Sam. 19:32); and it may mean no more here. The phrase is expressive of the power of wealth as sufficient of itself to entitle its possessor to greatness, although, in all other respects, he may be entitled only to execration.[1] In the first passage above quoted, it is applied to a man who had nothing but riches to recommend him. He was "churlish and evil in his doings" — a selfish, ungrateful, drunken wretch — "such a son of Belial that a man cannot speak to him;" of whom his wife, Abigail, was compelled to say, "Fool is his name, and folly is with him" (1 Sam. 25:3, 17, 25). Yet this odious churl,[2] universally despised, was "very great," because he had 3,000 sheep, and 1,000 goats. Sheep and goats were more than brains or a righteous character. It is so, alas, even now. This worship of Mammon is the most intense and universal of any worship, even in so-called Christian lands! Wealth covers more sins than charity ever did.

If this were her only title to greatness, the Shunammite is only

---

[1] A curse.
[2] Bad-mannered person.

one of a large company of women whose lives are warnings rather than encouragements. Cleopatra was "very great" in this respect, and, in addition, was possessed of a bright intellect; yet her name is covered with infamy. Look at the display of her greatness in her voyage to Tarsus, and her entertainment of Antony:

> *The tackling silk, the streamers waved with gold,*
> *The gentle winds were lodged in purple sails.*
> *Her nymphs, like Nereids, round her couch were placed,*
> *Where she, another sea-born Venus, lay.*
> *She lay and leaned her check upon her band,*
> *And cast a look so languishingly sweet,*
> *As if, secure of all beholders' hearts,*
> *Neglecting she could take them. Boys, like Cupids,*
> *Stood fanning with their painted wings the winds*
> *That played about her face; but if she smiled,*
> *A darting glory seemed to blaze abroad,*
> *That man's desiring eyes were never weaned,*
> *But hung upon the object! To soft flutes*
> *The silver oars kept time; and while they played,*
> *The hearing gave new pleasure to the sight,*
> *And both to thought. 'Twas heaven, or somewhat more:*
> *For she so charmed all hearts, that gazing crowds*
> *Stood panting on the shore, and wanted breath*
> *To give their welcome voice.*[1]

The feast to which, after her arrival at Tarsus, she invited Antony, was of such luxury and magnificence, that language is taxed to its utmost wealth of expression to describe it. So overpowering was the display, that the power and majesty of Rome, in the person of Antony, was prostrate at her feet. And yet — who covets the fame of Cleopatra? Her history and her tragic fate are read only as warnings of the utter vanity of the greatness of wealth and power. Better to live and die in the little village of Shunem, and leave no name — no heritage but the undying memory of virtue and piety.

> *O, what is woman, what her smile,*
> *Her lip of love, her eye of light?*

---

[1] Dryden

What is she, if her lips revile
The lowly Jesus? Love may write
His name upon her marble brow,
Or linger in her curls of jet;
The bright spring flowers may scarcely bow
Beneath her step; and yet — and yet,
Without that meeker grace, she'll be
A lighter thing than vanity.

We have intimated that we are not certain that wealth was all that was to be indicated in the expression, "a great woman," as applied to the Shunammite. The Chaldee gives, as the sense of the phrase, a *woman fearing sin;* and the Arabic, *a woman eminent for piety before God.* But, whatever sense it may express, it must, with a due regard to Scripture usage, be taken to *include* the idea of wealth. According to the standard of wealth in that neighborhood, she was rich — capable of indulging in comfort and luxury to an extent which poverty forbade to most if not all of her neighbors, and receiving their respect and homage as being much their superior in worldly condition.

It is important to note this element of greatness. Wealth gives power. It practically frees its possessor from the obligation to respect the conventionalities to which others are rigidly held. Nabal could despise the opinion of others, because he was "very great" in his wealth. The rich are largely a law to themselves, and, to a considerable extent, a law to others. Those who are inferior in wealth, wait upon their steps, ape their ways, and echo their opinions. "The poor useth entreaties; but the rich answereth roughly" (Prov. 18:23). Wealth becomes, therefore, a test of character. When it is made tributary to virtue, righteousness, and benevolence, it indicates the possession of incorrupt principles of humanity and piety, entitling the possessor to a real greatness which cannot be so readily awarded to the virtuous poor, who are held to right ways by a necessity which it is not safe to despise.

Let us see, then, what we can gather, from this brief narrative, as to the character of this Shunammite:

1. She lived to do good to others. — The instance which is recorded must be taken as typical. It is not given as a solitary and exceptional fact, but rather as the natural outflow of a benevolent heart. The prophet Elisha, in his official peregrinations,[1] frequently passed through Shunem. He was dependent on the good will of the people, wherever he went, for food and shelter; and, in that corrupt time, when the nation was fearfully demoralized by Baalism, there were none too many who cared to show kindness to a public enemy of Baal. Especially was this true of the rich, who were all too ready to yield to the sensuous charms and the sensual rites of this fake religion. This woman evidently knew much of the character and work of Elisha, for she styles him "a holy man of God" (verse 9) — not merely "a man of God," which would only recognize him in his official character as a prophet, but "a holy man of God," thus recognizing his *personal character* as a man of uprightness and piety. The very first time she noticed him passing through the village, "she constrained him to eat bread." Mark: "constrained him." It implies urgency on her part. Elisha did not thrust himself on the rich. He seems even to have been reluctant to accept this hospitality — so much so that it required constraint — urgent and persistent entreaty on her part — to induce him to yield to the hospitable invitation. Several things are suggested here.

(1). A desire to use her means for the good of others. She had abundance of bread — she would share it with those who were in need. Her wealth was not selfishly employed.

(2). She was *hearty* in her benevolence. It was not a formal, stiff response to a beggar's cry. It was unsolicited kindness, urged on the deserving. How much depends on the spirit in which our benefactions are bestowed!

(3). She reverenced goodness. She tendered her hospitality to Elisha because she knew him to be "a holy man of God." She showed no sympathy with the vain, the idle, the wicked, but paid her homage to truth and goodness and piety in the person of their needy champions and adherents.

(4). She was prompt and bold in throwing her influence on the side of right. She did not wait to see in what direction popular opinion would drift; but was forward to *lead* public opinion by committing herself to the cause of the prophet at the first opportunity. This, in view of the prevalence of idolatrous worship, supported as it was by the throne and the court, develops a moral

---

[1] Journeys.

courage, an independence, and a conscientiousness, which go far to establish her claim to the distinction of "a great woman."

(5). Her benevolence was thoughtful, judicious, and steady. It was no mere impulse. When, by frequently entertaining the weary prophet, and learning more fully the high aims of his mission, she had become deeply impressed with the value of his services to the imperiled cause of Jehovah, she proposed to her husband to prepare a room for the prophet, and furnish it, to which he might resort, whenever he passed that way, for rest, or study, or devotion. This we call *thoughtful* benevolence. It recognized the *needs* of the prophet, and provided that which would be most grateful to him, and most useful in aiding him in his work. This thoughtfulness in providing that which is best adapted to serve good ends is one of the richest charms of kindness: not lavish gifts, nor ostentatious displays of benevolence, but gifts which at once show personal regard and an aim of usefulness. Note that this proposition was made by the wife to the husband, not by the husband to the wife. He was probably well enough pleased that the prophet should be hospitably entertained at his house when he passed through Shunem; but beyond that, he does not appear to have bestowed a thought upon Elisha's welfare, or the interests of the great cause which he championed. The wife is the prime mover in this wise and benevolent proceeding. The controlling mind and heart are hers. Blessed is the wife who can charm her husband into goodness. The room was prepared, and henceforth the weary prophet could escape from the tumults of the outside world, and even from the annoyances of household activities, and from his own quiet room look out restfully on the beautiful plain of Esdraelon, or beyond to his beloved Carmel, and, alone with God, gird himself anew for the toilsome task before him.

2. *She was contented with her lot.* — There are few things more essential to happiness than a spirit of contentment. How feverish and restless we are — yea, and how thankless! — ever coveting what belongs to others, envious at the lot of others, murmuring at our inferior position or bad fortune, and eagerly grasping for more! But look at this "great woman." Elisha, touched with her cheerful and hearty hospitality, thought it but right to show his appreciation of it, and said to his generous hostess: "Behold, thou hast been careful for us with all this care; what is to be done for

thee? Wouldest thou be spoken for to the king, or the captain of the host?" Elisha at this time had great influence at court. The king was indebted to him for the preservation of his kingdom in a time of great peril, and could not easily resist any request that the man of God might make of him in behalf of his friends.

What selfish ambitions, what eager desire for place and power, such questions would stir in the hearts of the men or women of to-day! Even without such encouragements, what rage for office, what eager scheming, what desperate efforts for place and power, what worship at the shrine of Fashion, do we constantly witness! To most hearts, the poor little village of Shunem, the humble character of even its best society, the hum-drum of agricultural life, would at once have become contemptible. To dwell in populous and beautiful Samaria, to move in its glittering circles of fashion, to shine at court, to participate in its revelries and share in its gorgeous pomps, and live in the glamor of royalty — riding in chariots amid the huzzas and prostrations of the populace, or heading armies in glorious conflict and winning distinguished military honors: what woman's head would not have been turned with an offer of such a splendid future for her husband and herself? But the simple and prompt answer of this woman of Shunem was: "I dwell among mine own people." I am content. My cup is full. My husband and my house and my people are all that I desire. Courts and camps, and the glare of official honors, have no charm for me. Let me but live to do good where I am, and die and be buried among mine own people.

Wise woman! How few possess thy genuine greatness! One of the great lessons of the New Testament is to learn, whatsoever state we are in, therewith to be content (Phil. 4:11). It is the spirit within us, rather than our outward condition, that causes discontent, and a change of circumstances will not cure it. In the humblest condition, a contented spirit will extract honey from the rock, and make the wilderness bloom like the rose. A sour, restless, discontented spirit will lend its curse to wealth and fame, and transform an earthly paradise into a hell. There is quite as much to be done in a lowly sphere as anyone will be ready to account for when God calls him into judgment. True, such a lot has its ills, sometimes hard to be borne; but this is equally true of the lot of those we envy. The ills may be different, but not more endurable. Shakespeare makes Anne Boleyn say:

> 'Tis better to be lowly born,
> And range with humble livers in content,
> Than to be perk'd up in a glistering grief,
> And wear a golden sorrow.

And bitterly did she prove the truth of this in her subsequent experience. If our present lot is not that for which we are best fitted, the best way to prepare for escape from it is to discharge faithfully its duties and enjoy thankfully what blessings it affords; and in due time — quite as soon as we are ready for it — we shall be guided into another sphere of life. The eager and restless desire for change robs us of much that we might enjoy, is a sinful murmuring against Providence, and urges us on to changes that prove injurious, if not disastrous. Yet how this spirit of discontent insinuates itself into every heart, and poisons every cup of life! There is a story of a man who owned a magnificent farm, who posted by the wayside a notice that he would give this farm to the first person he found who was perfectly contented with his earthly lot. There were many applicants for the farm, but in every instance close and pointed inquiry developed the lack of perfect contentment. At last an applicant came who could not be shaken by the most searching and minute inquiry. He stoutly affirmed and maintained his perfect contentment with his home, his wife, his children, his pursuits, and all his surroundings, and vehemently claimed the fulfillment of the promise. But, said the man who made the offer: "If you are, as you say, perfectly contented with your lot, *why are you so eager to get my farm!*" That settled the question. Fairly content, perhaps, he was, until this offer waked him up to a new ambition and developed a restlessness of which he had not previously been conscious.

In nothing can we show a truer piety than in a cheerful acceptance of our lot, a patient endurance of its ills, a diligent improvement of its opportunities, and a thankful acceptance of whatever good it affords us. In this land of ours, with its powerful and numberless incitements to change, the eager ambition for gain that everywhere abounds, and the melancholy and often startling history of disappointment, disaster, and ruin that follows it, there is no lesson of more practical value to the Christian than this of contentment with the lot in which Providence has placed him. And this is one of the precious lessons of the narrative we are considering. No more genuine stamp of real greatness can be found than in this noble woman's answer to Elisha's questions: "I dwell among mine own people."

Teach us, gracious God, to be contented with the lot which Thou hast appointed for us, and to seek to serve Thee in the sphere in which we live. May we learn from this narrative how noble a character may be formed in tame and uninspiring scenes, and how tender is Thy care, how rich Thy blessing, to the humble and faithful. May we prize those virtues that make home pleasant, and those charities that, unseen of men, cheer the hearts and lives of the neglected children of poverty and toil. Teach us to be particularly kind to Thy servants who give up all for Thee, that they may preach Thy word and win souls to Thee, that we may hold up their hands in their conflicts with error and wrong.

A Great Woman (Part Two).

(2 Kings 4:8-37, 8:1-6)

The answer of the Shunammite to Elisha does not evince that she had no desires unsatisfied. The sequel shows to the contrary. But it does evince that she was so far contented as to be unwilling to seek any change beyond what God might providentially order, lest it should be for the worse. And this is true, natural, scriptural contentment — not indifference to our lot, but a cheerful acceptance of it as God's will.

Elisha rightly divined that there was one gift which would, above all others, gladden her heart. She was childless. Her home, while filled with peace and love, lacked the patter of little feet and the innocent, joyous prattle of children's voices; and her heart, though happy in a husband's love, and in the gratitude of those whom she blessed, had oftentimes trouble to suppress its maternal instincts. Although she murmured not, she keenly felt that, in this regard, her home was unblessed, and her life unsatisfied. When, therefore, according to the prophet's promise, a little boy came to gladden her home, her cup overflowed. To father and mother it was a new chapter of life, filled with tenderest interest, and as the years grew on, and page after page of this new life was opened with ever-increasing delight, they felt that they had received, in this precious gift, the crown of all their joys. This brings us to a new development of character which we discover, namely:

3. *Great self-control and strong faith in God.* — A day of bitter trial came. The darling boy followed his father to the harvest-field, and his gladsome presence lightened the toil of the fond father's hands and poured gladness into his heart. But the child, being overpowered by the heat, was sent to his mother, with the confidence that her nursing skill would soon restore him. She held him in her arms until noon, doubtless doing all for his relief that love could prompt and skill execute — but all in vain. The little life went out at midday; the mother was left with a lifeless form in her arms; all the bitterness of death was upon her. It is in such hours that opportunity is offered for the development of some of the noblest traits of character. Thousands of mothers might equal the Shunammite in their love of offspring, and yet, in such an hour of

bereavement, put no check on their grief. Forgetful alike of their obligations to others and their dependence on God, they would abandon themselves to the selfishness of grief, thinking of nothing and caring for nothing beyond their own suffering. Not so this noble Shunammite. She had shown, in prosperity, that she could moderate her ambitions and subdue all temptations to selfishness; she is to show now that she can moderate her grief also, and be calm and considerate, prompt and energetic in meeting the dreadful emergency, even when her heart is ready to break. Quietly she bears her dead child to the prophet's room and lays him on the prophet's couch. No one intrudes there. It is the *Prophet's* room; no one else must enter without permission. There the lifeless form will be secure against observation; no one will know that he is dead. She sends to her husband for a conveyance to Mount Carmel, that she may visit the prophet Elisha; but she says not a word of the death of the child. Her request seemed strange to her husband. "Wherefore wilt thou go to him today? It is neither new moon nor Sabbath." Here is another gleam of light on this woman's character. The Sabbaths and the new moons were observed at Carmel. The pious and faithful Israelites were in the habit of gathering there, at those times, to be instructed by Elisha in the law of Jehovah, and to honor Him by their worship. Of these, this woman of Shunem was one. Her husband would have expected to provide a conveyance for her on the Sabbath, or at the new moon; what perplexed him was, that, making such frequent visits to Carmel, there should be any necessity for an additional visit between the Sabbaths. Evidently, then, she was in the habit of paying weekly and monthly visits to Carmel. Twelve miles and back, every week and every month, she traveled, that she might honor Jehovah by steadfast worship at a time when the multitude had forsaken Him for Baal. Think of this, ye careless ones; who, within easy distance of houses of worship — nay, even under their shadow, are more frequently absent than present in the assemblies of the saints. In addition to her goodness of heart, benevolence of life, and beautiful spirit of contentment, we here discover a steadfast and bold faith in Jehovah — a *religiousness* which, like everything else about her, was calm and strong.

Her quiet answer to her husband is, "It shall be well." As much as to say, "Do not trouble me with questions now. Grant me what I ask. You will find it is all right." The acquiescence of her husband in her request, without farther questioning, is evidence of the confidence he had in her judgment, and of his great deference to her wishes. Her wisdom and her devotion to him gave her imperial sway. But what strength of mind — what self-control — was needful, to banish all outward signs of grief, and close her lips against even a whisper of the anguish that was gnawing her heart! She would not involve her husband in her own wretchedness, hoping that he might be kept in blissful ignorance of the calamity until the last possible effort was made to overcome it. Was she not "a great woman"?

4. *Her energetic action and passive submission.* — She sits not down to mourn away her opportunity, but rouses herself to immediate exertion, if, perchance, the dread calamity may be overcome. Away she hies[1] to Carmel, to consult the prophet. This precious life was given her from God, at Elisha's request; may it not, through the same channel, be restored? She will not yield until she has tested this. The prophet, from the summit of Carmel, sees her in the distance, and sends his servant Gehazi to make the customary inquiries after the welfare of the approaching visitor. "Is it well with thee?" asked Gehazi; "Is it well with thy husband? Is it well with the child?" And she answered and said, "It is well." What a faith was there! It has been objected that the answer was not true. But we observe, in reply, that there is a wide difference between an *incomplete* statement and a *false* statement. For some reason this woman did not care to give a detailed answer to Gehazi. Perhaps, in her eagerness to reach the prophet, she brushed the servant aside with this brief reply to his inquiries. Perhaps her woman's keen intuitions detected in Gehazi that rottenness of heart which was afterwards made manifest; and she did not care to waste words on him. But that she departed from the truth is not for a moment to be allowed. With a meaning to her words which Gehazi could not penetrate, she said, "It is well." Such was her faith in God, that, whatever the outcome might be, she would still cling to the assurance that it was well with the child, and well with them all. This beautiful spirit of resignation to calamity, while straining every nerve to overcome it, is a blending of the active and passive virtues

---

[1] Goes in haste, speedily.

not often witnessed, but furnishing a combination of qualities that must ever be admired.

But when she came into the presence of the man of God, she could no longer contain her grief. She prostrated herself, under a violence of distressful emotion, which told better than words her burden of anguish. It was but a momentary outburst. She soon subdued it so as to be able to speak. And when she spoke, it was with an indirectness — an avoidance of all direct mention of the calamity, as something too terrible to be uttered — which, more than anything else, reveals the intensity of her grief. "Did I desire a son of my lord?" and the awful truth flashed upon Elisha. At once he dispatches his servant with the prophet's staff, to be laid upon the face of the child. Whether he thought this would be successful in restoring life, or merely sought to quiet the mother's anxiety by a knowledge that *something was being done,* we are not able to say. Whatever was the intention, it did not succeed in soothing her anxiety. "As Jehovah liveth, and as thy soul liveth, I will not leave thee," she said to Elisha. He knew her firmness of purpose, and wasted no words in reply. "He arose and followed her." We may well believe that no time was lost in the journey. Gehazi, who had gone before them, returned and met them with the not encouraging tidings that he had done as he was commanded, but in vain. Still they pressed on, and reached the house, and the prophet went at once to his room, where the lifeless body lay. It was a tremendous task to which he was summoned, but by earnest prayer and anxious effort he accomplished it. The child was restored to life. He sent for the mother, and "she went in, and fell at his feet, and bowed herself to the ground, and took up her son, and went out." This is no hysterical scene; no rush to seize the child in transport; no forgetfulness of the courtesies due to the prophet; no word spoken. It was an occasion too sacred and too soul-thrilling for words. Indeed, she was not a woman of many words, and when she spoke, her words were weighty, because they were firm and full of meaning. With the same external calmness and self-control with which she had laid her dead boy on the couch when her heart was crushed, she now lifted him from the couch, alive and blooming, when her heart was thrilled with unspeakable joy.

Thus we see, associated with wealth, a strong faith in Jehovah, a steady and fervent piety, the domestic virtues that make home peaceful and bright, a wise benevolence, a self-reliance and independence, a self-control, a sweet spirit of contentment, and a wonderful energy, that combine to make her really "a great woman" and a model of her sex. Blessed be the memory of the Shunammite. Though her name has perished, and her grave is unknown, she lives through millenniums, to show what a woman of fair endowments is capable of becoming in goodness and usefulness, and what such a woman in the possession of wealth is capable of accomplishing in a quiet domestic sphere. To all the noble Christian women who are seeking, in a humble way, to glorify God and bless their fellow-beings, without neglecting their homes or failing in the duties of wives and mothers, we present this portrait as designed to cheer and strengthen them in their efforts.

It will not do to close this sketch without allusion to a tender and touching providence which encircles like a halo this beautiful life.

Trouble afterward came to this family. Good families are not exempt from trial, for they could not be educated into the highest goodness without them. A famine came upon the land for seven years. In view of its approach and its long continuance, Elisha advised the Shunammite to seek refuge among some other people. Probably before this she had been bereaved of her husband. It seemed a hard fate, for one who had been so liberal of her bread to others, to be compelled to leave her beloved home and go among strangers in quest of bread for her own household. But she confided in the prophet's counsel, and went to the land of the Philistines, and sojourned seven years. Through all these years her faith would feed on past mercies, and she could say to the God in whom she trusted, "Thou hast been my help; therefore in the shadow of thy wings will I rejoice." During her absence, her land had been appropriated by others who refused to restore it to her. She determined to appeal to the king. It seems that the king had met Gehazi, and was curious to learn from him of the wonderful works of Elisha. Among other wonders, Gehazi related the story of the Shunammite.

And it came to pass as he was telling the king how Elisha had restored a dead body to life, that, behold, the woman whose son he had restored to life cried to the king for her house and for her land. And Gehazi said, "My lord, O king, this is the woman, and this is her son, whom Elisha restored to life." And when the king asked the woman, she told him. So the king appointed unto her a certain officer, saying, "Restore all that was hers, and all the fruits of the field since the day that she left the land, even until now."

Thus what was dark before became light. The death of her son links itself with the heart of the king in the day of her calamity, and by means of it she obtains audience at the throne, and the restoration of her property in her day of need. Thus, through this painful bereavement God prepared the way to reveal himself as the Father of the fatherless, and the judge of the widow, in the day of distress. The righteous is not forsaken, nor is his seed left to beg bread. How often is it thus found that the providences of God are far-reaching in their aims, and that, however dark and mysterious they may be for a time, yet, when we see "the end of the Lord," we find "He is very pitiful and of tender mercy." "Many are the afflictions of the righteous, but the Lord delivereth him out of them all." "Weeping may endure for a night, but joy cometh in the morning." "Acknowledge God in all thy ways, and He will direct thy steps."

How faithful art Thou, righteous Father, to them that trust in Thee! Though darkness gathers about their paths, and they may be sorely tried, yet Thou dost not forget them. Thou causest light to spring up in darkness; when they pass through deep waters, they perish not; when they are placed in the fiery furnace, the flame does not kindle upon them; for Thou art Jehovah, their God, the Holy One of Israel, their Savior. May we learn never to be faithless. If, even for a long time thou seemest to forsake us, may we still be assured that, in the end, it will be seen that Thy mercy endureth forever.

A Group of Characters:
Elisha, Jehoram, Naaman

We have anticipated so much of Elisha's history, that what remains to be said of him can be best said in contemplating him as the center of a group of remarkable characters belonging to that period.

Elisha is introduced to us as "the son of Shaphat, of Abelmeholah" (1 Ki. 19:16). As Shaphat is the usual word for judge, it is inferred that his father was the local judge, and therefore a man of foremost position in the community. *Abel-meholah* means "the meadow of the dance," a well-known locality in the valley of the Jordan, where, in connection with his office of judge, the father of Elisha carried on farming operations. Here, with twelve plows at work under his direction, or, with twelve "yokes" of land already plowed,[1] and he busy with the last, Elisha was found by Elijah on his return from Horeb. Suddenly, and without warning, as usual, Elijah made his appearance, and, casting his sheepskin mantle on the head of the young farmer, in token of his investiture with the office of a prophet of Jehovah, hurried along without the utterance of a word. We presume there was some previous acquaintance between these parties. At least Elisha, as a true worshiper of Jehovah, could not have been ignorant of the wonderful career of Elijah, and from his appearance and his dress was able to identify him. He therefore ran after the stern Gileadite, now pale and worn with his long fasting and his burden of sorrows, and promptly accepted the call to this new and perilous task, asking only for time to close up his home affairs and bid farewell to his parents. There may have been previous intimations to Elisha of the work in store for him, and on his own part, a stirring of spirit — A pious ambition to stand in the front in defense of the persecuted and oppressed cause of Jehovah. At all events, the call came to him in such a way that he had no doubt of its genuineness, and the first gleam we get of his character reveals a promptness of decision and a resoluteness of purpose which leave us no room to doubt his courage or his lofty

---

[1] A "yoke" of land was what two oxen could plow in a day.

enthusiasm. "He left the oxen, and ran after Elijah, and said, Let me, I pray thee, kiss my father and my mother, and then I will follow thee." But he meets with no encouragement from the stern prophet. Elijah well knew, in his own bitter experience, that no one was fit to bear the responsibilities and do the work of his successor, who had to be helped to a decision to accept the role. It must be his own thoroughly free and self-determined response to the call of Jehovah. He therefore said to Elisha, "Go back again; for what have I done to thee?" But Elisha was not to be thus repulsed. He did, indeed, go back, but only to take an affectionate farewell of his parents and the servants of the household, and to offer a sacrifice of thanks and devotion to Him whose servant he had now become, and then "he arose, and went after Elijah, and ministered unto him." He took a servant's place. He was known as "Elisha the son of Shaphat, who poured water on the hands of Elijah" (2 Ki. 3:11). The best way to learn to rule is to learn to serve. He is greatest who is servant of all. There is here a valuable hint to young men who desire to excel in the ministry of the Word. Their first work should be that of subordinates, under the direction of an enlightened eldership, or under the guidance of an experienced evangelist. Not by the mere study of books can a young man be fitted for usefulness in the ministry. He needs before him some embodiment of wisdom and prudence, of energy, patience, meekness, gentleness, grace, and dignity, the quickening spirit of whose counsels and example will be worth more to him than mere book-learning, and whose advice respecting books — course of reading and study — may save him years of blind groping for the information and learning he most needs.

For the seven or eight years that Elisha served Elijah, the inspiration of Elijah's life and character was worth more to him than all beside. We know little of their history during that time. We have already intimated, in a previous study, that Elijah probably busied himself in reorganizing the schools of the prophets and preparing young men from all parts of the land to act as instructors of the people; and if so, Elisha, with the rest, underwent a long course of training for his future work. He was neither too proud to serve, nor too self-conceited to learn; in patient service and diligent study he laid the foundations of his future eminence as a prophet of Jehovah. If, even with the aids of inspiration, Elisha needed such a training, who that would be eminently successful in the Christian ministry can say that he does not need a thorough preparation for his work?

The call of Elisha was before the death of Ahab — probably four years before that event. He died in the reign of Joash, some sixty-five years afterwards; so that his career as a prophet extended over a period of from fifty-five to sixty years. So much was crowded into this long official life, and so many personal characteristics are brought out in this prophet's large experiences, that we may well watch his career.

The devoted friendship between Elijah and Elisha illustrates what is often witnessed — a close and strong attachment between persons almost antipodal[1] in disposition and characteristics. They supplement each other. Each seeks in the other that which he lacks in himself. Elijah was rough, stern, fiery; Elisha was smooth, gentle, complaisant. Elijah was fond of wild solitudes, and dwelt apart from courts and busy throngs; the free ranges of Gilead, the wilderness of Sinai, the cave at Horeb, were charming to him, while the thronged streets of Samaria and the splendor of the royal palace at Jezreel were detestable. Elisha loved men, delighted in society, was at home in crowded cities or by the camp-fires of armies. We find him at Jericho, Dothan, Samaria, and Damascus, and in the stirring scenes of military life with the armies of Israel and Judah on their march against Moab (2 Ki. 3:11). Elijah's spirit is symbolized by the earthquake, the tempest, and the fire; Elisha's by the "still small voice." If Elijah, in his spirit and power, foreshadowed John the Baptist in his asceticism and fiery energy, Elisha's spirit is rather suggestive of Him who would not break the bruised reed or quench the smoking flax. At first, indeed, something of Elijah's severity gleams forth in the mission of his successor. When, on his way to Beth-el, the profane youths[2] of that idolatrous city mocked him as they noted the contrast between his close-cropped hair and

---

[1] At opposite ends of the globe.

[2] The word is Naar, and is used of Solomon at his accession, when he was at least twenty years old (1 Ki. 3:7); of Jeremiah, when called to be a prophet (Jer. 1:6, 7), and the companions of Rehoboam, who himself was forty years old when he began to reign, are described by the word *yeled,* which is often translated by *child,* e. g., 1. Ki. 3:25, 17:21; (see 1. Ki. 12:8, 10, 14; 1 Chron. 10:14). — *Geikie.*

the flowing locks of Elijah, he "cursed them in the name of Jehovah" (2 Ki. 2:23-24). And when Jehoram, king of Israel, whom he greatly despised (see 2 Ki. 6:32), came with the kings of Judah and Edom to seek his counsel in a great peril, his answer would have been worthy of Elijah:

> *"What have I to do with thee? Get thee to the prophets of thy father, and the prophets of thy mother. As the Lord of hosts liveth, before whom I stand, surely, were it not that I regard the presence of Jehoshaphat the king of Judah, I would not look toward thee, nor see thee"* (2 Ki. 3:13-14).

But Jehoram was the son of Ahab, and a remembrance of the tremendous evils brought on Israel by Ahab and Jezebel, and of their treatment of Elijah, was enough to kindle the indignation of even as gentle a man as Elisha. Yet he did not reject the supplication of Jehoram, but afterward is found on friendly terms with him, and rendering him invaluable assistance. Apart from these sudden flashes of pious indignation at the beginning of his ministry, Elisha's public life was largely in contrast with that of Elijah.

> *He was not secluded in mountain fastnesses, but dwelt in his own house in the royal city (2 Ki. 5:9, 24, 6:32, 13:17); or lingered with the sons of the prophets within the precincts of ancient colleges, embowered[1] amidst the shade of the beautiful woods which overhang the crystal spring that is still associated with his name (the Ain es-Sultan, near Jericho, [is] often called Elisha's spring. 2 Ki. 2:18-22, 6:1); or was sought out by admiring disciples in some tower on Carmel, or by the pass of Dothan (2 Ki. 4:25, 6:14); or was received in some quiet balcony, overlooking the plain of Esdraelon, where bed and table and seat had been prepared for him by pious hands (2 Ki. 4:8-10). He was sought out not as the enemy, but as the friend and counselor of kings. One king was crowned at his bidding, and wrought all his will (Jehu. 2 Ki. 9:1-2, 6-10). Another consulted him in war, another on the treatment of*

---

[1] Being covered or surrounded.

his prisoners, another in the extremity of illness, another to receive his parting counsels (2 Ki. 3:11-19, 6:21, 8:8, 13:14-19). "My Father" was their reverent address to him. Even in far Damascus his face was known. Benhadad treats him with filial respect (2 Ki. 8:7-8); Hazael trembled before him (2 Ki. 8:11-13); Naaman hung upon his words as upon an oracle (2 Ki. 5:18). If for a moment he shows that the remembrance of the murder of Naboth and [of] the prophets of Ahab and Jezebel is burnt into his soul, yet he never actively interposes to protest against the idolatry or the tyranny of the court. Even in the revolution of Jehu he takes no direct part. Against the continuance of the worship of Baal and Ashtaroth, or the revival of the golden calves, there is no recorded word of protest... His deeds were not of wild terror, but of gracious, soothing, homely beneficence, bound up with the ordinary tenor of human life. When he smites with blindness, it is that he may remove it again; when he predicts, it is the prediction of plenty, and not of famine (2 Ki. 6:18-20, 7:1). The leprosy of Gehazi is but as the condition of the deliverance of Naaman... At his house by Jericho the bitter spring is sweetened; for the widow of one of the prophets the oil is increased; even the workmen at the prophets' huts are not to lose the ax-head which has fallen through the thickets of Jordan into the eddying stream (2 Ki. 6:5-7); the young prophets, at their common meal, are saved from the deadly herbs which had been poured from the blanket of one of them into the caldron, and enjoy the multiplied provision of corn (2 Ki. 4:38-44). At his home in Carmel he is the oracle and support of the neighborhood; and the child of his benefactress is raised to life, with an intense energy of sympathy that gives to the whole scene a grace as of the tender domestic life of modern times (2 Ki. 4:27-37).[1]

But if the spirit of Elisha was gentle and tolerant compared with that of Elijah, it was not less influential in rebuking sin and vindicating truth. Elijah's work of judgment was necessary. But for

---

[1] Stanley's *History of the Jewish Church*, Lecture 31.

Elijah, there could have been no Elisha. But if there had been no Elisha to succeed him, Elijah's work must soon have perished. The latter dealt in overpowering judgments on those who could be reached by no gentler means, and humbled the people in the dust before Jehovah; the former sowed the seeds of truth and righteousness in the hearts thus prepared for it, relying on the imperishable power of great principles diligently planted in the hearts of the people, and availing himself of opportunities as they occurred to make operative these principles, so as quietly to undermine the very foundations of false religion. In this he, more than any other prophet, seems to have anticipated the spirit and the work of Christ. As illustrative of the gentle but uncompromising and incorruptible spirit and comprehensive methods of working by which Elisha was distinguished, let us refer to his dealings with Naaman.

Naaman, captain of the host of the king of Syria, who had become famous for his military achievements, and was high in favor with the king, was afflicted with a leprosy that threatened to be to him a life-long curse. A captive Hebrew girl, who became slave to Naaman's wife, told her mistress of the wonder-working prophet who dwelt in Samaria. On the strength of this, Naaman is furnished by the king with letters and rich presents to the king of Israel, that he may go and be healed of a disease for which Damascus had no cure. The king of Israel regards the proceeding as a trick to involve him in a new war with Syria, by compelling him to reject an unreasonable demand. "Am I God, to kill and to make alive, that this man doth send to me to recover a man of his leprosy? Wherefore, consider, I pray you, and see how he seeketh a quarrel against me!" At this juncture Elisha interposes. He has none of the exclusiveness or bigotry that would withhold pity or help from an uncircumcised Syrian, enemy though he be to Israel, and base idolater. He sees how an act of beneficence may carry the knowledge of the true God into the heart of the city and court of Damascus, and he will not lose the opportunity. "Let Naaman come now to me," was his message to the king, "and he shall know that there is a prophet in Israel." Riding in pomp in his chariot, and surrounded by the flower of the cavalry of the Syrian army, Naaman proceeds to the humble abode of the prophet. It was conferring a great boon on the poor and humble Elisha to make him such a visit, and bring before his door the chariot of so eminent a foreigner, and his distinguished retinue.[1] The proud Syrian hero expected a flattering reception. His own personal greatness, and the splendid gift he bore, amounting to more than $50,000 would, he was sure, secure to him the most obsequious service of the prophet and the punctilious performance of the most elaborate religious rites. He knew that such a gift would purchase from any Syrian priest the profoundest reverence and the most imposing ceremonies. He thought Elisha would come out to him with fawning and flattery, and stand before him, and call on the name of Jehovah, his God, and strike his hand over the place, and recover the leper. But, no: Elisha is the servant and ambassador of a King of infinitely greater majesty and power, and he means that this proud idolater shall humble himself before the God of Israel. He will not so much as show himself in the presence of this leper, but simply sends him a message: "Go and wash in Jordan seven times, and thy flesh shall come again to thee, and thou shalt be clean" (2 Ki. 5:10). Naaman was wroth. Was it to wash in the muddy Jordan that he had come away from the clear and sparkling streams of his own country — Abana and Pharpar? Had he made this journey — he, the captain of the host of the king of Syria — to be flouted and insulted in this fashion? Alas! How often we glory in the tokens of wealth and fame, when the flaunting splendor that decks us does but cover foulness and loathsomeness! A disgusting leper enraged because the military dress and equipage that cover and surround his blotches and scales and hideous sores are not worshiped! He turned and went away in a rage. And how many, like him, who cover their moral leprosy with the gay robes of wealth and fashion, turn away from what they deem the humiliating demands of the gospel of salvation. But their leprosy clings to them, as did Naaman's, and will cling to them forever, unless, like him, they learn to listen to the voice of truth and mercy.

In a soberer moment, listening to the wise suggestions of his servants, he respected the command of the prophet, went to Jordan, dipped himself seven times beneath its waters, and was healed. He came back cleansed, humbled, converted, to the house of Elisha, avowing his faith in Jehovah, his profound gratitude for his deliverance from a fearful curse, and offering lavish gifts to the man of

---

[1] Followers.

God. But Elisha would not touch the tempting gifts; he would not sully the purity of his motive by the acceptance of a reward of gold and silver. He sent back to Syria not only a cleansed leper, the fame of whose healing would be sounded through the land to the honor of the God of Israel, but a happy convert to Jehovah, who, from his high official place, could send forth an undoubted testimony to the throne, the court, and the people, of the power and goodness of the one living and true God. It was in such quiet but effective ways that this gentle prophet diffused a knowledge of Jehovah, not only in Israel, but in surrounding countries. The still, small voice was mightier than earthquake, tempest, and fire.

When thou callest us, O Lord, may we be ready to leave at and go where Thou directest. Teach us to be willing to serve rather than ambitious to rule. Save us from pride, since the leprosy of sin gives us so much cause for constant humiliation. Let us not exalt our own vain conceits against the voice of Thy authority. Grant us that unquestioning obedience that falters at none of Thy commandments. May He who cured Naaman of his leprosy cleanse us from the fouler leprosy of sin.

A Group of Characters: Elisha And Gehazi

We have already, in treating of Elisha and the Shunammite, referred to Gehazi as Elisha's servant. Who he was, and under what circumstances Elisha was led to choose him for his attendant and receive him into the intimate and confidential relations which must necessarily subsist between a prophet and his minister, we have no means of knowing. It is thought by some commentators that as Elisha, the servant of Elijah, had been under training to succeed his master in the prophetical office, so it was meant that Gehazi, the servant of Elisha, should be successor to his master. He was probably one of the sons of the prophets whose abilities, character, and zeal were so superior that Elisha selected him as perhaps destined to reach high prophetical distinction. If this supposition is correct, it but shows that Elisha, like Samuel before him (1 Sam. 16:6-7) judged according to appearances, which are so often deceptive. Whether this supposition is correct or not, it is evident that Elisha showed little penetration in his favorable judgment of Gehazi. The woman of Shunem seems to have judged him much more correctly (2 Ki. 4:26, 30), for she evidently had so little confidence in him that she would confide nothing to him, nor put the least faith in him as worthy to perform a sacred trust. It is not improbable that, as the master and servant so frequently partook of the hospitalities of her house, she had detected moral obliquities in Gehazi. Or, by virtue of a woman's keen intuitions, and through the operation of the mysterious law of attraction and repulsion which is so influential in deciding our friendships and enmities, she had *felt* a dislike of him for which she could give no satisfactory reason, but which had to her all the force of a revelation.

Shakespeare, in making one of his female characters account for her opinion of a certain person, says:

> *I have no other but a woman's reason:*
> *I think him so, because — **I think him so**.*

It is not *thinking,* at all; it is *seeing — a penetrating* insight into character, in which women are superior to men.

Elisha was lacking in discernment. Like many other great men, he was free from suspiciousness and easily deceived in men. That he should have been so long in close contact with this false, selfish man, without the slightest suspicion of his moral unsoundness, indicates not only a nature of such remarkable innocence and integrity as to be incapable of suspecting wrong in others, but also a lack of that close observation and discernment so necessary in dealing with men. Such penetration into human character is quite as necessary, on one hand, to guard against imposition, as is an unsuspicious, charitable spirit, on the other hand, to guard against harsh and unjust judgment of our fellows. We doubt, however, whether Gehazi was ever thought of as Elisha's successor. Elisha was not Elijah's choice. He was called of God. But Gehazi was Elisha's choice, without a call from God, and we see no reason to believe that he was chosen with a view to anything beyond that of filling the place of a servant. Even in this view, the choice reflects no credit on Elisha's practical judgment; for, of all qualities needed for such a place, truthfulness and unselfishness are chief.

But let us take the most charitable view of Gehazi's case. It may be that he did not know himself — that under the repressive influence of his education and his environment, the demons of falsehood and avarice that possessed him were kept in a slumbering condition. Nothing in his surroundings had been sufficient to rouse them into life against the adverse influence of his associations and his pursuits. It is possible for men to go far along in manhood, in an even course of life, braced up by their family, their church, their social affiliations, enjoying the confidence of their fellows and complacently regarding themselves as of saintly spirit and character, when all the while there are evil passions lurking in them which, *under a change of circumstances,* break loose from their concealment, dethrone faith and reason, usurp the sway of life, and drive it furiously on to wreck and ruin. "The heart is deceitful above all things, and desperately wicked; who can know it?" The possibilities that slumber within us, waiting their opportunities to be translated into terrible realities, are often not even suspected. The bewitching influence of self-conceit, the narrow limits of experience, the constant pressure of our surroundings, the attractions of the outside world charming us away from all serious introspection, the gratifying but ensnaring influence of the admiration and flattery of friends, combine to blind us to a proper knowledge of our own weaknesses and frailties; while the exceedingly subtle and bewitching play of the passions that stir within us is seldom understood aright. There is a glamor thrown about the workings of passion that betrays us into acquiescence, hiding from us the hideousness of evil impulses and wicked suggestions. Not until these evil impulses and suggestions have grown into unsuspected strength, and a favorable opportunity occurs for an assertion of their power, is one likely to discover the ensnaring, captivating, destructive energy of these hitherto hidden forces, and he is the bond-slave of his own wicked desires at their first open assault on his virtue and integrity. No wonder that Paul should admonish us: "Let him that thinketh he standeth, take heed lest he fall." No wonder that the Psalmist should cry out, under fearful discoveries of the treacheries that lurked within him: "Search me, O God, and know my heart; try me, and know my thoughts; and see if there be any way of wickedness in me, and lead me in the way everlasting." No one who knows himself will walk otherwise than humbly before God, working out his salvation with fear and trembling, and clinging for comfort to the assurance that God works in him to will and to work.

We take it that Gehazi had not been long in the service of Elisha — perhaps two or three or four years. He had previously been, in all probability, at one of the schools of the prophets, to which he had gone from one of the humble, pious homes that still remained faithful to Jehovah amidst a general apostasy. He had been carefully housed from the corruptions that prevailed on every hand; nay, his family may have been driven, by the persecution that prevailed, and by the voice of the popular sentiment, into seclusion and poverty; and thus his early years may have been guarded from the power of temptation. In the school of the prophets he would be subject to influences repressive of all unholy impulses — so that in the study of the law of Jehovah, the play of those holy raptures that were wooed and cherished in those sacred colleges, and the stern discipline of poverty to which these students were subjected, there was not likely to be temptations to falsehood or to avarice; and this young man may have been all unconscious of the defects of his moral nature. But when Elisha called him into his service, a new world opened to him. A knowledge of camps and courts — the

blare of trumpets, the glare of royalty, the excitements and gran-
deurs of public life, the restless play of ambition, the splendors and
pomps and hilarities of life in Samaria, contact with kings and
princes and generals, and a knowledge of the wealth and fashion,
the pride and extravagance of the favorites of fortune — for Elisha
was a man who mingled with men, and was on familiar terms with
kings and nobles and military commanders and the nabobs[1] of the
land — all these were new and bewitching influences, and they
kindled a flame within him, or they found a flame already kindled,
of unholy ambition — a passion for wealth, and for the luxury and
splendor and distinction which wealth could purchase. True, his
master was poor, and likely to remain so; but he laid the rich and
the great under heavy obligations by his services to the throne and
the people — and Gehazi began to watch for an opportunity to secure to himself the riches which the prophet so firmly and persistently rejected. His avaricious desires grew upon him, for from
their first budding he secretly nursed them into stronger life. Like
Judas Iscariot, who was willing for a time to share the privations of
the ministry of Jesus, and be purse-bearer to the poverty-stricken
company that gathered about Him, hoping that in a little while the
Messiah would set up His kingdom in great power, and he, the
humble treasurer of the apostolic band, would become lord-
treasurer of a universal empire; Gehazi was willing to be for a time
the slave of the moneyless Elisha, in hope that by virtue of his relation to the prophet of Jehovah, so familiar with kings and the great
and honorable of earth, he might in the end grasp some portion of
that wealth which was pressed upon his master in vain.

The opportunity came. Naaman, the proud Syrian chieftain,
came to Elisha to be healed of the leprosy. He was healed; and in
pious gratitude he returned from the Jordan to Samaria — a distance of some thirty-two miles — to acknowledge his new-born
faith in Jehovah, and to make a suitable present to the prophet at
whose word he had been redeemed from so fearful a curse. He had
brought with him from Damascus, as a present to the king of Israel,
"ten talents of silver, six thousand shekels of gold, and ten changes
of raiment" (2 Ki. 5:5). The money, apart from the raiment, would
amount to from $35,000 to $60,000. It is hardly supposable that the

---

[1] Rich people.

king of Israel, scornfully rejecting the message that accompanied the present, would receive the money. Out of this treasure, therefore, Naaman was at liberty to bestow on the benevolent prophet whatever amount he thought proper of the present rejected by the scornful king; and we may be sure that the healed leper and the noble chieftain would bestow his gifts with lavish hand. But Elisha would receive nothing. He would not debase the gift of God by making it a thing of barter, or bring his own prophetic work on a level with the impositions of greedy and venal heathen priests, by the acceptance of a gift. Naaman must understand that he sought not *his*, but *him*; this idolater must be won to Jehovah by a free gift of Jehovah's grace, unsmirched by even a suspicion of selfishness or venality.[1] And so he sent his distinguished guest away with his benediction, leaving him to meditate not only on the greatness of the cure wrought on him, but on the marvelous disinterestedness of the prophet of Jehovah.

Gehazi watched all this proceeding with absorbing interest. His heart had already become dead to all interest in the cause of Jehovah — if, indeed, it had ever been genuinely alive to the interests involved in the great controversy between Jehovah and Baal — except as it might be made to minister to his own advantage. Elisha's noble disinterestedness was to him the merest folly. What recked[2] he of the honor to be won for Jehovah's name in Damascus and Syria by this unsullied benevolence in Naaman's behalf? What concern was it of his, if the prophet's work should be degraded to the base level of the greed of idolatrous wonderworkers? What was it to him that Jehovah's name should be dishonored in the eyes of the heathen? Nothing. Here is the money he had so long craved, and this he will have at all hazards. He said to himself, "Behold, my master hath spared this Naaman the Syrian, in not receiving at his hands that which he brought: as Jehovah liveth, I will run after him and take somewhat of him." It is not surprising that profanity — for, under the circumstances, the use of the phrase "As Jehovah liveth" can only be regarded as a profane utterance — should be joined with his wicked purpose. Sins grow in clusters. A wicked thought utters itself in wicked speech. Stealing away, as he

---

[1] Being open to bribery.

[2] Concerned, cared, regarded.

thought, unobserved from his master, he followed after Naaman, concocting a lie on the way with which to ensnare him. There is something worthy of note in the manner of his reception by the Syrian captain. As soon as Naaman perceived his approach, he halted his chariot and came to meet him — this eminent chieftain alighting to meet a slave — thus honoring the prophet in the person of one whom he took to be his messenger. It is difficult to imagine how this lying, covetous wretch could stand in the presence of such gratitude and courtesy, and receive such an unspeakable honor on the strength of his master's worth, without extreme embarrassment or relenting in his wicked purpose. But he knows no relenting. "Is it well?" anxiously inquired Naaman — for he evidently feared some evil tidings from Elisha. "It is well," calmly replied Gehazi. "Only, two young men of the sons of the prophets from the hill country of Ephraim have come unexpectedly, and my master, unprepared to care for them, begs for a talent of silver (about $1,800) and two changes of raiment." This, for the purpose named, was a large amount, but it was probably small in comparison with the amount offered to Elisha. It was the design of Gehazi to satisfy his greed as far as he could, without exciting suspicion of his own infamous purpose. Naaman, only too glad of the opportunity to render a grateful service, doubles the amount asked for; and sends his own servants to bear the burden of silver and the changes of raiment, which Gehazi carefully stowed away, and returned to his master's presence, apparently as unconcerned as if nothing had occurred. But Elisha, as if merely conscious of his absence for an unusual length of time, asked him, "Whence comest thou, Gehazi?" And now another lie must be added, to cover up the sins already committed — for when one begins an evil course, not only does one sin beget another, but every sin necessitates additional sins to support it, to conceal it, or to justify it. One of the most fearful things in sinning is the power and the necessity of sin to multiply itself. "Thy servant went no whither," responded Gehazi, and he evidently thought that this lie would cover up the whole wicked business, and leave him free to enjoy his ill-gotten gains without farther trouble.

This leads us to note another inherent characteristic of sin — *its tendency to reveal itself*. By the everlasting laws of the moral universe, wrong perpetually works to the surface and *crops out*.

"Be sure your sin will find you out." Efforts to hide it may be partially or temporarily successful; but sooner or later, and generally in unexpected ways and at unexpected times, it comes into view, and that which was spoken in the ear is proclaimed on the housetops. In this case, the end was reached right speedily, and in a way altogether unexpected. "Went not mine heart with thee," said Elisha, "when the man turned again from his chariot to meet thee? Is it a time to receive money, and to receive garments, and olive-yards and vineyards, and sheep and oxen, and men-servants and maid-servants?" Elisha now understood that his servant's covetous heart was going out after all these things — that he meant to gather about him, if not by fair means then by foul, all that could minister to pride, luxury, and self-aggrandizement. "The leprosy therefore of Naaman shall cleave unto thee and unto thy seed forever. And he went out from his presence a leper as white as snow."

It requires but a few minutes to read all that is said about this in the sacred narrative, but it is worthy of long pause and serious reflection, and should lead to heart-searching, introspection. Look at the developments of covetousness in this case.

1. *It made Gehazi false to Jehovah.* — It was a time of exceeding humiliation in Israel. The nation had been humbled and despoiled by its enemies. The court was corrupt. The people were idolatrous, with all of moral degradation that idolatry implies. Clouds of doom were gathering over the land. Elisha's ministry, while in many respects successful, was yet feeble to counteract the popular tendency to apostasy. He well said, "Is *this* a time to receive money?" Yet, insensible to all these calls to humiliation and renewed devotion to the law of God, this man, hardened by covetousness, had no desire but to riot in wealth and luxury!

2. *He was false to Elisha.* — He knew his master's grief over the prevailing corruptions, and his all-absorbing desire to preserve his own ministry free from even the suspicion of evil; yet he was willing to bring dishonor on the prophet's name and work, if only he could serve his own selfish purposes.

3. *He was false to Naaman.* — He deceived him, and preyed on his generous spirit by cunning falsehood for his own advantage.

4. *He was false to himself.* — He made his whole life a living lie, and carried about with him the awful consciousness of deliberate and labored hypocrisy — knowing that for the sake of present

advantage he was sacrificing his own integrity and murdering his own peace. No man can do a greater wrong to himself than to abandon his soul to falsehood, for he subverts the very foundation of all virtue; there is nothing left in him that can be trusted, or that can inspire self-respect.

Such are the hideous results of covetousness. It leads to falsehood, ingratitude, dishonesty, impiety, infidelity; blunts all the sensibilities, and wrecks all that is manly and noble and generous in the character of its victim.

If we have seemed to dwell too long on this ungainly picture, it is because we are impressed with the conviction that the sin of covetousness is the fountain of much — very much — of the mischief and wretchedness that curse society. It brutalizes its victims. It curses families with selfish ambitions, deadly strifes, degrading vices, and even appalling crimes. It robs churches of spirituality, freezes the fountain of charity, hushes the thunders of the pulpit against sin and wrong, and deafens the ears of its victims against the cries of the perishing. It fills communities with selfish strifes, with wrongs and crimes of every shape and hue. It corrupts governments; encourages fraud and embezzlement; prevents the faithful execution of the laws; promotes drunkenness, gambling, and licentiousness; kindles wars; corrupts legislatures; hardens the hearts and blinds the eyes of statesmen; leads to robberies, forgeries, suicides, and murders. Its bitter fruits are found in the slain on battle-fields; in criminals in our prisons; in the oppression and degradation of the children of toil; in the control of politics, commerce, and manufactures for the injury of the many and the aggrandizement of the few; in the broken hearts and shattered fortunes of the innocent, who have become a prey to the cunning and unscrupulous. It bars the way in millions of hearts to the entrance of God's saving truth. There is no crime that has not been committed under its accursed inspirations, no imaginable wrong, or injustice, or cruelty, that has not been wrought at its bidding. Take away from all hearts the insane craving for wealth and what wealth can purchase, and what a transformation society would undergo! Will the day ever come, of which the poet dreams, when

Wealth shall no more rest in mounded heaps,
But, smit with freer light, shall slowly melt

In many streams, to fatten lower lands;
And light shall spread, and man be liker man,
Through all the seasons of the golden year.

The love of money is not, as our common version asserts, "the root of all evil," but it is, as a better translation reads, "a root of all *kinds* of evil;" and it is true, from age to age, that "they that desire to be rich fall into a temptation and a snare, and many foolish and hurtful lusts, such as drown men in destruction and perdition."

If nothing in the hideous deformities and the monstrous wrongs wrought by this passion is sufficient to repel us, we ought yet to be awed by a view of the ultimate ruin it inevitably works to one's self. Gehazi coveted gold and silver, changes of raiment, sheep and oxen olive-yards and vineyards, men-servants and maidservants. He might have said, in the language which Shakespeare puts into the mouth of Malcolm:

There grows
In my most ill-composed affection, such
A staunchless avarice, that, were I king,
I should cut off all the nobles for their lands
Desire his jewels, and this other's house;
And my more having would be as a sauce
To make me hunger more; that I should forge
Quarrels unjust against the good and loyal,
Destroying them for wealth.

And what did he reap from all his eager avarice? *Leprosy* — a rottenness of flesh and bones, that rendered him incapable of any joy of life, and made his existence a perpetual curse. This was the bitter fruitage of the infidelity, impiety, ingratitude, falsehood and hypocrisy into which his covetousness led him. Nor is this an exceptional case. It is rather a typical case; and for this reason we have dwelt at length upon it. The blight and curse inherent in this unholy passion is sure to assert itself sooner or later — a curse that will eat into the very center of life, consuming all that is healthful and beautiful in one's nature, rendering him incapable of enjoying what his avarice acquired, and degrading him into a hopeless outcast in the moral universe. It was in tender mercy as well as divine wisdom that our Lord said, "Take heed and beware of covetousness."

Most earnestly do we pray Thee, who art Love, that we may never so far wander from Thee as to be guilty of worshiping mammon. Keep us from all idolatry. Save us from covetousness, which is idolatry. Guard us from a passion so absorbing in its nature, so captivating in its pleadings, so corrupting in its power, so ruinous in its consequences. And when we see how one sin leads to another, may we tremble at the thought of submission to any evil influence. We pray not only that we may be saved from covetousness, but that we may so share in Thy beneficence that it shall ever be a delight to do good in Thy name; that we may thus be children of Him who causes His sun to shine on the evil and on the good, and sends rain on the just and on the unjust.

A Group of Characters:
Elisha, Jehu, Athaliah, Jehoshaphat, Jehoiada

If Elisha did not generally appear in the sternness and fiery zeal of Elijah, he nevertheless wrought, in a quieter way, but with terrible effect, a work of justice and judgment. He not only gave information to the kings of Israel of the plans and purposes of their foes, thereby defeating their intentions; but sometimes he inspired great movements which resulted in crushing disaster to the enemies of Jehovah, whether of other nations, or of the apostate sons of Israel. Elijah received a commission to anoint Jehu, son of Nimshi, King of Israel. The time for this did not arrive during Elijah's life, and he handed over this commission to his divinely appointed successor (1 Ki. 19:16-17). The time at length came. Alike in Israel and in Judah, Baal triumphed. Ahab's successor, Joram, was largely under the spell of his mother's idolatrous fanaticism. In Samaria and in Jezreel, Baal-worship flourished; and while it is not apparent that the open adherents of this idolatry were numerous outside of these cities,[1] the people at large were only nominally on the side of Jehovah. The influence of the court, if it did not win adherents to Baal, at least paralyzed the faith of the people in Jehovah, and succeeded in producing a general indifference on religious questions. Such a condition of things must ultimately result in bringing the land under the sway of the religion of Phoenicia, especially as Jezebel's untiring zeal and relentless purpose, backed by the power of the throne, the patronage of the court, and the zealous propagandism of a powerful priesthood, would never cease while this end remained unaccomplished. Elisha made no open war on the throne and the priesthood, as Elijah had done; and this imperious and fanatical queen carried on her work without opposition, save such as came from the unobtrusive labors of Elisha and the sons of the prophets to educate the people in the knowledge of the true

---

[1] The temple of Baal in Samaria held all the open followers of that God that could be found in all the land (2 Ki. 10:21).

God. Doubtless, the personal influence of Elisha, and the educational work of the sons of the prophets, held the mass of the people from open adhesion to Baal-worship; but their faith in Jehovah was feeble and uninspiring.

But, more than this: Jerusalem had also become a center of this abominable idolatry, and Judah as well as Israel had been brought under its accursed spell. And this had come about through the culpable[1] weakness of one of Judah's most pious and faithful kings — Jehoshaphat. Firm as he was in his attachment to the law of God and His true worship, he was led into an alliance with the infamous Ahab; and his son and heir, Jehoram, married Athaliah, the daughter of Ahab and Jezebel, who had much of her mother's decision of character and superstitious devotion to Baal (2 Chron. 18:1-3, 21:5-6, 22:1-4). Jehoram permitted Baal-worship to be established in Jerusalem, and his queen continued her encroachments on the national worship until the whole power of the throne and the court was arrayed in support of this hideous idolatry. Elisha understood the crisis. There was no hope for the ancient faith but in the sword. The day of judgment had come, when the accumulated sins and crimes of the house of Omri must be visited with a vengeance more fearful and a calamity vastly more sweeping than any that had belonged to the fiery mission of Elijah.

Jehu was now at Ramoth-gilead, commander of the forces that defended it against the assaults of Hazael, king of Syria. We have already caught a glimpse of him in his young manhood as one of Ahab's bodyguard (2 Ki. 9:25-26), accompanying the king to Jezreel, when Elijah met the royal chariot and pronounced the divine judgment on the wicked and cruel house of Omri (1 Ki. 21:20, 24). He has since worked his way up to the chief military command. He is now in the prime of life. He is popular with the army, and stands next in military authority to the king. Under a calm exterior, he had concealed a bitter hate of the house of Omri from the time he had heard Elijah pronounce its doom, and had patiently waited for the hour when that doom should be executed. The time came. The king had gone to Jezreel to be healed of wounds received from the Syrians at Ramoth-gilead. Jehu is, in the king's absence, supreme in military authority. At this juncture, Elisha remembers the unful-

---

[1] Guilty.

filled commission transferred to him from Elijah: "Jehu, the son of Nimshi, shalt thou anoint to be king over Israel," and he privately dispatches a young prophet to Ramoth-gilead to perform the anointing.

While Jehu is sitting in council with his officers — or perhaps indulging in a revel with them — a young man, in the coarse garb of a prophet, and flushed with the heat of rapid travel, suddenly appears, and, selecting Jehu from the company of officers present, led him away into the innermost and most secluded room of the house, and poured on his head the flask of oil Elisha had given him, saying:

> *Thus saith Jehovah, the God of Israel, "I have anointed thee king over the people of Jehovah, and over Israel. And thou shalt smite the house of Ahab thy master, that I may avenge the blood of my servants, the prophets, and the blood of all the servants of Jehovah, at the hand of Jezebel. For the whole house of Ahab shall perish; and I will cut off from Ahab every man-child, and him that is shut up, and him that is left at large in Israel. And I will make the house of Ahab like the house of Jeroboam the son of Nebat, and like the house of Baasha the son of Abijah. And the dogs shall eat Jezebel in the portion of Jezreel, and there shall be none to bury her" (2 Ki. 9:6-10).*

Then the young prophet opened the door and departed as hurriedly as he came.

When Jehu returned to the council-room, he was asked, "Wherefore came this mad fellow to thee?" Too much meaning, we think, has been extracted from this language. It does not justify the idea of a raving enthusiast or fanatic. Rude soldiers are not apt to look with favor upon religious teachers. The sudden appearance of this young prophet, his excited manner and action, his mysterious movements, and his unceremonious departure, led these rude men of the camp to style him — half in ridicule and half in superstitious fear, for the prophets at this time, as the men of overpowering influence with the people, were held in awe — a mad or wild fellow. The strangeness of his action excited their curiosity and awe. When Jehu, with apparent modesty, gave them an indirect answer, saying, "Ye know the man and what his talk was," we are furnished in their response with a specimen of that rude frankness so characteristic of the camp. "It is a lie," they answered, "tell us now." As soon as Jehu, under this pressure, made known the prophet's errand, he was enthusiastically proclaimed King by the army, and instantly proceeded to execute his commission. Gathering silently and speedily a sufficient military force, the Mad Driver set out on his journey of sixty miles — northward, past Jabesh-gilead to the ford at Bethshean; thence across the Jordan and up the wide opening of the valley between little Hermon and Gilboa, he hasted, until the clouds of dust raised by his approaching forces attracted the attention of the watchman on the tower of Jezreel. Then followed the last act in the awful tragedy, in the last scene of which we hear the crashing fall of the house of Omri, and witness the terrible fate of Jezebel, the royal family, the worshipers of Baal, and of Baal's image and temple — which we have already described in a previous study. It was a terrible vengeance — one of those righteous retributions which, here and there, in the warfare between right and wrong, amidst the bewildering confusions of human affairs, redeem us from utter despair of a final triumph of righteousness, and reassure us that the Lord God Omnipotent reigneth. Ah! could the despairing Elijah have known all that was involved in his commission to anoint Jehu to be king over Israel, with what a light and joyous step would he have gone on his way! But he was disheartened, as we all too often are, because sentence against an evil work was not executed *speedily* (Eccles. 8:11-13). God's ways are not as our ways. His counsels are far-reaching; His patience is divine; His purposes often flow in subterraneous channels so long and so far that we forget to believe in Him: but the moment of destiny arrives; the clock strikes; the hour and the man appear, and the long-concealed purpose breaks forth in desolating wrath upon the unsuspecting offenders, and sweeps away the evil-doers from the face of the earth.

But the polluting influence of Baal-worship had extended beyond the kingdom of the ten tribes into Judah, and into Jerusalem itself. Bravely and faithfully as the prophets and some of the kings of Judah had contended for the true religion, the pestiferous[1] influence of this base idolatry had not only insinuated itself into the

---

[1] Annoying or troublesome.

hearts of many of the Jews, but Jerusalem itself became a center of idolatrous worship under royal protection. This disastrous result of a spirit of compromise should teach a great lesson to all who are entrusted, to any extent, with the interests of true religion. Jehoshaphat, one of the most zealous of royal reformers, who had used all the power and authority of his throne to protect, defend, and make practically effective the laws of Jehovah, was nevertheless led, for reasons that we can only guess at, into an alliance with the weak and corrupt Ahab. Perhaps his fear of the encroachments of Syria, and his appreciation of the facilities which the rivalries of the two kingdoms of Judah and Israel gave to invaders, led him to abandon the warlike policy of his predecessors towards Israel, and to pursue a peaceful policy instead — hoping by cementing the interests of the two kingdoms, to make them strong against their common enemies. While this may redeem his policy from dishonor, it only adds another to the numerous illustrations of the fatal consequences of any compromise between that which is radically true and right, and that which is radically false and wrong. Jehovah and Baal stood for ideas, principles, laws and aims that were radically antagonistic. Any attempt to reconcile them could only result in the triumph of falsehood and wrong — for truth and right are omnipotent only when they stand on their own merits and reject all entangling alliances. The result of this alliance between Jehoshaphat and Ahab was the marriage of Jehoram, son of Jehoshaphat, to Athaliah, daughter of Ahab and Jezebel — a true daughter of her mother in ambition, energy and cruelty, and in thorough devotion to Baal. Her influence over Jehoram was like that of her mother over Ahab.

She was a power behind the throne greater than the throne itself; and all that power was used to defy and dishonor Jehovah and glorify Baal. Jehoram, like Ahab, yielded to his wife's influence. Jerusalem became a seat of idol-worship. A temple of Baal was raised hard by the temple of Jehovah, and a vile priesthood, of the members of which but a solitary name survives — Mattan — (2 Chron. 23:17), supported doubtless by many of the adherents of Baal that flocked in from the northern kingdom, made the City of God as hideous as Samaria or Jezreel with their debasing and licentious performances. It does not appear that the worship at the temple of Jehovah was suppressed — that was impracticable; but the worship of Baal was openly and shamelessly practiced, and was known to enjoy the protection and patronage of the throne. Jehoram died. Ahaziah, his son, came completely under the influence of his mother, but after a brief reign fell under the avenging stroke of Jehu (2 Ki. 9:27-28). The Philistines and Arabians (2 Chron. 21:16-17), and Jehu (2 Ki. 10:13-14) had so far destroyed the heirs to the throne of Judah, that at Ahaziah's death only his own children were representatives of royalty, and none of these were fit to reign (2 Chron. 22:9). Then the heartless and crafty Athaliah caused all her grandchildren to be murdered, and usurped the kingdom. This abominable idolatress sat on the throne, and used all her cunning and authority to win the people to the glittering and pompous, but false and demoralizing, religion of the Phoenician Baal and Astarte. But the echo of the crashing fall of Baal at Samaria was heard all over Judea, and so were the thrilling reverberations of Jehu's glorious victory; and they who feared Jehovah were stirred by a holy ambition to avenge the insults offered to the one living and true God in His own chosen city.

We have said that Athaliah had destroyed all the seed royal. Not all; for the half-sister of Ahaziah, Jehoshabeath, wife of Jehoiada, the high priest, had snatched the youngest child of Ahaziah from death, and secreted him in the temple. He was a mere babe, and the only legitimate heir to the throne — so near was the lamp of David to utter extinction!

Jehoiada was already an old man, and inherited the faith and loyalty of earlier and better times. Prudently and vigilantly he watched over the precious life of the infant Joash, and waited through six long years of the swaggering and defiant heathenism that ramped in the streets of Jerusalem and flaunted its vile symbols on God's holy hill of Zion. But in the seventh year of Athaliah's usurpation his arrangements were completed for a revolution. At a solemn festival, and on a Sabbath day — when least of all would any measures of violence be suspected — he brought into the temple the officers of the queen's body-guard, whom he had won over; the priests and Levites — not only those then in service at the temple, but all that could be gathered out of the cities of Judah; also "the chief of the fathers of Israel." These he armed, and appointed them their stations and their duties. "Then they brought out the king's son and put upon him the crown, and gave him the testimony, and made him king; and Jehoiada and his sons anointed him and said, God save the king." Then the Levitical choir broke forth in a triumphal chant; musical instruments filled the air with exultant strains, in which the trumpeters broke in, ever and anon, with gay and loud flourishes of joy; and the multitude rent the air with their enthusiastic shouts.

Athaliah, attracted by these noisy demonstrations, came to the temple to learn their cause. There she saw the crowned king, encompassed by her own bodyguard, the priests and Levites, and enthusiastic crowds of the best people of the land. Instantly she read her doom. But, bold and defiant — one cannot but admire the fearlessness and firmness which belonged alike to mother and daughter — she rent her clothes and cried, "Treason! Treason!" And then, proudly and scornfully she stood at bay, awaiting the doom that she saw must come.

There is a marvelous calmness and dignity in the administration of justice in this instance, revealing the masterly hand and just heart of Jehoiada. Calling out the proper officials, he said, "Have her forth between the ranks;" that is, guard her on all sides, that none kill her as she is passing out, and thus pollute the temple with her blood. Instead of "they laid hands on her," the Revised Version says, "they made way for her." The officers cleared a way for her, and the people fell back on either side, so that she walked out untouched by any violent hand, until they reached the chariot-gate of the royal palace — and there, at the proud entrance to the seat of her usurped greatness, she was ignominiously[1] slain. Then the people went to the temple of Baal and demolished it, and broke his altars and images in pieces, and slew Mattan, the priest, before one of the altars.

Then the temple was placed under guard, and an imposing procession of those in authority and of all the people of the land, conducted the boy-king from the temple to the royal palace, and set him upon the throne of the kingdom. "So all the people of the land rejoiced, and the city was quiet: and they slew Athaliah with the sword" (2 Chron. 23:21).

Thus we see that Elisha, though in a very quiet way, put forth an avenging power equal to that of Elijah. He set in motion all the

---

[1] Having all dignity removed.

ministries of judgment by which Baalism in Israel and in Judah was overthrown.

To the one living and true God be honor and glory everlasting. Thy word, O Lord, never fails. Thy promise to David, which seemed so sure to be made void through the vigilance and hate of Thy foes, is still performed, and the wrath of man is made to praise Thee. In Thy judgments, as in Thy mercies, Thou art adorable. Nay, Thy judgments are mercies, for through them Thou workest out merciful and gracious purposes. May we behold alike Thy goodness and Thy severity with humble and earnest gratitude and trust. May we learn to say, with Thy ancient servant, "Seven times a day will I praise Thee, because of Thy righteous judgments."

A Group of Characters:
Elisha, Jehoiada, Jehosheba, Joash

We have already seen that the power of Elisha reached into the kingdom of Judah, and had much to do, indirectly, in shaping its fortunes in a period of extreme peril. We must not suppose, because his long life was devoted almost exclusively to the kingdom of the ten tribes, that he had no interest in the affairs of the neighboring kingdom of Judah. Witnessing, as he did, the overthrow of the house of Omri, alike in Israel and in Judah, and living through the entire regency of Jehoiada, and the forty years' reign of Joash — in that intensely interesting period when the "lamp of David" was burnt down to its socket, and a single rude breath might have extinguished it utterly — we cannot possibly regard him either as an indifferent spectator of the usurpations and revolutions in Jerusalem, or as destitute of power, effectually though quietly exerted in shaping the course of events which snatched the royal family of David from extinction. Even Elijah, supremely devoted to Israel, did not fail to watch with keen anxiety the encroachments of the house of Omri on the house of David; and when he saw that by the unholy marriage of Jehoram, king of Judah, to Athaliah, daughter of Ahab and Jezebel, the safety of the house of David and the integrity of the law of Jehovah were imperiled, his sleepless vigilance dictated a letter of warning and denunciation to Jehoram (2 Chron. 21:12-15). Not less could have been the anxiety and vigilance of Elisha at that critical period when, through the corrupt influences emanating from his own kingdom of Israel, Baal was so near to a complete victory over Jehovah in Judah and Jerusalem. We have seen, too, how the reign of Jehu, inaugurated by Elisha, reached over in its influence to Judah, thrilling the hearts of the patriotic and God-fearing with new hope and courage, and preparing the way for the overthrow of the usurpations of the daughter of Ahab. We may, therefore, properly introduce, in the outer circle of the group of characters of which Elisha is the center, Jehoiada, Jehosheba, and Joash, of the kingdom of Judah.

Of Jehosheba, or Jehoshabeath, we have but little recorded, but that little leads us to a desire to know much more of a character evidently noble. She was the daughter of Jehoram, king of Judah, and sister of Ahaziah (2 Ki. 11:2). It is generally conjectured that while she was the daughter of Jehoram, she was not the daughter of Athaliah. While this may be true, it is only a conjecture. On the other hand, it is at least quite as probable that she was the daughter of Athaliah, and that the name of the mother is not mentioned by the chronicler because it was held in such universal detestation. She was married to Jehoiada, the high priest (2 Chron. 22:11) — the only instance on record of the marriage of a princess of the royal house with a high priest. This is significant. Jehoiada, the high priest, was the boldest and truest representative of the true religion, and of loyalty to the throne of David. Her acceptance of him as her husband, at a time when the royal house was saturated with Baalism, and the court was either in sympathy with false religion, or indifferent to the honor of Jehovah and the supremacy of His law, shows that she had decided for herself in this great controversy, and had made a right decision. A great crisis in her life had come. She must decide between the true and the false. Her parents and the reigning influences of the court were secretly, if not openly, in favor of Baal, and poisonous streams were flowing out over all the land from the throne and the royal palace. On the other hand stood Jehoiada, the noblest representative of the ancient faith and loyalty of Judah. The influence of her position as a member of the royal family would have much to do in weakening or strengthening the faith of the people in Jehovah in this time of peril. She turned her back to her parents and the royal court, and gave her heart and hand to the highest and noblest representative of the law of Jehovah. We see here moral courage, a noble independence, strong faith in Jehovah, a supreme regard to truth and righteousness. While there had been no open breach, as yet, between Jehovah and Baal, it was evident that, with such a man as Jehoiada on one hand, and such a woman as Athaliah on the other, war must sooner or later be declared between the throne and the altar — and Jehosheba forsook the throne and clung to the altar. The noblest elements of character are here in full bud. If, as stated in 2 Chron. 24:15, Jehoiada was one hundred and thirty years old at his death, and he died five years before the end of Joash's reign of forty years, he must have been ninety-five years old when he overthrew the reign of Athaliah; and as Jehoram, the father of Jehoshabeath, was thirty-two years old when he began to reign (2 Chron. 21:5), which was fifteen years before Joash was crowned, Jehoiada must have been eighty years old at the beginning of the reign of Jehoram. All of which goes to show that Jehosheba had married an old man. It cannot be regarded as a love-match. She became his wife that she might most effectually serve Jehovah, and, like Esther, was raised up for such a time as this (Est. 4:14). This brings her noble character out into clear view.

As Baal was represented by a woman — idolatrous, determined, unscrupulous, fanatical; so Jehovah raised up a woman — pure, devout, strong-minded, vigilant, and supremely devoted to His honor, to represent Him in this tremendous controversy. Jehovah's representative triumphed. Athaliah undertook one bold and desperate movement to end the strife and secure a permanent victory for Baal — the destruction of all the heirs to the throne. She ruthlessly murdered, as she supposed, all her grandchildren (2 Ki. 11:1). By previous calamities, all the heirs to the throne of David had been destroyed, with the single exception of the family of Ahaziah (2 Chron. 21:4, 17; 2 Ki. 10:12-14). Ahaziah himself was slain (2 Chron. 22:8-9). If, now, this cruel and ambitious woman could destroy all that remained of the seed-royal, the light of David would be quenched, and she could safely occupy the throne

But Jehosheba was in a position to learn of this murderous purpose, and, quick and resolute in her decision, while the bloodthirsty excitement was raging, and all was tumult and rage, she quietly took possession of Ahaziah's youngest child — a babe but two months old — and hid him away, and for six years watched over this precious young life, waiting an opportunity to produce him as the rightful heir to the throne! Thus was the craft and cruelty and fanaticism of one woman balked by the vigilance, tender mercy, and enlightened faith of another woman. It would intensify our interest in the outcome of this struggle, and give peculiar emphasis to the retribution finally visited on this monster of cruelty, if we could be sure that the woman by whom her diabolical scheme was defeated was her own daughter.

Forever blessed be the memory of Jehoshabeath, through whose fidelity to Jehovah the flickering flame of the lamp of David was guarded, and nourished again into brightness.

Jehoiada the high priest must have belonged to the latter part of the reign of Jehoshaphat, and evidently partook largely of the spirit of loyalty and piety that prevailed under the sovereignty of that illustrious monarch. His course during the reigns of Jehoram and Ahaziah, and the usurpation of Athaliah, was marked by faithfulness combined with great prudence. As the worship of Jehovah was not forbidden, he contented himself with the zealous maintenance of that worship, waiting patiently for the dawning of a brighter day, when the worship of Baal might be overthrown. When the infant Joash came under his protection, he did not at once proceed to extremities with the usurping Athaliah. In quietness and in confidence was his strength (Isa. 30:15). He waited until the patriotic spirit kindled by Jehu's overthrow of the house of Ahab in Israel should be inflamed by the bold impieties of Ahab's daughter in Jerusalem. The devotees of Baal soon grew bolder, and their number was doubtless largely increased by idolatrous fanatics coming from the northern kingdom, where they were no longer safe. Jerusalem and Judaea were rapidly taking on the character of a Phoenician province. The people, looking to Jehoiada as their leader, year by year became more impatient for an uprising against the impudent and insulting authority that had been so wickedly imposed on them. When this feeling became universal and intense among the priests and prophets and people, Jehoiada proceeded to open revolution. The quietness with which all the preparations were made; the skill with which all the forces at his command were distributed; the time chosen for decisive action; the orderly manner in which the revolution was conducted; and the swift yet deliberate vengeance visited on the usurping queen, all tell of a master spirit at the head of the revolutionary movement. How it must have cheered the heart of Elisha to learn of the glorious outcome of the mission of judgment he had set on foot by the anointing of Jehu!

Jehoiada was for many years regent of the kingdom. The extirpation of the worship of Baal, the repairing of the temple, which had been profaned and desolated by Athaliah (2 Chron. 24:7), and the general prosperity of the kingdom, indicate that in addition to his well-worn priestly dignities, he was fairly entitled to the honors of superior statesmanship. It is no wonder that, at his death, after so long a life of pious and patriotic service, he received the singular honor of a burial in state within the walls of Jerusalem, "among the kings, because he had done good in Israel, both toward God and toward his house" (2 Chron. 24:16). He had destroyed the power of heathenism, preserved the Davidic dynasty, restored the national worship to its integrity and something of its former glory, and exalted the priesthood to an influence it had never known before. His long life testifies to his temperate habits, and his whole official career to honesty, ability, prudence, patriotism, and an uncompromising devotion to the honor and glory of Jehovah. His is one of those perfectly rounded, symmetrical characters, which we never tire of contemplating as a thing of beauty.

Joash, under the loving tutelage of Jehoiada and Jehoshabeath, grew into a fair character. His anxiety for the repairing of the temple seems to have exceeded even that of Jehoiada, and his effective measures to overcome the failure of an indolent and corrupt priesthood in raising the necessary funds for this object, prove that he was well gifted in practical wisdom (2 Chron. 24:4-14). But he lacked strength of character. His was one of those weak natures which readily take the impress of present influences, whether they are good or evil. This is evident from the fact that no sooner was Jehoiada dead than a new environment developed an entirely different character. The "princes" of Judah — the leaders of the proud aristocracy of the land — were still in sympathy with Baalism. Though they had been held in subjection by the strong, wise hand of Jehoiada, they secretly longed for the reestablishment of the worship of Baal as the *fashionable* religion. Their highest ambition was to ape the follies and licentiousness of Tyre, Samaria, and Jezreel. They were doubtless alarmed by the growing power of the Jewish priesthood under Jehoiada. As soon as Jehoiada was out of the way, they approached the flabby[1] king with offers of support to his throne, if he would but allow them to restore the worship of Baal. And, in defiance of his education, of the whole tenor of his past life, and of all his obligations to God who had preserved him, and to the people who had crowned him, this king weakly yielded to their flatteries! "And they forsook the house of Jehovah, the God of their fathers, and served the Asherim and the idols; and wrath came upon Judah and Jerusalem for this their guiltiness" (2 Chron. 24:17-18). Prophets were sent to denounce this great iniquity, but no heed was given to their rebukes and warnings. At length Zecha-

---

[1] Weak.

riah, the high-priest, successor to Jehoiada his father, who had been from childhood the companion of Joash, and was related by blood to him, was moved to cry out from the altar against this monstrous disloyalty and impiety, and to warn the king and the court of the dire consequences of encouraging and fostering such iniquity. Even a weak and pliant nature may become bold and stubborn when it has committed itself to falsehood and wickedness. Joash, in his rage, gave command to kill Zechariah on the spot. Right there, "between the temple and the altar," Jehovah's high-priest, the son of Jehoiada and Jehosheba, to whom this ungrateful wretch owed his life, his throne, and all his prosperity, is commanded by his own cousin to be slain! "And they conspired against him, and stoned him with stones at the commandment of the king in the house of the Lord." With calm dignity Zechariah submitted to his fate, merely saying to his murderers, "Jehovah look upon it and require it." Every circumstance of this murder is horrible. The rejection of God's own message; the indignity heaped on Jehovah's own representative; the outrage on justice in condemning a man to death without a hearing; the defilement of God's house with the blood of murder; above all, the monstrous ingratitude that not only suffered but *commanded* the murder of the son of parents to whom the guilty king owed everything, even to life itself: stamp it as one of the most hideous of crimes. But this weak king was in the hands of his flatterers, and was deaf to every voice of reason, of honor, and of conscience. His ductile[1] nature was bent to their wishes; he had no strength to resist; in one hour he allowed his name to be covered with an infamy from which it can never be redeemed.

It is worthy of note that the chronicler, in pointing out the special horror of this crime, does not speak of the dishonor done to the priesthood, or to the house of God, but of the ingratitude of the king. "Thus Joash the king remembered not the kindness which Jehoiada had done to him, but slew his son" (2 Chron. 24:22). Ingratitude is the blackest of sins. He who is capable of casting off the obligations of gratitude, is capable of any crime. He is a lump of hideous selfishness, dead to every sense of right, and capable of being wrought into any deformity, persuaded to any injustice or

---

[1] Easily influenced.

outrage that selfishness may dictate. Let us most earnestly pray God to preserve us from this awful sin.

But vengeance came, and came speedily. The few remaining years of Joash's reign were dark with the curses provoked by his faithlessness, impiety, and cruelty. Hazael, king of Syria, came against Judah. Although he came against Jerusalem with only a small force, the large army of Judah was completely routed. The "princes" who seduced the king from his fidelity to Jehovah and provoked the king to murder Zechariah, were all slain, and Hazael was only bought off by Joash's surrender to him of "all the hallowed things that Jehoshaphat, and Jehoram, and Ahaziah, his fathers, kings of Judah, had dedicated, and his own hallowed things, and all the gold that was found in the treasures of the house of the Lord, and of the king's house" (2 Ki. 12:18). Joash was then afflicted with diseases that made him helpless. And while in this helpless condition, — his reign a terrible failure, his body racked with pains, and his conscience with guilt — amid the execrations of a people who had come to despise and hate him, he was murdered by two of his guards. Not only was there no lamentation over the murder of the accursed ingrate, but, while he was buried in the city of David, the universal indignation of the people forbade his burial in the royal sepulchers (2 Chron. 24:23-26).

To the honor of human nature be it recorded that the general horror at this ingratitude and impiety lived on through more than eight hundred years, and finds utterance from the lips of Jesus in the New Testament. The Jewish tradition concerning it, while it bears the stamp of extravagance which belongs to so much of the Talmudical writings, is still eloquent in its picturing of a crime too monstrous to be wiped out.[1] In the New Testament Joash's crime

---

[1] They committed seven sins in that day. They killed a priest, a prophet, and a judge; they shed the blood of an innocent man; they polluted the court; and that day was the Sabbath day, and the day of expiation. When therefore Nebuzaradan (the officer appointed over Jerusalem at its capture by Nebuchadnezzar), went up thither, he saw the blood bubbling. So he said to them, "What meaneth this?" "It is the blood," said they, "of calves, lambs, and rams which we have offered on the altar." "Bring, then," said he, "calves, lambs, and rams, that I may try whether this be their blood." They brought them and slew them, and that blood still bubbled, but their blood did not bubble. "Discover the matter to me," said he, "or I will tear your flesh with iron rakes." Then they said to him, "This was a

caps the climax of unrighteous murders for which the sleepless vengeance of God was to be poured out. "That upon you may come all the righteous blood shed upon the earth, from the blood of Abel the righteous unto the blood of Zechariah the son of Barachiah,[1] whom ye slew between the temple and the altar" (Matt. 23:35).

The practical lessons suggested by these various exhibitions of character — strong and weak, good and bad — are too obvious to require from us any formal statement. No thoughtful reader can contemplate them without finding abundant material for reflection, and gathering encouragements and warnings that should make him wiser and better.

Elisha lived more than fifty years after he gave Jehu his commission, outliving Jehu and Jehoahaz his successor, and was still active in the first part of the reign of Joash, king of Israel. To what extent he mingled in the affairs of the nation, we are not informed. But judging from the quiet but effective part he took against the Syrians (2 Ki. 6-7), and in commissioning Jehu and Hazael, and also from the great grief of king Joash at his death, as losing one who was of more worth to him than all the horses and chariots of Israel (2 Ki. 13:14), we may conclude that during all his long life he was busy giving counsel, shaping events, protecting the forces of Israel from dangers, and directing their movements in such a way as to baffle the enemy and execute upon him the just judgments of Jehovah. We may properly conclude these chapters on Elisha by pointing to the closing scenes of his life

The Syrians had sorely vexed and oppressed Israel. The com-

---

priest, a prophet, and a judge, who foretold to Israel all these evils which we have suffered from you, and we rose up against him and slew him." "But I," said he, "will appease him." He brought the Rabbis and slew them upon that blood, and yet it was not pacified; he brought the children out of the schools and slew them upon it, and yet it was not quiet. So that he slew upon it 94,000, and yet it was not quiet. He drew near to it himself, and said, "O Zacharias, Zacharias! thou hast destroyed the best of thy people: would you have me destroy them all?" Then it was quiet and did not bubble any more. — Quoted from the Talmud, by *Lightfoot,* on Matt. 23:35.

[1] This Zacharias was the son of Jehoiada. The son of Barachias was another person (Zech. 1:1). There is an error in the text, probably from incorporating into the text a marginal gloss from some scribe who confounded the prophet Zecharias, with the son of Jehoiada.

mission which the prophet, with tearful eyes, had given to Hazael, for the chastisement of Israel, had been terribly fulfilled; and, after all his long and valuable services to his own people, Elisha was about to die in a time of disorder and gloom, leaving his beloved Israel a prey to a foreign foe. The king, hearing of the prophet's extreme illness, went to his humble abode, to obtain, if possible, some light on his own dark and troubled pathway. He wept over the prostrate form of the dying man of God, and said, "O my father, my father! The chariot of Israel and the horsemen thereof!" Elisha understood his anxiety. It would be cheering to the prophet, as well as to the king, if this dying hour should be lighted up with prophetic visions of a brighter day for Israel. By a symbolical action Elisha was inspired to reveal that the day of deliverance from Syria was at hand. The king was directed to shoot arrows eastward, in the direction of territory which the Syrian king had subjugated; and as he did so, the prophet cried, "The arrow of the Lord's deliverance, and the arrow of deliverance from Syria: for thou shalt smite the Syrians in Aphek until thou hast consumed them." In the kindling enthusiasm of his soul, he directed another symbolical action. He gave a bundle of arrows into the hands of the king, and directed him to smite upon the ground — meaning thereby to express how Syria would be smitten by Joash. Evidently, if the king had entered into the spirit of this symbolical action he would have smitten lustily, and kept on smiting until the prophet should bid him cease. But he smote only three times, and stayed. "And the man of God was wroth with him." Yes, the dying man flushed with anger at the halfhearted zeal of this whimpering monarch. "Thou shouldest have smitten five or six times," he said indignantly; "thou hadst then smitten Syria till thou hadst consumed it: whereas now thou shalt smite Syria but thrice" (2 Ki. 13:14-19). Thus, cheered with a dying vision of returning prosperity to his country, and vexed and angered at the wretched trifler who was so unworthy to enjoy it, — earnest and heroic to the last, he closed his eyes upon this troubled world, winding up a long life of toil and anxiety, but of eminent usefulness, with a calm trust in Jehovah and a burning desire for the welfare of Israel.

When we see, O Lord, that not only Athaliah, trained from infancy to hate Thy name, but Joash, reared from infancy to fear Thy name, turns away from Thee and bows down to idols, we may well tremble at the treacheries that lurk in the human heart, at the wickedness which, unknown to us, conceals itself within us. O, deliver us from the deceitfulness of sin. Teach us to abhor and detest ingratitude. May every recollection of the pious counsels and examples that blessed our childhood, every memory of kindness shown to us, bind us to that which is good, and inspire us to walk in Thy ways. And may we be encouraged by the long life and placid death of Elisha, to serve Elisha's God. "Let me die the death of the righteous, and let my last end be like his."

Jonah and the Ninevites

Not long after the close of Elisha's career, another prophet loomed into view, whose brief history forms perhaps the most singular, and, in some respects, one of the most profoundly interesting, books of the Old Testament. It is among the earliest, if not the very first, of the writings known as prophetical, in the Jewish Scriptures. It is so unique, and some of its statements are so marvelous, that a mixture of levity and incredulity is often noticeable in the treatment it receives, even at the hands of professed believers. Yet we think it may, without difficulty, be shown that in this remarkable fragment of history and biography are found truths of largest scope, and instruction in righteousness, forming a valuable part of the heritage of those "on whom the ends of the ages are come."

Jonah belongs probably to the eighth century B.C., though it is impossible to reach strict chronological accuracy. That he figured in the reign of Jeroboam II is certain from 2 Ki. 14:25; but whether at the beginning, or close, or through the whole of that long reign, or whether his life belonged in part to the previous or succeeding reign, we cannot positively determine. According to the accepted chronology, Jeroboam II began to reign B.C. 825, and occupied the throne 41 years.

According to Jewish tradition, Jonah was (1) the son of the widow of Zarephath, whom Elijah restored to life, (1 Ki. 17:17-24), and who afterwards became Elijah's servant; (2) the prophet whom Elisha sent to anoint Jehu as king of Israel (2 Ki. 9:1-10). We know nothing concerning these traditions that entitles them to respect. The statements concerning him for which we find a historical basis, are (2 Ki. 14:25):

1. He was the son of Amittai, of Gath-hepher, a town of lower Galilee, within the limits of the tribe of Zebulun.

2. As a prophet, he was conspicuous in the reign of Jeroboam II.

It was at his instance that Jeroboam undertook his bold and remarkably successful military enterprises, which resulted in the recovery of large portions of territory and the uplifting of the kingdom of the ten tribes to a prosperity and glory greater than it had ever known. His is the most glorious reign in the entire history of that kingdom. Syria had subjected Israel to fearful oppressions. Jeroboam's father, Joash, had begun to mar the military prestige of the haughty and relentless Syrians, but it belonged to the son to work out a great deliverance for his people and restore to them not only peace, but broad dominion and unparalleled prosperity. In this he was inspired by the cheering prophecies of Jonah, who appears to have been an intense patriot as well as an inspired prophet. The presumption is, from his influence with the king in determining these great military movements, that as a man and a prophet, he had reached an eminent position.

We have also a reference to Jonah in the apocryphal book of Tobit, which is worthy of notice. Tobit was among the captives carried by Shalmaneser from Israel into Assyria. As his long, chequered life was drawing to a close, he called his son Tobias and gave him his dying charge: "Go into Media, my son, for I surely believe those things which Jonah the prophet spake of Nineveh, that it shall be overthrown" (Tobit 14:4). This is repeated in verses 8, 10. And of Tobias, the son, it is declared (verses 14-15) that he "died at Ecbatane in Media, ... but before he died, he heard of the destruction of Nineveh, which was taken by Nebuchadnezzar and Assuerus: and before his death he rejoiced over Nineveh." This goes to show (1) that Jonah's prophecy against Nineveh was well known among the pious captives in Assyria; (2) that while it had not been immediately fulfilled, on account of the repentance of the Ninevites, it was understood to await fulfillment when their cup of iniquity should be full.

It is fairly presumable, from Jonah's access to the court and the throne at Samaria, and from his share in shaping the conduct of the king in the gravest matters at a momentous crisis in the affairs of the kingdom, that he had been for a considerable time known as a prophet, and had grown up, through his prophetical ministrations, into prominence as a steadfast patriot and a man of God; but of the extent or duration of his prophetical career the record is silent. At some point in this career — whether before or after the delivery of his prophecy to Jeroboam, we know not — he received a charge as startling as it was unwelcome: "Arise, go to Nineveh, that great city, and cry against it; for their wickedness is come up before me." There were many reasons why Jonah should feel a repugnance to undertake such a mission. The long and toilsome and perilous journey it involved would be a serious objection, especially to one whose sympathies and affections were so intensely localized — who, narrowed and warped by his lifelong confinement to the little territory of Israel, which was all the world to him, had not a spark of sympathy with, or anything but contempt for, the great outlying world. Then to enter, alone and unfriended, the great capital of a vast empire, and face the throne with prophetic wails and threats, was certain, he doubtless thought, to doom him to torture and death at the hands of the uncircumcised. Yet this repugnance might have been overcome. Could he have been sure that his mission would result in the overthrow of the proud capital and mighty throne of that vast idolatrous empire, he might have accepted it to gratify his own patriotic and religious hate of accursed Gentiles. The shadow of that great conquering power had perhaps already been cast over the land. Binnirari had crushed Damascus, and Phoenicia, Edom, Philistia, and even the kingdom of Israel had felt, more or less, the weight of Assyrian authority. Jonah's beloved land was open to Assyrian invasion. Glad would he be if Nineveh were destroyed. But stern and awful as his message seemed to be, he understood it — and he understood correctly — to be a call to repentance — an offer of salvation (see Jonah 4:2). He knew that in every divine rebuke and threat there lingered a mercy ready to spring forth in tender offers of pardon, if rebuke and threat awakened the guilty to repentance. The divine proclamation (Ex. 34:6-7), "The Lord, the Lord God, merciful and gracious, longsuffering, and abundant in goodness and truth, keeping mercy for thousands, forgiving iniquity, transgression and sin," he was well assured was as true then as when Jehovah uttered it in the ears of Moses; and to go on a mission of mercy and salvation to that distant country, to the enemies of his people, to the despised and abhorred heathen — his whole soul, aflame with bigotry and wrath, rose up against it: he would not go. Rather than bear such a message to such a people, he would turn his back to Jehovah, and run away from His presence!

Let us not do injustice to Jonah. In his proposal to flee to Tarshish from the presence of the Lord, we must not attribute to him the folly of supposing that the presence of Jehovah was confined to the land of Israel, or to the region round about. With all his Jewish narrowness and bigotry, he had worthier conceptions of Jehovah than this, as is evident from his language to the mariners (chap. 1:9). But that presence of Jehovah which had clothed him with the spirit of prophecy and sustained him in the performance of his prophetical work, he probably thought, would not follow his flight into a vile heathen land; and to make sure of this, he proposed to get as far away as possible from the center of these prophetical inspirations. He therefore fled from the hills of Galilee to the seaport of Joppa, and took passage in a vessel just ready to leave there for Tartessus, in Spain,[1] that he might make the breach between Jehovah and himself as wide as possible, and render himself unfit for the mission to which he had been appointed.

We need not linger on the familiar details of this attempted flight. The deep sleep into which, from physical and mental exhaustion, Jonah subsided; the rising and raging of a fearful tempest; the extreme peril of the vessel; the despair of the seamen, and their wild cries to their various gods for deliverance; the awaking of the sleeper, the casting of lots, the confession of the offender; the magnanimous and heroic efforts of the heathen sailors to preserve the life of the guilty man, and their final reluctant consent, under the spur of a terrible necessity, to cast their guilty passenger into the sea: all this is graphically described, and is familiar to all Bible readers. Three things, however, are especially worthy of note in this thrilling portion of the narrative:

1. The heroism and magnanimity of these heathen sailors must have touched the heart of Jonah. He was inspired in his flight by an intense, all-controlling hate of the Gentiles — all of whom, according to his notion, were under the curse of God. Yet he has hardly stepped off his own territory until he is brought face to face with Gentiles whose beautiful and touching exhibition of tenderness and goodness is a new revelation to him. How often we shut ourselves up in the narrow spirit of sect, or caste, or race, and make ourselves miserable in hating or despising all outside our own charmed circle, when those whom we despise are our superiors in genuine worth!

2. It must have been equally a surprise to the sailors to find in

---

[1] While it is not certain that this is the "Tarshish" mentioned in the text, the probabilities are, in our judgment, in favor of this conclusion.

Jonah such downright honesty, and so high a sense of justice. He conceals nothing. He frankly owns his guilt and his folly, pronounces the sentence of justice against himself, and insists on its execution. He will not involve others in destruction on account of a sin which is all his own. This atones for much that is unlovely in Jonah. We can deal leniently with very serious faults, if only a man is truthful, honest, and just. Jonah is narrow-minded. He is a bigot. He is heartless in his bigotry. He knows not the meaning of philanthropy. He would exult over the destruction of the whole Gentile world. But he is truthful; he is honest; he is just, according to his understanding of justice. Let us bless him for this. There is always hope of a man, whatever his faults, who has truthfulness for the basis of his character.

3. It is silly, as well as unmanly, to attempt to escape from duty. A man may run away from dangers, from evil associations, from unhappy strifes and embroilments; it may be wise to do so. But he cannot run away from God, nor can he run away from himself. His guilt and wretchedness go with him wherever he goes, and God's avenging justice will follow him to the ends of the earth. The only safe way is to face duty manfully, however unwelcome it may be, and leave the results with God.

Here we come to a part of the narrative which provokes incredulity with so many, and which has led to so many attempts at special interpretation. According to these perplexed interpreters, it is fable; or, it is an attempt to load the true history with the ornaments of fancy; or, it is an apologue,[1] founded on a history; or, it is based on the Phoenician fable of Hercules, who was represented as swallowed by a sea-monster, and then restored, etc., etc. The only reason for such strained interpretations is to get rid of the miraculous element in the narrative; but under a dispensation marked plentifully through the larger part of its duration by miraculous demonstrations and interpositions, it is vain to attempt to make an exceptional case here. Let us say, however, that there is not so much of the miraculous here as is generally supposed. The swallowing of Jonah by a sea-monster has nothing of the miraculous in it. The white shark, which is not uncommon in the Mediterranean, is not only capable of such a task, but there is evidence that it has successfully

---

[1] A moral fable.

performed it; and it is even claimed by naturalists that this shark has the power of "throwing up again, whole and alive, the prey it has seized."[1] The preservation of Jonah's life in the belly of the fish for three days and nights, or for one whole day and night and parts of two other days and rights, can only be explained as miraculous; but it is not more difficult to believe than the preservation of the three Hebrews in the fiery furnace, or the resurrection of Jesus from the dead. Indeed, the reference of Jesus to the facts in Jonah's history shows that he regarded this preservation and restoration of Jonah as a grand miracle of power, akin to that by which he was himself to be raised from the dead and his acceptance of the facts in the Book of Jonah as historically true forbids us to yield to any but the historical interpretation (Matt. 12:38-41). The swallowing of Jonah by the sea-monster is as historical, in the estimation of Jesus, as the preaching of Jonah to the Ninevites.

Released from his strange and awful imprisonment, and having celebrated, in fitting strains, his deliverance out of a hopeless grave — "out of the belly of Sheol" — Jonah is so far subdued by his terrible and wonderful experiences as to accept the duty laid upon him — to go to Nineveh and proclaim its destruction. There is too little that is trustworthy in the writings of the ancients concerning Nineveh to enable us to speak accurately of its size and population. If we take the statement in chap. 4:11, to refer to infants, then we may safely conclude that the city had a population of about 600,000. And if the expression "an exceeding great city of three days' journey" has reference to its circumference, then the statements of the area of the city by Diodorus Siculus and Strabo may be regarded as correct. Unquestionably, as the capital of a, mighty empire, it was "an exceedingly great city,"[2] and, like all great cities, especially capitals and centers of corrupt systems of idolatry, it was reeking with sin and crime. Into this great city the lonely prophet entered, in foreign garb, with all the weirdness of appearance and manners that characterized the prophets of the olden time, and, amid the hum of business, the rumbling of chariot-wheels, the shouts of revelry, the ceaseless tramp of pedestrians, the clatter of

---

[1] See Dr. Pusey's "Minor Prophets," on Jonah; *Smith's Bible Dictionary*, Art. "Whale."

[2] See Layard's *"Nineveh and its Remains."*

marketplaces, and the jeers of curious throngs that gathered about the eccentric foreigner, lifted up his voice in a sad wail that seems to have awed all other voices and noises into silence, and went echoing through the streets, and over the parks and gardens, and up to the entrance of the royal palace, as a voice of doom: "Yet forty days and Nineveh shall be destroyed!" It reminds us of the voice of the son of Ananus, at the siege of Jerusalem under Titus, when he proclaimed, in tones of thrilling terror, through the streets of Jerusalem, day by day, "A voice from the east, a voice from the west, a voice from the four winds, a voice against Jerusalem and the holy house, a voice against the bridegrooms and the brides, a voice against the whole people: Woe be to Jerusalem!" But briefer, with an eloquence more compact, intense, and terrifying, was this piercing cry of Jonah, "Yet forty days, and Nineveh shall be destroyed!" It was sustained by no evidence. It was upheld by no argument. It was confirmed by no miracle. It was enforced by no acknowledged authority. It came from the lips of a stranger who had nothing in common with them. And yet it swept over the city with the might of heaven's resistless thunders, and shook it to the foundations. Every voice of mirth was hushed. Every jeer, every note of ridicule or of defiance, was awed and silenced. The hum and roar of business died away, and the shouts of revelry, and even the murmur of tongues in the streets and in places of concourse. The city's life-pulse ceased to beat, except in feverish flutters. The penetrating wail of the prophet smote the heart of the king on his throne, and the gay, proud, luxurious court of Nineveh and the members of the royal household bowed down in dust and ashes. Soon the whole city was robed in sackcloth, and to the prophet's weird voice succeeds the mighty cry of the guilty and prostrate population — a cry to heaven for mercy!

How such overwhelming results were produced from a cause so apparently feeble and inconsequential, we may not be able to tell. How far the Ninevites were acquainted with the fame of Jonah as a prophet, or with the peculiar circumstances attending his special mission to Nineveh; or what their previous knowledge of the achievements of the God of Israel may have had to do in impressing them with the truth of Jonah's message, we can only conjecture. One thing is quite probable; another is altogether certain.

It is *probable* that the confused and threatening condition of affairs in the city and in large portions of the empire, had much to do in preparing king and people to listen reverently to this voice of warning. Provinces had been in revolt — revolts taking on such a magnitude as to threaten the integrity of the empire. For a period of forty years, up to the accession of Pul, B.C. 745, there had been a constant succession of bloody revolts, which severely taxed the strength of the empire; and away back of that the peace and safety of the government had been frequently and seriously threatened. At such a time of general disquiet and widespread fear and distrust, the throne trembling, and the capital rocked with disturbances, or surging with agitations that threatened calamity to the city and the empire, the appearance of a prophet of such unearthly aspect, with such a message, might readily impress itself on an agitated and distressed people and alarmed monarch, as a voice from heaven not to be disregarded.

The *certain* thing is this: there are crises in the lives of nations, as of individuals, when influences long at work gather to a head — when sin itself, without the aid of argument or appeal, becomes disgusting in its terrible fruitage, and hideous in all its aspects, and horrible in all its workings, and men feel and know that they are on the edge of dreadful retributions, and every pulse is a pulse of fear and anguish. At such a time the one thing needful is a *voice of thunder to the conscience.* Before this, everything gives way. It needs no labored argument. The stony hearts have already been drilled; the dynamite has been placed; the wires have been laid; the battery is prepared, and all the connections have been established. It wants but the touch of a finger to let in the power that has been stored up for the hour of catastrophe, and instantly comes the terrific explosion that rends the rocks and tosses them like playthings into the air. It was at such a crisis that Jonah appeared at Nineveh. Everything was ready. It needed but his electric message to produce the explosion that shattered the pride and broke the hearts of that vast population, and laid Nineveh's Hell-gate in ruins.

How often we argue when argument is vain — when what is needed is the stern voice of truth that speaks with resistless authority, and compels a response from the heart that is already self-condemned, and the conscience that cannot repress its answering thunders.

Preserve us, O Lord, from bigotry. Teach us not to despise our fellow-men. Grant that we may never flee from duty, and vainly think to hide from Thy presence. May we learn that the path of duty is the path of safety, and that they that walk uprightly, walk surely.

Jonah and the Ninevites (Part Two)

How long Jonah continued to preach to the Ninevites, we do not know. We are told of but one day's preaching. Whether he went the "three days' journey" necessary to compass the entire city, preaching as he went; or, produced such a universal impression the first day that no further preaching was necessary; no one can now tell. But, the more we study his character, the more unlovely does it appear. He was not only a preacher of wrath, for which he had no responsibility, since his message was given to him from the Lord; but he was a wrathful preacher — and here he *had* responsibility, for he was under no instructions to deliver his message in a hateful spirit. It seems to us impossible to imagine a spirit more utterly divorced from the duty laid upon it.

1. He hates to go on this mission. He determines not to go. He seeks to run away from duty and from God.

2. He goes, at last only because he is compelled to go. There is no escape from it. Like a galley-slave scourged to his task, his unwilling feet go on this hateful errand.

3. He merely obeys the letter of his instructions, without an effort to enter into the spirit of his mission. He was well aware that Jehovah's purpose was to bring the Ninevites to repentance and save them from the impending doom (chap. 4:2): and had he sympathized with this gracious purpose, there would have been tenderness in his heart and an exquisite pathos in his pleadings. But, without one spark of sympathy with this guilty population, over which was brooding a dire vengeance, he thundered the message of doom in their ears in a spirit of wrath that added to its terrors. He was indeed a *foreign* missionary — a missionary foreign in every thought, in every heart-beat, in every prejudice and passion of his nature, in every tone of his voice, in every look of his eye, to the interests and sympathies of the people to whom he was sent.

4. One would have thought that when he witnessed the quick and hearty response of the whole city to his preaching — when he saw the entire population, from the king to the beggar, turning from their sins, and humbling themselves in the dust, and heard their piteous cries for mercy — his stubborn heart would melt, and he would join his prayers to theirs that the threatened wrath might

155

be averted. It seems impossible that any human heart could remain unmoved by this startling spectacle of a great city of half a million souls sitting in ashes, covered with sackcloth, and, in penitence and shame, crying out of the dust for the mercy of God. But we are not authorized to believe, from any hint given to us in the Scriptures, that so much as one kind look or word went forth from this preacher to any one of this city full of broken hearts.

On the contrary, as soon as he had fulfilled the letter of his commission, he "went out of the city" — separated himself from all these penitent throngs, as if dreading the least contact with them — "and sat on the east side of the city, and there made him a booth, and sat under it in the shadow, till" — till what? Till he might learn whether this universal humiliation and repentance was a mere gust of emotion to last only for a day? Till he could ascertain whether, in the event of the repentance proving sincere and permanent, there was further work for him to do in instructing and encouraging these benighted heathen souls, and in transforming this capital of earth's greatest empire into a City of God, a habitation of Jehovah's praise? Oh no: "till he might see what would become of the city!" Waiting for the forty days to expire, that he might see thunderbolts red with uncommon wrath descend on palace and temple, with crashing vengeance, and feel the earth rock with earthquake violence under the city's walls and towers, and look upon the smoke and blaze of a mighty conflagration, and listen to the shrieks of half a million fellow-beings perishing in the flames! And then, after "treading the ashes of the wicked under the soles of his feet," and walking with exultant step over the charred ruins of earth's mightiest city, he could return cheerily to his own beloved land and tell God's elect people — faithless and corrupt as they were — how Jehovah had spread death and ruin among the uncircumcised! Was ever piety perverted and disgraced by a more heartless bigotry than this?

We are drawing no fancy picture. Although the story is told in few words, there is no need to mistake its meaning. Jonah found shelter from the oppressive heat in the shade of a rapidly growing tree — perhaps the *Palma Christi*, or Castor-oil plant — which, growing and unfolding its broad leaves rapidly during the forty days of his waiting, became to him a grateful retreat, to which, in the absence of all human associations and sympathies, he became greatly attached. With a prophet's limited wants and self-denying habits, it was to him equal to a royal palace — nay, far superior: for, while the forked lightnings should descend on the battlements of the royal mansions, and the thunders should crash over the whole doomed city, not even a rough wind should visit the leafy bower[1] where dwelt the prophet of Jehovah! So here he dwelt for one full moon and more, nursing his wrath and counting the days until the day of Nineveh's doom should come.

The forty days came and went. We can well imagine that no eye was closed in Nineveh on the night of that fortieth day. With sleepless anxiety they waited to learn whether their repentance had availed to turn aside the threatened destruction. Nor is it likely that Jonah closed his eyes. Doubtless he watched the heavens for some token of the approaching tempest of wrath. He waited with unsleeping vigilance to know if Jehovah would set the seal of truth to his ministry by fulfilling the threat which, by divine authority, he had published. What were the lives of five hundred thousand heathen dogs, and all the glory of Nineveh, compared with the honor of a circumcised prophet of Jehovah? But the fortieth night and the forty-first day came and went, and the heavens were calm and bright, and the earth was beautiful and fragrant. The birds sang, and the waters babbled gaily along, and the soft breezes came laden with the breath of flowers, and the sun shone on Nineveh in all its brightness; and the sackcloth was laid aside, and over the walls of the great city came hymns of thanksgiving and anthems of praise that drowned the wails of anguish which for forty days had filled the air — for God had repented of the evil that he had pronounced against the wicked, but now repentant, city.

Everybody was happy but Jonah! He was "very angry" — angry because Jehovah had been merciful to repenting sinners! He broke out in a strain of mortified pride and disappointed hate — in what the writer of this book calls a prayer. Such a prayer! — a piety of gall and wormwood, of mean selfishness and unmerciful hate. Well is it for us that God is so much better than our prayers.

I pray thee, O Lord, was not this my saying when I was yet in my country? Therefore I fled before unto Tarshish:

---

[1] Shelter.

for I knew that thou art a gracious God, and merciful,
slow to anger, and of great kindness, and repentest thee of
the evil. Therefore, now, O Lord, take, I beseech thee, my
life from me; for it is better for me to die than to live!

Is this *praying?* Or is it not rather mere *fuming?* It is a petulant and insulting arraignment alike of the justice and mercy of God — and all because this selfish, ill-natured bigot felt that his reputation was at stake! He had no objections to proclaiming wrath, if only the wrath would come and sustain his reputation as a prophet. But to utter words of warning that might lead Gentiles to repentance, so that mercy might rejoice against judgment — never! Better that all Nineveh should perish, than that Jonah's wrathful prophecy should be unfulfilled! Better, far, to die than to have anyone saved contrary to his narrow creed. "Take, I beseech thee, my life from me, for it is better to die than to live." There are, alas, many Jonahs, even yet!

"Doest thou well to be angry?" is the gentle inquiry of the patient Jehovah: and then, for a time, He left the wrathful prophet to his own reflections. But the next morning Jonah awoke to find that his beautiful, shady bower was all withered; and when an oppressive east wind came, and the intolerable heat of the sun beat upon his unsheltered head, he again cried out for death. "Doest thou well to be angry for the *kikayon*?" — the gourd, or the Palma Christi bower. "Yes," said the wretched man, "I do well to be angry, even unto death." The way is now open to expose and rebuke his mean selfishness and bigotry. "Thou hast had pity on the gourd, for which thou hast not labored, neither made it grow; which came up in a night and perished in a night;[1] and should I not spare Nineveh, that great city, wherein are more than six score thousand persons that cannot discern between their right hand and their left hand, and also much cattle?" Whether Jonah answered, and if so, what his answer was, we are not informed. The narrative breaks off abruptly here. Let us hope that he went home, if a sadder, yet a wiser, man.

Let us suggest some of the lessons taught in this singular narra-

---

[1] There is no need to press these words to an exact literalness; it was probably a proverbial expression to express speedy growth and speedy decay — just as we speak of short-lived pleasures as "the pleasures of an hour."

tive, by which we may profit:

1. Jonah is a typical Jew. His narrowness and bigotry were those of the Jews at large. The conceit that they alone were the favorites of heaven has been the conceit and the curse of sectarian bigots in every age. There is, in the Old Testament, a gradual unfolding of God's gracious purposes in behalf of the Gentiles. "The inspiration of the Gentile world," says Dean Stanley, "is acknowledged in the prophecy of Balaam, its nobleness in the Book of Job, its greatness in the reign of Solomon. But its distinct claims on the justice and mercy of God are first recognized in the Book of Jonah." We may add that it was a hundred years after Jonah's time before Isaiah and Micah received their glorious visions of "all nations" flowing unto the mountain of the Lord. Looking back now, from the summit of God's mountain, we can see how the way was prepared, through the ages, for the salvation of all peoples, and that the Jewish nation was simply God's agent to bring about this glorious consummation. Yet there are many, even now, who think that for four thousand years all outside of the Old Testament covenants perished; and many reject the Old Testament because they regard it as teaching that for ages God doomed all the human race to destruction, except a handful of His covenant people on a little patch of land in Palestine! To all such, this Book of Jonah ought to be a great revelation. It is a book of sublime importance, as intimating the scope of God's mercy.

2. Closely akin to this is the lesson, that so eternal and unalterable is the purpose of God to forgive the penitent ("His mercy endureth forever"), that even when unexpressed, it is always implied. It was unexpressed in Jonah's preaching; the proclamation of destruction was apparently unconditional; yet no sooner did the Ninevites repent than the doom was withdrawn. See Jer. 18:1-10. The only sin that hath never forgiveness is the sin unrepented of.

3. "Take we heed that we place not our felicity in the enjoyment, or please ourselves too much in the confidence, or allow ourselves overmuch freedom in the use, of any creature; but as Jonah was overjoyed when the gourd sprang up, and overvexed when it withered, so the loss of what we overvalued when we had it, overwhelms us with grief and impatience when we must part from

it."[1]

4. Let us beware how we exalt our thoughts and ways against the thoughts and ways of God. "Are we not disposed to murmur at God's dispensations, and in a hasty spirit wish ourselves out of the world? Is there no gourd, no earthly comfort, on which we have foolishly placed our affections, and for the loss of which we are inconsolable? Are we not ready to say, 'What good shall my life do me, since the desire of my eyes is removed?' We ask again, 'Doest thou well to be angry?' O vindicate not such pride and petulance, but confess your guilt and implore forgiveness."[2]

5. Let us cherish a *philanthropic* spirit. Love of family, of friends, of country, of race, of those of kindred faith: all these may be virtuous. But if we stop at any of these, and fail to reach the love of man *as man,* we dwarf our nature, and fail to conform to the image of God. A man may be honest and pious, and yet, from the narrow range of his sympathies and fellowships, have an unlovely character. Jonah was honest and pious, but his character is exceedingly deformed by his narrowness of sympathy, his fierce bigotry, his intense hate of all outside the little circle of Judaism. A thoroughly genuine Christianity will never be seen until an uncompromising devotion to truth and a universal philanthropy shall be superior to creed, sect, or nationality.

6. Not the least important lesson to be learned is our obligation, in view of our superior advantages, to give heed to the word of God. "The men of Nineveh," said Jesus, "shall rise in judgment with this generation, and shall condemn it; for they repented at the preaching of Jonah, and, behold, a greater than Jonah is here." Think of these Ninevites: raised in heathenish darkness; hearing a preacher who hated them, who preached but one sermon, and that sermon full of wrath. They saw no miracle, heard no argument or exhortation, received no encouragement, had no promise of pardon — yet they repented and turned to God. Yet how many — perhaps even among those who read these pages — in a land full of Bibles, with all religious surroundings in their favor, with voices of pleading from home and Sunday-school and church, and from the graves of beloved ones, sounding in their ears, beseeching them to be rec-

---

[1] Bishop Sanderson
[2] Robinson's *Scripture Characters.*

onciled to God; who have heard hundreds of earnest sermons, and listened to numberless private entreaties, and whose hearts and consciences have been touched many times by the lessons of Providence and the invitations of God's grace — still fail to repent and turn to God! Yes, the men of Nineveh will condemn you; and, what is worse than this, you will stand self-condemned before the judgment-seat, if you do not repent.

After all has been said, this little book of Jonah is a wonderful and a wonderfully instructive book.

O God of mercy! We know not how to praise thee as we ought for that mercy which endureth forever. Wherever the humble and contrite heart is found, there Thy presence is also found. Thou hast never turned a deaf ear to the cry of the penitent, blessed be Thy name! Teach us to sympathize with the perishing, and to seek their salvation. And not only at home, but wherever there are sinners to be rescued from the ways of death — however corrupted and degraded they may be — may we be ready to reach forth a heart of compassion and a hand of help to them. Let us not, like Jonah, be so wrapped up in home interests as to be opposed to foreign missions. Save us, not only from all hate of our fellow-men, but also from all indifference to their wants and woes.

Royal Reformers: Asa

(1 Kings 15:9-24; 2 Chron. 14-16)

Every careful reader of Old Testament history must be struck with the contrast between the monarchies of Judah and Israel. Each of these kingdoms had nineteen kings; but the nineteen kings of Israel reigned only about two hundred and fifty years, while the nineteen kings of Judah reigned about four hundred years. One family in Judah holds the throne through nearly four centuries, while within two and a half centuries there are nine changes of dynasty in Israel. Asa, who ascended the throne of Judah in the last year of Jeroboam, witnessed the overthrow of Nadab, Baasha, Elah, Zimri, Tibni, and outlived Omri's reign of twelve years. There are several reasons for this.

1. The prestige of the reigns of David and Solomon remained with Judah, and loyalty to the throne was the popular sentiment; while the other kingdom sprang out of a rebellious spirit, which was readily reawakened with every popular discontent.

2. Judah had the temple, the priesthood, and the ordinances of divine appointment; while the religion of Israel was a mongrel affair, devised by Jeroboam, and was incapable of inspiring respect or reverence.

3. Not only the Levites, but the most enlightened and pious of the other tribes, forsook the territory of Israel and cast in their lot with Judah and Benjamin, because of their attachment to the true religion. And while, from other than religious motives, the bitter rivalry between the two kingdoms led the people of Judah to exalt their own worship against the false worship of Beth-el and Dan, those who, from religious conviction, forsook their own homes, were intense in their hate of, and uncompromising in their opposition to, everything that tended to corrupt the law and the worship of Jehovah. On the other hand, the people of Israel, who had already consented to a gross corruption of the religion in which they had been educated, were open to the seductions of the pompous, sensuous, idolatrous, and licentious worship of neighboring heathen kingdoms and tribes. See 2 Chron. 13:4-12.

4. The Messiah was to come in the line of David. In a special sense, therefore, the throne of David was under the covenant pro-

tection of Jehovah. See 2 Chron. 21:7. All the sacred traditions of the nation, all the proud patriotism nourished for nearly a century by the magnificent triumphs of David and the splendor of Solomon's peaceful reign, all the strength and enthusiasm of the religious devotion that centered in the Temple and the Priesthood of Jerusalem, and all the high hopes of an all-conquering Messiah who should possess the throne of David and sway an undisputed scepter over all the world, combined to strengthen the loyalty and piety of the people of Judah alike against rebelliousness and idolatry. But the kingdom of Israel was essentially military in spirit, and was subject to the violent and bloody revolutions to which military governments are always exposed. The history of military governments is a history of assassinations and revolutions.

Yet, notwithstanding all these conservative influences, Judah was continually subject to the invasions of idolatry, and at last was so completely overpowered that one of the prophets declared, "Neither hath Samaria committed half thy sins; but thou hast multiplied thine abominations more than they." See Ezek. 16. The defeats of sin and iniquity are never final. The unclean spirit may be exorcized from the body politic, as from the human body, and the temple he polluted may be emptied of its defilements, and swept and garnished; but the dislodged demon will return with seven other spirits more wicked than himself, and strive again to enter. The heroes of righteousness can never repose[1] on their laurels. There is no discharge in this war. "Eternal vigilance is the price of liberty." Let us never dream that because, in our personal history, or in any public movement against error and wrong, we have fought a battle and won it — complete as the victory may seem to be — the war is over. Often the greatest danger is the self-security that victory occasions. You may fight and win, fight and win, a hundred times, and be conquered at last through the over-confidence that victory inspires and the cessation of vigilance against a sleepless foe.

The corrupting influence of idolatry that darkened the close of Solomon's reign was not diminished during the succeeding reigns of Rehoboam and Abijah. While the prevailing sentiment was strongly against idolatry, the influence of the court was largely in its favor. These invasions of heathenism were largely owing to

---

[1] Rest.

women, and, grew out of unlawful marriages with foreigners by members of the royal family. It was through the blandishments of his heathen wives that Solomon was persuaded to permit idolatrous worship in Jerusalem. The wisest of men became a base fool through the bewitchments of the harem. Maachah, the favorite wife of Rehoboam, was a daughter or grand-daughter of Absalom (2 Chron. 11:20-21), and the mother of Absalom was the daughter of Tamar, king of Geshur (2 Sam. 3:3), and the wild heathenish blood that flowed in the veins of Absalom, flowed also in the veins of this favorite wife of Rehoboam, whose devotion to the grossest forms of idolatry became a prime source of hideous corruptions in Judah (2 Chron. 15:16). Jezebel, Maachah, Athaliah: — these three names stand for everything that is false, iniquitous, cruel, and revolting in the idol-worship of Israel and Judah; and their power to curse the people of God *came through unwise and unlawful marriages with unbelievers.* There is a great lesson here, which we cannot now pause to enforce; we merely drop a hint which may start the reader into reflection.

We have already written of Jezebel and Athaliah; let us say a word concerning Maachah, worthy to take the third place in this trinity of evil powers. She was the wife of Rehoboam, the mother of Abijah, and the grandmother of Asa. It is evident, from passages already referred to, that she had a supreme influence over Rehoboam, and during the reign of Abijah was the Queen Mother, — a position next in influence to that of the King, and often, when female blandishments were combined with wicked ambition and talent for intrigue, the Queen Mother was a power behind the throne greater than the throne itself. We need not be surprised, therefore, to learn that, under her influence, her son Abijah "walked in all the sins of his father, which he had done before him" (1 Ki. 15:3). She seems to have retained her official dignity after the death of her son. Perhaps, owing to the tender age of Asa, her grandson, she acted as regent for several years. At all events, she managed to retain a commanding position in the government, and used it for the promotion of her vile superstitions. What is recorded of her is in few words, but they are very significant. We quote 2 Chron. 15:16 from the Revised Version:

"And also Maachah, the mother of Asa, the king, he

removed her from being queen [marginal reading: *queen mother*] *because she had made an abominable image for an Asherah; and Asa cut down her image and made dust of it, and burnt it at the brook Kidron.*"

This idol, or abominable image, is called in Hebrew a *horror*. It was an image employed in the worship of Astarte, and was so hideously obscene in its expression as to be styled *abominable* even in comparison with such images generally — and the least offensive of them were altogether vile. She was, therefore, not only by virtue of her official rank, an enthusiastic patron of the licentious rites in the worship of Ashtaroth, but was personally one of the most degraded slaves of heathen superstition.

How Asa came to be so superior to his environment is something of a mystery. His grandmother was a fanatical devotee at the vilest of heathen shrines. His father's character was not commendable. It is said (1 Ki. 15:3) that "he walked in all the sins of his father, which he had done before him; and his heart was not perfect with the Lord his God, as the heart of David his father." Yet in the narrative in 2 Chronicles, he does not appear as altogether bad. His speech to Jeroboam and Israel (2 Chron. 13:4-12) indicates strong faith in Jehovah, and devotion to His law. It appears also that he dedicated liberally to the house of Jehovah of the spoils he had taken in his great victory over Jeroboam, although these were misappropriated by the heathen priests, with the connivance of the queen-mother, for the benefit of the goddess Astarte, and did not reach their proper destination until the fifteenth year of Asa (2 Chron. 15:10, 18). As Abijah reigned only three years, he had not opportunity for a full development of his character. As far as we see it, it was a mixed character — half Jewish, half heathenish. Perhaps he began well, with full intent to be faithful to Jehovah, but under the influence of his mother's blandishments and machinations, and the flatteries of heathen courtiers, was led into at least a partial abandonment of his integrity. Or, as a mere matter of policy, he may have been tempted to court the favor of both heathen and Jewish religionists, subordinating everything religious to the strength of his throne while that throne was in peril on account of his wars with Jeroboam. If so, he was not the first nor the last to build his hopes of success on a policy of duplicity — crying Good

Lord, or Good Devil, as his political interests dictated. Mark the men who make religion simply a thing of policy to subserve their own selfish interests. They are rotten at heart — the vilest of hypocrites.

It is evident that Asa could not have received any encouragements to piety from such a father, especially at the tender age at which he came to the throne. Did he receive his faith and piety from his mother? We do not know. Her name is not so much as mentioned. The bad preeminence of his grandmother overshadowed the mother's name and fame. We read, indeed, that "Abijah waxed mighty, and married fourteen wives, and begat twenty and two sons and sixteen daughters" (2 Chron. 13:21); but which of these fourteen wives was the mother of Asa, we know not. It is not unlikely that we are indebted to some humble, pious daughter of Israel, whose very name has perished, for all that is noble and glorious in the reformation wrought by Asa, and that while the name of the grandmother Maachah has won an infamous immortality, the name of the faithful mother who trained him to honor Jehovah and fear His law, is known only in heaven. How many of God's faithful ones have gone uncrowned, unhonored, unsung, serving Him grandly in obscurity, in lives all uninspired by human praise! Though "shining unobserved," their light is "not of essential splendor less." Perhaps the brightest crowns of heaven will rest on the brows of those who knew on earth no crown but one of thorns. "Ye good distressed" who toil on in the ways of righteousness uncheered by human sympathy, take courage. Your lives are not in vain. They may reach out in great blessing, as in the child Asa, though you live and die unknown. Whether they do or not, you are the richer for your work of faith, and shall in no wise lose your reward.

From whatever source, Asa obtained a faith and courage that enabled him to overcome the corrupting influences then prevalent at the court. The heart of the nation was still loyal to Jehovah. It wanted but a leader to sound the trumpet, and the people were ready to respond to the call. When the leader was found in the king himself, the people were enthusiastic in answering to his call.

> *He took away the altars of the strange gods, and the high places, and brake down the pillars (or obelisks), and*

hewed down the Asherim,[1] and commanded Judah to seek the Lord, the God of their fathers, and to do the law and the commandment. Also, he took away out of all the cities of Judah the high places and the sun-images; and the kingdom was quiet before him" (2 Chron. 14:3-5).

Prospered in all this, he employed years of peace in rebuilding and fortifying the cities of Judah and strengthening his army. But such work is never allowed to go long undisturbed. Zerah the Ethiopian — perhaps the same as Osorkon, a king of the twenty-second Egyptian dynasty — came against him with an immense army that threatened to sweep everything before its resistless march. Asa went out to meet him with a firm reliance on the protecting arm of the one living God. His prayer to Jehovah is as sublime in spirit as it is simple in expression: "Lord, there is none beside thee to help, between the mighty and him that hath no strength: help us, O Lord our God; for we rely on thee, and in thy name are we come against this multitude. O Lord, thou art our God; let not man prevail against thee." And in this faith he made an assault upon the apparently invincible forces of Zerah, and smote them with an overwhelming defeat. Thus alike in peace and war were Asa's faith and courage rewarded. It was upon his exultant return from this great victory that the prophet Azariah met him, and seized the opportunity to strengthen him in his noble reformatory purposes.

Hear me, ye Asa, and all Judah and Benjamin: the Lord is with you while ye be with him; and if ye seek him, he will be found of you; but if ye forsake him, he will forsake you.

A very simple, but rational and true theology, albeit it lodges a heavy responsibility with man for his own failures and woes — heavier than most men are willing to accept. He then proceeds to point out the work of reformation that remains to be done:

Now for long seasons Israel hath been without the true God, and without a teaching priest, and without law: but when in their distress they turned unto Jehovah, the God of Israel, and sought him, he was found of them. And in

---

[1] Probably the wooden symbols of a goddess Asherah.

those times there was no peace to him that went out, nor to him that came in, but great vexations were upon all the inhabitants of the lands. And they were broken in pieces, nation against nation, and city against city: for God did vex them with all adversity. But be ye strong, and let not your hands be slack; for your work shall be rewarded.

Thus encouraged, Asa proceeded with all zeal, not only to root out the prevailing corruptions and abominations, but to establish anew the laws and ordinances of Jehovah. He is but half a reformer — a mere iconoclast — who contents himself with *destroying*. The true reformer not only tears down, but builds up; not only destroys, but recreates. Asa not only "put away the abominations out of all the land of Judah and Benjamin, and out of the cities which he had taken from the hill country of Ephraim," but he renewed the altar of Jehovah, and restored the sacrifices, and brought into the temple the things that his father had dedicated, and that he himself had dedicated; and, assembling Judah and Jerusalem, with all that had come to them out of Ephraim and Manasseh and Simeon, "they sacrificed unto Jehovah of the spoil which they had brought; and they entered into a covenant to seek the Lord, the God of their fathers, with all their heart, and with all their soul, and that whosoever would not seek Jehovah, the God of Israel, should be put to death, whether small or great, whether man or woman. And they sware unto the Lord with a loud voice, and with shouting, and with trumpets, and with cornets. And all Judah rejoiced at the oath: for they had sworn with all their heart, and sought him with their whole desire; and he was found of them; and Jehovah gave them rest round about" (2 Chron. 15:9-15). And to crown this work of reformation with an illustrious act of impartial justice, Asa cut down the abominable image that his grandmother had set up, and "made dust of it, and burnt it at the brook Kidron," and deposed the guilty queen-mother from her official dignity and authority — that it might be seen that no considerations of kindred, or of family pride, should interfere with the just demands of the law of God.

But there is a deep shading to this picture. It is important, in these noble efforts at reformation, to note the imperfections that marred them — the failures as well as the successes that characterized them; for there are important lessons in both.

1. While we read that Asa took away the high places," we read again, "but the high places were not taken away out of Israel." The reform was but partial. Asa purposed to take them all away, but he succeeded only in part. The high places, which had been tolerated in days of adversity, when the tabernacle had no permanent abiding place and when the people were unable to resort to it as a place of worship, owing to the possession of the land by hostile forces — though these high places had afterward been prostituted to idolatrous worship — had become sacred to the people by long usage; and although, after the building of the temple and the reign of peace in the land, they were no longer necessary, *attachment to usage* continued to have all the force of divine authority, and it was next to impossible to win the people from their venerated customs. And thus it has been in all reformations. In the reformatory efforts of Luther and Calvin and Wesley, ancient usages, entirely unsupported by Scripture, have maintained their places among the laws and ordinances of God, with nothing better to support them than the sacredness and power of *custom* and *prejudice.* At the end of every history of Christian reformation it may be written, "But the high places were not taken away out of Israel." Let us beware.

2. Asa's faith in God did not grow with his growth. Baasha, king of Israel, had seized Ramah — only five or six miles distant from Jerusalem — "that he might not suffer any to go out or come in to Asa," for the pious Israelites had in multitudes fled into Judah (2 Chron. 15:9). Such a fortification, so near the capital of Judah, would be a continual menace to Jerusalem. But Asa seems to have lost his strong faith in Jehovah, that it was "nothing for God to help, whether with many, or with them that have no power;" and in place of looking to Jehovah for deliverance, he sent great treasures to the king of Syria, to bribe him to break his league with Baasha and fight against him. The scheme was successful, and Baasha was compelled to abandon Ramah. But it was, after all, not a success. Nothing unrighteous is ever a success, however successful it may, for the time, seem to be. Hanani the prophet came to Asa, just when we may suppose him to have been priding himself on the success of his diplomacy, with a message from the Lord: "Because thou hast relied on the king of Syria, and not relied on Jehovah thy God, *therefore is the host of the king of Syria escaped out of thine hand:*" intimating that had Asa been true to his earlier faith in Je-

hovah, not only would Baasha have been conquered, but Syria would have been subjugated also. "Were not the Ethiopians and the Lubims a huge host, with very many chariots and horsemen? *Yet because thou didst rely on Jehovah,* he delivered them into thine hand. For the eyes of Jehovah run to and fro throughout the whole earth, to show himself strong in behalf of them whose heart is perfect toward him. Herein hast thou done foolishly; therefore from henceforth thou shalt have wars." Is it not strange that when our faith in God is rewarded, we should allow it to be supplanted by self-sufficiency or by a reliance on human policy? The danger to one's spiritual life, or to the prosperity of a work of reformation, is not in the time of weakness when we are driven to trust in God in the absence of all other help; but when the day of prosperity comes, and human resources multiply, and we forget the Hand that has blessed us, and begin to say, "Is not this great Babylon that I have builded, by the power of my might, and for the honor of my majesty?" Then, in self-exaltation, or in a reliance on human expedients, we are apt to dishonor God and bring disaster on ourselves. There is a great lesson here.

But more than this: Asa, although he knew that all the prophet had said was true, "was wroth with the seer, and put him in a prison-house, for he was in a rage with him because of this thing. And Asa oppressed some of the people the same time." Thus as pride increases with prosperity, we not only depart from God, but grow intolerant when our sins are rebuked. Successful reformers are apt to grow intolerant. Witness Luther in his dealings with Zwingli, and Calvin with Servetus. What a blot on the character of Asa as a reformer! And how many such blots defile the reputation of bold and brave and righteous men, who have done great things for God and humanity! Let us learn from these sad failures to guard against the blinding influence of prosperity — against pride, self-sufficiency, and intolerance.

3. Asa does not seem to have recovered from this lapse into unbelief; for the last we learn of him, toward the close of his reign, is, that he was "diseased in his feet until his disease was exceeding great; yet in his disease he sought not unto the Lord, but unto the physicians." Not a high compliment, surely, to the physicians; but they were probably unprincipled quacks — pretenders to the possession of magical powers. There was good reason, at that time, for

seeking unto the Lord rather than unto the physicians, for there was no science of medicine, and physicians were merely shrewd pretenders. Even yet, what we call the science of medicine is largely empirical. That Asa should resort to the impudent pretenders of that time, and fail to seek unto the Lord, who had so signally blessed him, is sad evidence that his faith, instead of growing and abounding with his ever-increasing accumulations of experience in the service of Jehovah, had been overshadowed by his pride and arrogance, until the glory of his early religious life was sadly dimmed. Forty-one years of almost absolute power was too much for him. Great power and prosperity had spoiled him, until he was deaf to the voice of God and gloried in his own strength. The greatest peril to spiritual interests is large and long-continued prosperity in earthly things. There are few who can resist its corrupting influence, for it is a subtle and blinding influence.

We mourn over our afflictions, and murmur at the calamities that befall us, when they are probably the greatest mercies with which a wise and kind Father could visit us. "Jeshurun waxed fat and kicked."[1] There are Jeshuruns in every generation — nations, churches, as well as individuals. Alas! how often, in our national and church troubles, when we are weak and distressed, in place of seeking unto the Lord, we seek unto the political and ecclesiastical quacks, and by a resort to every human device seek relief from the troubles which are curable only by a return to truth and righteousness — by submission to the unerring law and the unfailing mercy of God. Evermore the divine complaint salutes us: "My people have committed two evils: they have forsaken me, the fountain of living waters, and have hewn out unto themselves cisterns, broken cisterns, that can hold no water."[2] It may be to us a means of rescue from eternal ruin, if we heed the words of Azariah: "The Lord is with you while ye be with him; if ye seek him, he will be found of you; but if ye forsake him, he will forsake you:" and the words of Hanani — precious words that should be written in every heart: "For the eyes of Jehovah run to and fro throughout the whole earth, to show himself strong in the behalf of them whose heart is perfect toward him."

---

[1] Deuteronomy 32:15.
[2] Jeremiah 2:13.

O that our hearts may be perfect towards Thee, blessed Father! When we read of the errors and sins of good men may we fear and tremble lest we too be thus guilty. May we never cease to trust in Thee. Keep us from a vain trust in man. Preserve us from all intolerance. When our sins are rebuked, may we humbly accept reproof and turn from our evil ways. And while we earnestly contend for Thy truth, and rebuke the errors of others, may we also consider ourselves, lest we also be tempted into wrong.

Royal Reformers: Jehoshaphat

Jehoshaphat, as a reformer, had a decided advantage over his father Asa, in that he had only to perfect a work already successfully begun. His education and his environment were highly favorable to the perfecting of a reformation, the chief obstacles to which had already been removed. But it is an evidence of the inveteracy[1] of evil habits, and especially of established wicked usages, that much of the work of Asa had to be repeated by Jehoshaphat and succeeding reformers. Thus we read (2 Chron. 14:3, 5) that Asa took away the high places and the sun images; yet we are informed (15:17) that "the high places were not taken away out of Israel." And so Jehoshaphat had to renew the war against the high places (17:6); yet we are told (20:33) that "the high places were not taken away." In the subsequent reign of Hezekiah, we learn that the high places were thrown down, and the altars out of all Judah and Benjamin, in Ephraim also and Manasseh, until they had utterly destroyed them all (31:1). Surely we have reached the consummation of this reformation now? No — turn to 34:3-6, and you will find that the war against the high places was renewed by Josiah! Cavilers parade these texts as involving contradiction, and therefore falsehood, and point to them triumphantly as evidences that the Old Testament records are untrustworthy, and therefore uninspired. But this is a very shallow sophistry. These various passages simply unfold a truth of great practical value: that deeply rooted sins and usages are not easily extirpated; that, make war against them as you may, even to gaining a victory that seems to be complete and final, the deep and many-branching roots of these evils have been but partially destroyed, and will send forth new shoots, and reappear above the surface in a new and vigorous growth. We have something analogous to this in the history of Temperance reformations. Again and again it has been proclaimed that Prohibition has triumphed in Maine; and as often it has been followed by the announcement that "the high places are not taken away" — that drinking and drunkenness abound. The same is true concerning Kansas. And more recently, the glad news of the triumph of Prohi-

---

[1] Deep rooted customs, which fight against removal.

bition in Atlanta, Georgia, has been followed by the sad tidings that Prohibition does not prohibit. But these are not *contradictions,* Some of the Statements may be, and doubtless are, the exaggerations of interested parties; yet, on the whole, it is but a repetition of the Old Testament history: the high places were destroyed, yet they were not destroyed. Victory after victory was succeeded by defeat after defeat. And this teaches us a great lesson as to the inveteracy of evil habits, and the exceeding difficulty of rooting them out. We must never be so sanguine[1] of complete success as to cease our efforts in any work of moral or religious reform; nor must we become so discouraged by defeat, that we cannot begin anew the work of reformation. The battle against wrong never ends. There is no discharge in this war.

Jehoshaphat was wise in this: he saw that the work of reformation under his father did not reach to the root of the evils that cursed the nation; it was merely or mainly an *external* change, while the *sources* of iniquity still remained untouched. Asa had sought to dry up the streams, but left the fountains still flowing. Jehoshaphat therefore determined on an advance movement. He saw that the people were profoundly ignorant of the law of Jehovah, and were consequently an easy prey to superstition. They were ignorant of the glorious history of their own nation, and consequently were destitute of the enlightened patriotism without which there could be no enthusiastic devotion to their own laws and institutions. He accordingly arranged a system of general instruction — of national education. Under the direction of five of the princes of the land, he sent forth priests and Levites "to teach in the cities of Judah." Here are the germs of a system of national education (a system far in advance of our boasted system of public schools; for, in our pride and self-sufficiency, we are banishing the Bible from our public schools, and tabooing in a large degree all moral and religious instruction, relying on merely intellectual culture to produce and foster the intelligence and virtue which are the two great pillars of the temple of liberty — although it is rapidly becoming evident that we are thus leaning vainly on a broken reed). Jehoshaphat saw that moral and religious culture was essential to a true patriotism, and therefore was careful to have the peo-

---

[1] Confident.

ple "taught in the book of the law of Jehovah." We are not forgetful of the fact that the government of Judah was a theocracy, and
that Jehoshaphat could therefore properly insist on a popular education in the law of the Lord which, in our Republic, in theory divorced from religion, and made up of all sorts of people, where the
irreligious and atheistic and Jewish and pagan elements are potent,
is impracticable. We see and acknowledge the difference; yet we
record our conviction, in the face of this tremendous difficulty, that
by some means — if not by the action of the State, then by the missionary zeal and voluntary efforts of the Church, our population
must be morally and religiously educated, or our glorious Republic
will perish. Its interests cannot be conserved by the godless culture
of our public schools. Intellectual culture — *head* education —
may and does consist with moral obliquity[1] and degradation, and
depraved hearts are only armed with additional power for evil by
what is now popularly styled education. Such education furnishes
claws to the tiger and talons to the eagle, for a work of destruction.
We must see to this in time, or our free institutions are destined to
become a prey to untamed passions and unchastened and unsanctified ambitions.

Of the salutary[2] results of the system of popular moral and religious instruction introduced by Jehoshaphat, we have this testimony: "And the fear of the Lord fell upon all the kingdoms of the
lands that were round about Judah, so that they made no war
against Jehoshaphat (2 Chron. 17:10). Partial and temporary as was
this popular education — for, in the great scarcity of books, the
instruction was oral and largely perishable — an *educated* people
was more dreaded by hostile nations and tribes than an *armed* people. The light from the schools of Judah struck terror into the benighted and superstitious tribes and kings round about them. Brain-
power is superior to mere muscular force, and *heart-power* is
greater than all. An enlightened faith in Jehovah, and an intelligent
patriotism, made Judah more terrible than an army with banners.
Hence, even the haughty and scornful Philistines bowed before Jehoshaphat with presents to conciliate him, and the lawless Arabs
came with tribute to purchase his favor (2 Chron. 17:11) — splen-

---

[1] Deviation from a straight line.
[2] Beneficial, praiseworthy.

did testimonials to the superiority — the invincibility — of an enlightened people.

So intent was Jehoshaphat on this work of education, that he went a second time over the whole land, "from Beer-sheba to the hill-country of Ephraim," renewing the course of instruction and winning the people to an intelligent devotion to the service of Jehovah (2 Chron. 19:4). Had this educational movement been wrought into permanency, it might have been the salvation of Judah; but Jehoshaphat's successor, Jehoram, by his marriage with the daughter of Jezebel, was ensnared into idolatrous ways, and the work of the pious father was undone by the impious son.

Another reformatory movement of the wise and good Jehoshaphat was the purgation of the civil and ecclesiastical courts, and the reestablishment of a just administration of law (2 Chron. 19:5-11). The corruption of courts of justice is one of the signs of a nation's decadence. It is one of the evil signs of the times in our own land. The delays in bringing criminals to trial; the packing of juries; the infamous tricks resorted to by reckless criminal lawyers to defeat the aims of justice; the consequent failure of juries to convict the guilty; the guilty higgling[1] of the judges of superior courts, in deciding appeals — reversing the decisions of justice in the cases of notorious criminals by a resort to the most trifling technicalities — in virtue of which criminals of the deepest dye, released on bail, walk the streets of our cities for years, a menace to the peace and security of society; and the final defeat of justice in the acquittal of such guilty wretches after the lapse of years has allowed their crimes to pass into forgetfulness and the righteous indignation of the public has spent itself: all this has given license to lawlessness and crime, and brought our courts into contempt. It was after the public patience had been worn out by a repetition of these iniquities in our so-called courts of justice, and at their culmination in a verdict of manslaughter in the case of a self-confessed murderer, whose deliberate act of murder solely for the sake of gain was universally known, that the public indignation of Cincinnati gave birth to a fearful riot, resulting in the burning of the court-house with its invaluable records, and in the loss of sixty lives, and the wounding and maiming of two hundred persons. It is notorious that, in view

---

[1] Peddling, being open to haggling and compromise (and oftentimes bribery).

of the extreme uncertainty of righteous decisions in our criminal courts, Lynch law is frequently resorted to, with a silent acquiescence and approval even on the part of the virtuous and law-abiding. A painful commentary on the corrupt condition of our courts is found in the fact of a general outburst of admiration on the part of the press and the people when an exceptional instance of the administration of prompt and full justice occurs — admirable because it is rare! It has come to this: that an honest discharge of duty has to be celebrated because of its exceptional character! No nation is secure when its laws have fallen into contempt and the voice of its courts is a mockery in the ears of the people. Liberty is then sure to degenerate into licentiousness.

Judah had been sorely afflicted through the corruption of its courts. What was said by Zephaniah some time later was true even in the reign of Jehoshaphat: "Her princes in the midst of her are roaring lions; her judges are evening wolves; they leave nothing till the morrow" (Zeph. 3:3). Jehoshaphat undertook a reorganization of the courts. Judges of civil and criminal cases were appointed to sit in all the fenced cities of Judah, "city by city," as these were the centers of population. A solemn charge was given to these judges, which it would be well for all the judges in our land to commit to memory and repeat every morning: "Consider what ye do: for ye judge not for man, but for Jehovah; and He is with you in the judgment. Now therefore let the fear of Jehovah be upon you: take heed and do it: for there is no iniquity with Jehovah our God, nor respect of persons, nor taking of gifts" (2 Chron. 19:6-7; see also Psalm 82). An ecclesiastical court was established in Jerusalem, composed of skilled Levites, priests, and heads of houses, with the high-priest as presiding officer, to hear all appeals that might come up from local courts; while "the prince of the house of Judah" was the head of all the civil and criminal courts. Thus did the king seek, by an upright administration of justice and a scheme of popular education, to overcome the tendencies to apostasy and train up a generation of intelligent, law-loving subjects, armed and steeled against the seductions of idolatry.

In all this Jehoshaphat was rewarded with peace and prosperity. The awe of him was upon the surrounding tribes and nations, so that, free from wars, he gave himself to strengthening his kingdom, and he "had riches and honor in abundance." If idolatrous foes threatened the security of his kingdom, as when the Moabites, Ammonites, and Meunim combined to attack him, he was rewarded with a bloodless victory over their multitudinous armies (2 Chron. 20). Never since the time of the revolt of the ten tribes, had Judah been lifted to such strength, or commanded such respect among the nations.

It is painful to mar so beautiful a picture; yet it would be false and mischievous to leave it unmarred. The truth must be spoken. If it be saddening, it is yet wise, to learn how every human work is marred by imperfections and soiled by sins; otherwise we should ever be inflated by a false self-sufficiency, and fail of watchfulness against the dangers that beset us even in our best endeavors after righteousness.

Strange to say, Jehoshaphat, with all his unaffected devotion to the honor of Jehovah, became the intimate friend and devoted ally of the infamous Ahab (2 Chron. 18). This is a deeply interesting history, as illustrating the subtle play of *policy* in State affairs, against the stern demands of *righteousness*. We cannot suppose Jehoshaphat to have had the least sympathy with the idolatrous court of Ahab and Jezebel, so far as religion and morals were concerned. This is evident from the honor bestowed on him by Elisha even after the death of Ahab, when Jehoram was king, and Jehoshaphat joined his forces with those of Jehoram to fight against Moab. Jehoram sought unto Elisha for counsel in a time of extremity. It is one of the few instances in which the gentle Elisha was stirred to indignation. "What have I to do with thee? Get thee to the prophets of thy father, and the prophets of thy mother." But the sight of Jehoshaphat subdued him. "As the Lord of hosts liveth, before whom I stand, surely, were it not that I regard the presence of Jehoshaphat the king of Judah, I would not look toward thee nor see thee" (2 Ki. 3:9-19). For Jehoshaphat's sake, he opened to the allied kings the way of deliverance. It is thus evident that, notwithstanding Jehoshaphat's folly in entering into this alliance with the house of Ahab, Elisha respected him as a good man and a righteous king, having no fellowship with the iniquities of the house of Omri.

How, then, did so good and pure a man become entangled in such an unholy alliance? Just as honorable men among politicians and statesmen have, in hundreds of instances, in modern as well as in ancient times, been similarly ensnared — by the plausible and captivating pleadings of *policy*.

The rival kingdoms of Judah and Israel had largely consumed each other in raids and wars. Even Jehoshaphat began his reign by fortifying himself against the neighboring kingdom (2 Chron. 17:1-2). But he saw that while the two kingdoms had been preying on each other for sixty years, the kingdom of Syria — their common foe — and the tribes on their eastern frontier, had been growing into power, and would soon subdue them both. It became, therefore, his policy to cultivate peace with Israel, and make common cause with Ahab against these powerful enemies. It was an honorable ambition, to put an end to suicidal strifes among the twelve tribes, and unite their forces against a common enemy. But Jehoshaphat did not pause to consider that policy is only warrantable *within the limits of truth and righteousness;* and that, outside of these limits, he ought to throw policy to the winds, and put his trust in Jehovah, who had always been his refuge and strength against all odds. Is it not strange, that after all the lessons taught us in our experience of the perfect safety of those who cling to Jehovah's law, we should be perpetually reaching out after human expedients and policies which ever prove but broken reeds that pierce and wound them that lean upon them, and forsaking the fountain of living waters for broken cisterns that can hold no water? It is surely a humiliating evidence of the ingratitude and faithlessness of the human heart. Yet this is the perpetual tendency in Church and State. Doubtless considerations of policy, within the limits we have mentioned, are often weighty, and it would be folly to disregard them; but when we push these considerations beyond these limits, and adopt expedients and policies at war with truth and righteousness, divorcing either Church or State politics from the law of God, we venture on forbidden ground, and are sure to pluck down a curse on our own heads.

Jehoshaphat, deceived by the plausible character of his scheme for peace, was content to be blind to the fatal results of his unauthorized and unrighteous compromise. He shut his eyes against all the abominations of the court of Ahab and even when the bold and honest Micaiah gave warning against the proposed advance of the allied forces against Ramoth-gilead, he closed his ears against the warning, and went out with Ahab to battle. Once ensnared in schemes of policy, we are apt to go from bad to worse. After the disgraceful defeat at Ramoth-gilead, the prophet Jehu met Jehoshaphat on his way back to Jerusalem with words of stern reproof. "Shouldest thou help the wicked, and love them that hate Jehovah? for this thing wrath is upon thee from Jehovah." Yet, although the case was thus plainly put before him as one of moral dereliction, he clung to his peace-policy, and, to make it secure, went so far as to marry his son Jehoram, heir to the throne, to the daughter of the fierce, haughty, cruel, devotee of Baal, the infamous Jezebel (2 Chron. 21:6). We have already seen, in our sketches of Ahab, Jezebel, Athaliah, Jehoram, Jehoiada, and Maachah, the results of this unhallowed marriage. The lamp of David was burned to its socket. The succession to the throne hung by a single thread. Jerusalem and the land of Judah were steeped in idolatry. All the interests of the kingdom of David were fearfully imperiled. And all this as the legitimate result of that deceitful *policy*, on which Jehoshaphat prided himself. All his work of reformation was ruined by the very policy which he imagined would permanently establish it. And, notwithstanding the rebukes of Jehu, he persisted in this policy with Ahab's successors, Joram and Ahaziah, uniting with the former in wars, and with the latter in commercial enterprises (2 Chron. 20:35-37), until a fresh rebuke from the prophet Eliezer, and a fresh disaster from the hand of God, put an end to the unholy and calamitous alliance.

The lesson here taught is of immense value, if we will but heed it. Our very successes engender temptations that may land us in disastrous failure. One may work faithfully and bravely for many years in building up a good character, and then wreck it by some act of folly. Also, he may engage in some public work of reformation, and pursue it faithfully and successfully until it is about to culminate in complete success, and then, under the spell of some captivating delusion, or through the blinding power of some cunning sophistry, betray it to destruction. And the tempter, in these cases, is apt to assume the form of an angel of light. The surrender of *principle* is very likely to be accomplished by the bewitching temptations of *policy* — by the promise of achieving some great good through yielding just a little of one's uncompromising hostility to falsehood and wrong. There is never a time when we are in such peril as when we are on the verge of a great success; for then all the powers of evil are taxed to their utmost to bewitch or bewilder or corrupt us through some splendid and cunning sophistry, and to deceive us into some false step from which we may never recover. We need to be perpetually on our guard against the wiles of Satan. We are disposed to regard the wisdom for which an apostle teaches us to pray (Jas. 1:5) as just that spiritual wisdom that will enable us to detect and overcome these subtle temptations to a surrender of all we have gained in the battle of life. Jehoshaphat, by one false step, in behalf of what he honestly regarded as a most praiseworthy purpose, brought more trouble and evil on Judah than could be compensated by all the wise and righteous acts of his entire life. Let us watch and pray that we enter not into temptation. Especially let us be on our guard against the glittering sophistries of *policy*, and wed ourselves rather to *duty*, however stern and forbidding her aspect may sometimes be.

Jehoshaphat entered on his reign when he was 35 years old — the beginning of a noble prime of manhood — and reigned 25 years. In view of his antecedents and his surroundings, his should have been a glorious reign; and indeed, it was the most glorious of all the reigns of the kings of Judah from the time of Solomon. It would have been immensely more glorious, but for the one infatuation which led him into an unseemly and stubborn alliance with an apostate throne, which involved him in ruinous snares. Heaven save us from entangling alliances with the world, the flesh, and the devil. But as there was no intentional departure from right, and as, all life long, he resisted temptation and personally adhered to the law of Jehovah, he was honored in life and in death by the nation, and by Jehovah, who, while He chastened him for his errors, still blessed him to the last as an honest and faithful servant.

Grant, Lord, to preserve us from entangling alliances with evil doers. While avoiding all self-righteousness, as being hateful to Thee, may we not fail to separate our affections and our interests from those of wicked and ungodly men, lest we expose Thy name to dishonor and betray the sacred interests Thou hast committed unto us. May we rather stand alone with Thee, than to stand with all the world against Thee.

Royal Reformers: Hezekiah.

Hezekiah was twenty-five years old when he ascended the throne.[1] He was the son of a wicked and apostate father. It is strange that one who grew up in the midst of such corruptions as are described in 2 Chron. 28 could be so thoroughly devoted to the law of Jehovah as to win the remarkable encomium,[2] "After him was none like him among all the kings of Judah, nor any that were before him" (2 Ki. 18:5. See also in Apocrypha, Ecclesiasticus 49:4). Perhaps his religious training was due to his mother. Her name was Abi (2 Ki. 18:2), or Abijah (2 Chron. 29:1) — there being, in Hebrew, the difference of but a single letter in the two names. She was "the daughter of Zechariah." She may have been the daughter of the prophet so eminent in the reign of Uzziah (2 Chron. 26:5). We can readily understand that the daughter of such a prophet would educate the heir to the throne most carefully and diligently in the fear of God and the knowledge of His law; that she might thus most effectively subvert the idolatries and iniquities of Ahaz. Or, Zechariah may have been the "faithful witness" spoken of in Isa. 8:2. In either case we may count on it that Hezekiah would be thoroughly educated in loyalty to Jehovah. To this end other potent influences would contribute — especially the assistance and encouragement of the true prophets of God. Joel most certainly flourished in the reign of Uzziah, and, along with Zechariah and Isaiah, so far leavened the public sentiment as to prepare the way for the great reformation that took place under Hezekiah, and may well be supposed to have exerted a special influence over the mother of Hezekiah, and over those who were entrusted with his education. Isaiah, especially, who asserted so direct, controlling, and constant an influence over Hezekiah's reign, and whose pious and patriotic zeal led him to penetrate into every avenue of court influence, would, we may be sure, take a special interest in

---

[1] There is probably an error in 2 Kings 18:2, or in 2 Chronicles 28:1. As Ahaz, his father, died at the age of thirty-six, he could have been but eleven when Hezekiah was born. It is therefore suggested that in 2 Chronicles 28:1, we read "twenty-five" in place of "twenty," as we find it in the LXX and in the Syriac and Arabic Versions.

[2] High praise.

guarding the heir-apparent to the throne from every corrupt influence, and in imparting to him his own hate of the prevailing idolatries, and his own spirit of reverence for the law of Jehovah. Nahum, too, flourished at this time,[1] and Micah also. It is evident, from Jer. 26:17-19, that Micah not only prophesied to Hezekiah, but that the king hearkened to his rebukes, and it is even thought by many that the mighty strides in reform during Hezekiah's reign were prompted and inspired by this prophet. We are left to infer from these facts that during the minority of Hezekiah these vigilant prophets surrounded him with all possible holy influences, and aided in training him for the great reformatory work which he was predestined to accomplish. That Hezekiah responded to these counsels, and successfully resisted all the open and subtle influences of a corrupt court, as well as the bad example of his royal father, entitles him to peculiar honor.

Hezekiah came to the throne in an evil time. The feeble religious character of Jotham, and the open apostasy of Ahaz, had almost obliterated Judah's loyalty to the God of Israel. The conspiracy of Pekah, king of Israel, and Rezin, king of Syria, against Jotham, had been productive of great calamity to Judah; and these adversities, instead of humbling the heart of Ahaz, had driven him into worse apostasy, and against the remonstrance of Isaiah, he sought an alliance with the king of Assyria, and accepted a vassalage to that king which was productive only of disaster. According to the testimonies of the prophets we have named, the political, moral, and religious condition of Judah was most deplorable. A ruinous tribute had to be paid to Assyria; the court party was not only destitute of patriotism, and favored the oppressions of Assyria, but ambitiously sought to overrule the throne in the management of the affairs of the kingdom. The priests and the prophets were corrupt, and the judges also; the masses of the people were impoverished, superstitious, and debased, and the rich were selfish and oppressive. See Isa. 9:13-20, 29:21, 30:8-13; Micah 3:8-12;

---

[1] For the right understanding of Nahum's prophecy, it should be read in connection with the book of Jonah, of which it is a continuation. The two prophecies form connected parts of the same moral history; the remission of God's judgments being illustrated in Jonah, and the execution of them in Nahum. — *Blaikie and Angus.*

Hos. 9:7-10. Their enemies were ready to take advantage of their weakness and their internal strifes. One faction was bent on an alliance with Egypt; another insisted on courting the favor of Assyria; a third pleaded for national independence; and amid these factious clamors, the true prophets pleaded in vain for national repentance and a renewal of trust in Jehovah. The kingdom of the ten tribes was nearing its destruction, thus exposing Judah more completely to the despoiling power of Assyria. Egypt and Assyria, as rival powers, sought to embroil all the tributary nations that lay between them with the governments to which they were tributary, and there was apt to be found, in all these tributary powers, a party ready to listen to the seductive voices of these great monarchies, and to accept the temptations of these rival powers, luring them to alliance or to rebellion.

Under these perplexing and discouraging circumstances Hezekiah began his reign. He seems, from the first, to have penetrated beneath the troubled surface of things to the root of all the evils that afflicted or threatened his people. He realized that it is *righteousness,* and not playing at games of policy, that exalteth a nation. Hence he began at once a work of religious reformation. The promptness with which this work was undertaken is worthy of notice. "In the *first* year of his reign, in the *first* month, he opened the doors of the house of the Lord, and repaired them" (2 Chron. 29:3). This was, however, no sudden impulse. It was a settled purpose, based on a thorough conviction that it was the true way to a return of national prosperity, as may be seen from his admirable speech to the priests and Levites (2 Chron. 29:4-11), in which he urged them to purge the temple of its pollutions and reestablish the pure worship of Jehovah. We are apt to regard with peculiar interest the first acts of a new reign, as likely to foreshadow its character and furnish its keynote. The prompt and public committal of the throne to the reestablishment of Jehovah's authority leaves no doubt as to the intentions of the new monarch, and justifies what is said of him in a passage already referred to: "*He trusted in the Lord God of Israel;* so that after him was none like him among all the kings of Judah, nor any that were before him" (2 Ki. 18:5). Nothing but a profound, cultivated trust in the living God, and a thorough conviction of the dependence of the nation on righteousness as the only effectual remedy for its weakness and perils, could have led him to begin his reign in this way.

But not only did he purge and rehabilitate the temple, and restore the public worship according to the law, stirring up the lazy and corrupt priests to a performance of their duties; but, when this was accomplished, his reign was formally inaugurated by a sin-offering "for the kingdom, and for the sanctuary, and for Judah" — thus making a public confession of sin on the part of the throne, the priesthood, and the people, and invoking the mercy of heaven on all, from the king on the throne down to the lowliest in the land. The king, as well as the elders, seems to have laid hands on the heads of the sacrificial animals.

And this was accomplished with a service of song. "And when the burnt-offering began, the song of the Lord began also, and the trumpets, together with the instruments of David, king of Israel. And all the congregation worshiped, and the singers sang, and the trumpeters sounded; all this continued until the burnt-offering was finished. And when they had made an end of offering, the king and all who were present with him bowed themselves and worshiped." Thus, with penitence for sin and thanksgiving for divine mercy, did the young king enter on his difficult task of governing and reforming a disobedient and gainsaying people.

Let us learn that if we are to be temples of God, we must cleanse the sanctuary from all defilements, and in penitential confession of sin and the abandonment of all idolatrous and perverse ways, woo the return of the Divine Guest, whom our sins and follies have grieved away from us.

The king then prepared for the celebration of the greatest of the national festivals — the Passover. In doing this, his enlightened judgment and largeness of heart come into view, especially in two particulars.

1. The proper time for the observance of the Passover was the fourteenth day of the first month (Lev. 23:5). But the cleansing of the temple was not completed at that time (2 Chron. 29:17). A stickler for the sacredness of *usage,* a literalist clinging to the letter of this law as final in its authority, would have said, "We can have no Passover until next year; the law forbids it." But it was important to take advantage of the present public awakening, and lose no time, if, indeed, it could be done *without a violation of the law. Usage* could be sacrificed to the pressing necessities of the time;

mere prejudice in behalf of the usual time of observing the great feast could be surrendered, if only no dishonor was done to the authority of Jehovah. It was found, on examining the law, that in exceptional cases, such as legal defilement, or necessary absence from home at the legal time of the festival, the Passover might be kept on the fourteenth day of the *second* month (Num. 9:9-12). Now, as *the whole nation* was legally unclean, and as the failure to observe the Passover at the proper time was not willful, but unavoidable, the king had no scruples in regarding this provision of the law for exceptional cases as fairly applying to the whole nation in the present instance; and he therefore sent out a proclamation of a Passover observance for the fourteenth day of the second month. In this we say he exhibited enlightened judgment in a wise interpretation of a special provision of the law. He would not contravene the divine law — for his great object was to bring the people into submission to the authority of God. But, on the other hand, he would allow no mere prejudice, no superstitious attachment to a particular time, hallowed by long observance, as well as by divine authority, to shut him out from an opportunity which the law clearly sanctioned, and which the necessities of the time made urgent.

2. The invitation to "all Israel and Judah" to come to the festival. Here is largeness of heart. In view of all the bitter feuds and wars of the past, and especially in view of the fact that only a few years before, during the reign of Ahaz, the conspiracy against Judah of Israel and Syria had resulted in the slaughter of one hundred and twenty thousand in one day, and in the captivity of two hundred thousand more (2 Chron. 28:6-8), besides all that were carried captive to Damascus, none but a truly magnanimous nature could triumph over revengeful feelings and answer these wrongs with a brotherly invitation to "all Israel" to come up to Jerusalem and share as brethren in the solemnities of the great national festival. Israel at this time was on the brink of ruin, and anarchy prevailed in all her borders. Repeated Assyrian invasions had brought the kingdom of the ten tribes into extreme weakness and wretchedness. The Syrian kingdom, by whose aid Israel had inflicted such terrible punishment on Judah, had been subjugated by Assyria, and Samaria was now completely exposed to Assyrian vengeance. Hoshea, the king, was now nothing more than a feudal dependent of the all-conquering Assyrian power. The darkness of the day of doom was

already settling down on Samaria. It would have been natural for Judah, smarting under her grievous wrongs, to have exulted in the calamities of Israel. But the great-hearted Hezekiah flings to the winds all such barbarous suggestions, and, with a generosity and magnanimity far ahead of his age, he sends forth messengers through all the land, "from Beer-sheba even unto Dan," to invite *all* to "come to keep the Passover unto the Lord God of Israel at Jerusalem." Could even *this* age, whose sectarianism is evidently on the wane, be trusted to show a like magnanimity? Alas, not even all the sects ranged under one common name can be prevailed on to sit down together at one communion-table! Read the message (2 Chron. 30:6-9), and learn how the most sacred memories of the past, when the twelve tribes were a united people, and the glowing hopes of a God-blessed future for a united people, overpowered all selfish pride and vindictiveness by a catholic[1] piety and patriotism worthy of even a Christian age.

We do not read of any attempt on the part of Hezekiah to aid the neighboring kingdom in her last desperate struggles with a foreign foe. He doubtless had all he could handle to take care of his own kingdom in those perilous times, nor would any Jewish army have been easily prevailed on to give assistance to the cruel spoilers who had so recently afflicted them. But he did what was far better: he held forth the olive-branch of peace, and entreated them to come back to the God they had forsaken, as the only possible means of escape from the dire calamities that threatened them.

Hezekiah's magnanimity did not meet with the success it deserved. His invitation was like the cry to God's people in Babylon: "Come out of her my people, that ye be not partakers of her sins, and that ye receive not of her plagues" (Rev. 18:4). It seems strange that, in the last extremity of Israel's national existence, that doomed people did not hail the invitation as the very voice of God, and rush *en masse* to the long-forsaken altar of Jehovah for refuge from overhanging judgments. But, as "the posts passed from city to city through the country of Ephraim and Manasseh, even unto Zebulun, they laughed them to scorn and mocked them." "Ephraim is joined to his idols; let him alone." Yet it was not altogether in vain; for "divers of Asher and Manasseh and Zebulun humbled

---

[1] Universal.

themselves, and came to Jerusalem." In 2 Chron. 30:18, we read of many also from Ephraim and Manasseh and Issachar who came; so that five of the ten tribes gave some heed to the invitation. Dan was no longer a distinct tribe; Reuben and Gad were already in captivity (1 Chron. 5:26). Simeon and Naphtali alone seem to have been utterly incorrigible, and we judge from what is mentioned of Josiah's proceedings against them (2 Chron. 34:5-6), that they were wholly given to idolatry.

May we not find a lesson here? In these days of sectarian division and strife, when Satan triumphs largely through the alienations and corruptions of God's divided and scattered people, we sometimes think that a generous invitation to them all to come back to Jerusalem would be responded to by universal acclamations and a speedy return of these weary and scattered hosts to the city of God, that the highways and byways would all be thronged with pilgrims asking the way to Zion with their faces thitherward, saying, "Come, and let us join ourselves to the Lord in a perpetual covenant that shall not be forgotten" — that "the children of Israel would come, and the children of Judah together, going and weeping" (Jer. 1:4-5). We have known not a few who, on learning the simplicity of the gospel and the broad apostolic basis of union, were inspired with the most enthusiastic hopes that the whole Protestant world, as soon as the teaching of the New Testament should be unfolded to them, would immediately cast their party idols to the moles and to the bats, and return to the old paths of apostolic teaching and practice, and with one mind and one heart glorify the God of their salvation. But, alas! When the posts pass from city to city through the country of Ephraim and Manasseh, even to Zebulun, the people laugh them to scorn and mock them. Some will be found to listen to the message, and "divers of Asher and Manasseh and Zebulun and Ephraim and Issachar" will humble themselves and come to Jerusalem. But the great mass will continue to be joined to their idols, and many will be discovered to have gone into a hopeless captivity. The great reason of this lamentable result is hinted at in a verse already quoted: "Nevertheless divers of Asher and of Manasseh and of Zebulun *humbled themselves,* and came to Jerusalem." Only those who "humbled themselves" returned. It was pride, then, that stood in the way — that accursed passion through which Satan fell (1 Tim. 3:6), and by means of which he has wrought his greatest achievements against the kingdom of God and the welfare of our race. The Israelites were too proud to forsake their petty idolatrous shrines at Beth-el and Dan and return to God's holy hill; too proud to even imply that a religion good enough for their fathers was not good enough for them; too proud to admit that Samaria — though clouds surcharged with divine wrath were even then gathered over her, ready to burst with appalling vengeance upon her guilty population — was inferior to Jerusalem; too proud to say, "I have sinned," and turn away from transgressions which, because of the longsuffering of Jehovah, had long gone unpunished. And this pride led them on to utter destruction.

And is not this, even now, the great trouble? Sectarian pride, denominational pride, traditional pride, intellectual pride — how it yet leads Ephraim and Manasseh and Zebulun to laugh the messengers of good will to scorn, and to mock them! "Is not my father's religion good enough?" "Do you want me to dishonor my parents' memory by even implying that they did not understand the Bible, or that they have not gone to heaven?" "Do you mean to say that the glorious history of my Confession of Faith must be laid in the dust and trampled on?" "Have all the eminent men in my party been mistaken?" "Thou art but of yesterday, and dost thou teach us?" And rather than humble themselves by an acknowledgment of past errors, they curse the light that dawns on their confused paths, and the voice of heavenly truth and love that would guide them into God's own highway. Yes, it is *pride* that stands in the way. The proud Jews in our Lord's time reasoned after the fashion we have described. So reasoned pious Roman Catholics in Luther's time. So do multitudes of sectarians feel and talk now. "God resisteth the proud, but giveth grace to the humble." "The proud he knoweth afar off." Only the humble and meek will God guide in judgment and teach to them His way. The worst of it is that the multitudes are not only *ruled* by pride, but they are *deceived* by it. They think they are humble. They are offended if you intimate that they are proud. Yet, touch one of their party idols, and see!

We can think of no better preparation for a reunited Israel than the appointment and serious observance of seasons of humiliation, fasting, and prayer, the religious world over, with a view to the discovery and forsaking of pride — spiritual pride, denominational pride, pride of opinion — and penitential confession of the sin and evils of sectarianism, until God shall visit those who are of a contrite spirit and who tremble at His word.

> *"In those days, and at that time," saith the Lord, "the children of Israel shall come, they and the children of Judah together, going and weeping: they shall go and seek the Lord their God. They shall ask the way to Zion with their faces thitherward, saying, 'Come ye, and let us join ourselves to the Lord in a perpetual covenant that shall not be forgotten.'"*

O that there may be a heart in us to love Thy testimonies, O Lord, and to walk in Thy commandments. Let us not be lifted up with pride, lest we fall into the condemnation of the devil. May all who fear Thy name be humbled in the dust when they look on the desolations of Zion. May no partisan spirit, no denominational pride, no blinding prejudices of education, no reverence for tradition, make them deaf to the voice of Thy Word which calls them back to the faith and fellowship and practice of apostolic times. May we all ask the way to Zion with our faces thitherward, saying, "Come ye, and let us join ourselves to the Lord in a perpetual covenant that shall not be forgotten."

Royal Reformers: Hezekiah (Part Two)

We have somewhere in previous papers remarked that mere iconoclasm[1] is not reformation. It is not enough that we extirpate the false and the evil; we must supplant it with the true and the good. We are now to say, in the light of Hezekiah's proceedings, that the true reformer, in seeking to establish that which is true and good, will, with iconoclastic zeal, endeavor to uproot that which is false and evil. There are dreamy theorists who argue that the evil and the good, like the tares and the wheat, should be allowed to grow together; that true virtue — itself a military term — can only be found in the resistance of evil, and that it is the evident purpose of the present constitution of things to furnish healthful discipline to the soul by compelling it into perpetual wrestlings with vice and sin, for its own development of strength and mastery. We have heard religious men argue stoutly against the prohibition of the manufacture and sale of intoxicating drinks, on the ground that it is an attempt to subvert the divine order of things, which requires the presence of evil that we may combat it; and that one ought to drink wine and brandy for the very purpose of training one's self into the government of the appetites! There is some truth in this, but not enough to redeem the argument from sophistry. Doubtless this world of ours is to some extent a moral gymnasium, where the moral nature is to be trained to manly vigor by exercise — a battle-field where courage and endurance and self-denial and unconquerable energy and all high virtues are to be developed by steady and toilsome conflict with antagonistic forces. But of these antagonistic powers, there will always be sufficient to serve this purpose after we have done our best to annihilate them, and without our help to create new ones or to foster those already in existence. It were as sensible to say that in a battle for liberty against cruel and crafty oppressors, we should be careful not to interfere with the strength of the foe, lest we should no longer have an opportunity to show our mettle; or, when traitors are found in the camp, that we should

---

[1] The destroying of idols.

not put them to death, lest the spirit of loyalty should die out for lack of opportunity to fight treason!

The truth is there are odds against which truth and virtue cannot maintain a successful contest. In individual cases they may; but in society at large, they cannot. It is fearfully perilous to all the higher interests of our nature to tolerate dangerous evils when we have it in our power to destroy them. It is nursing in one's bosom the serpent that is sure to make return in a deadly bite. Our only complete safety against powerful temptations is to annihilate them when they are in our power. So reasoned Hezekiah. He had seen and known too much of the deadly influence of idolatry to allow any compromise with it. So, after he had aroused the people to a holy enthusiasm by the renewal of the Passover — which was protracted to double its usual time of observance — "all Israel that was present went out to the cities of Judah and brake in pieces the obelisks, and hewed down the Asherim, and brake down the high places and the altars out of all Judah and Benjamin, in Ephraim also and Manasseh, until they had destroyed them all" (2 Chron. 31:1).

When it is remembered that this was a sweeping and crushing condemnation of his own father's conduct, it will be seen that there was not only high moral courage, but supreme loyalty to Jehovah in Hezekiah's proceeding. Not even the fear of dishonoring a father's memory could check this furious devastation of the shrines of idolatry. Whether Hezekiah commanded it or not, the newly kindled enthusiasm of the worshipers who had come up from the territory of the ten tribes swept over the borders of Judah into the territory of Israel, and the high places and the altars in Ephraim and Manasseh, as well as in Judah, were defiled and desolated by these iconoclastic hordes. If this was before the fall of Samaria, it was in the midst of troubles and perils that did not allow Hoshea to contend against the indignity offered to his authority; and it may be that his indifference to the established worship of his kingdom was such that he took no offense at this raid upon the idols of Israel (2 Ki. 17:2).

It is a notable evidence of the thoroughness of Hezekiah's conviction of the bane of idolatry, that he did not spare even a venerable relic which for nearly eight centuries had been preserved among the most sacred of the nation's memorials. The brazen serpent which Moses lifted up in the wilderness (Num. 21:9) had been carefully guarded through all changes of the kingdom's fortunes, and was still preserved in Jerusalem. As a memorial of Jehovah's great mercy, there was no more impropriety in preserving it than in keeping the golden pot of manna and Aaron's rod that budded (Ex. 16:33; Num. 17:10). But it had been perverted to base uses; and that which is innocent, and even commendable in itself, when it is perverted to evil and becomes a source of mischief, must be abandoned. How often it is urged, as an apology for dancing, card-playing, theater-going, and other popular amusements, that they are innocent in themselves, and, that it is only their perversions to evil purposes that should be condemned. If this were granted, it by no means justifies indulgence in these pleasures. The brazen serpent was not only innocent in itself, but as a national memorial, about which clustered memories dear to the heart of the Jewish patriot and well calculated to quicken pious and patriotic sentiments, was valuable. But, from being an object of historical and national interest, it became an idol. An altar was erected to it, and incense burnt thereon. *It was impossible to dissociate it from this wickedness,* even as it is now impossible to dissociate the popular amusements we have referred to from the follies and wickednesses and madnesses of the fashionable idolatry to which they have been subjected. Therefore Hezekiah, in the face of the popular sentiment, in defiance of the national veneration of this sacred relic of antiquity, perhaps against the pleadings of his own heart in behalf of a venerated memorial, doomed it to destruction. It is evident from the language used that the idolatry, or semi-idolatry, connected with this object, was deeply-rooted; it had continued from the days when the twelve tribes were known as "the children of Israel." It was useless to attempt to extirpate idolaters from the land while this feeder of superstition was allowed to remain. It was easy to go from the semi-idolatry of burning incense to the brazen serpent, to a heathen temple, to bum incense to Baal. So Hezekiah "broke it in pieces." The people did not call it a serpent — that would have called up unpleasant suggestions; nor did they call it a God — that would have been an effrontery too brazen; they sought to cover up the idolatrous feature of their devotion under the euphemism *Nehushtan* — a piece of brass. "Yes," said the king, stripping the euphemism to utter nakedness, "a piece of brass; only a piece of brass: therefore let us break it in pieces. No more incense to a piece of brass!" Glorious iconoclast! Would that we had more Hezekiahs to smash with strong hand all the pieces of brass to which incense is burned in the temple of God!

It is not surprising, after all this, to read that "Jehovah was with him, and prospered him whithersoever he went forth." From the record of his reign after the defeat of Sennacherib, we learn of a greatness and glory which must have been, in part at least, characteristic of the earlier portion of his reign.

> *And many brought gifts unto the Lord to Jerusalem, and precious things to Hezekiah king of Judah; so that he was exalted in the sight of all nations from henceforth. And Hezekiah had exceeding much riches and honor: and he provided him treasuries for silver, and for gold and for precious stones, and for spices, and for shields, and for all manner of goodly vessels; store-houses also for the increase of corn and wine and oil; and stalls for all manner of beasts, and flocks in folds. Moreover he provided him cities, and possession of flocks and herds in abundance; for God had given him very much substance* (2 Chron. 32:23, 27-29).

So true was it, under that economy of temporal rewards and punishments, that earthly prosperity was sure to reward the willing and obedient. See Deut. 28:1-14.

With this prosperity Hezekiah was emboldened to make the perilous attempt to realize his cherished ideal of an independent nation, subject only to its Divine Sovereign, and depending solely on Him for protection. We call it a perilous attempt, because, situated between the rival powers of Egypt and Assyria, furnishing a highway along his western border for the march of their armies, and being but one of several inferior powers whose safety was sought in alliance with one or the other of these great sovereignties, it was impossible, from any merely political point of view, for a small kingdom like Judah to remain free from entangling alliances. His father had become tributary to Assyria (2 Ki. 16:7), and he must still pay the annual tribute, or provoke the wrath of that all-conquering power. This was the more perilous, for Syria had been conquered, and Israel carried captive, and Hezekiah's territory lay exposed to the ravages of armies with which it would be vain to contend. Yet we think it was in a true religious spirit, and with firm faith in that Supreme Power that had never failed him, and which he desired to glorify, that he "rebelled against the king of Assyria and served him not."

It is not needful to our object to enter into all the curious, complicated, and confused details of the reigns of Shalmaneser, Sargon and Sennacherib as bearing on the interests of the kingdom of Judah. It is enough to say that Sennacherib, one of the mightiest of Assyria's monarchs, came against Judah. He had reduced Phoenicia, recovered Ascalon, and at Ekron had met and defeated a great army of Egyptians and Ethiopians. He then proceeded towards Jerusalem, subjugating and spoiling on his way a large number of fenced cities, and towns and villages without number, capturing their inhabitants to the number, according to the Babylonian inscriptions, of two hundred thousand. He encamped against Jerusalem on its northern side, and began the siege. To this period of distress we presume Isaiah refers in that remarkably vivid description in chap. 24:1-12.

Hezekiah made a brave resistance for a time, of which we have an account in 2 Chron. 32:1-8. He cut off the supplies of water from the enemy, repaired the walls, increased the height of the towers, and made weapons and shields in abundance. He then sought to inspire the people with his own religious faith. "Be strong and of a good courage," said he, "be not afraid nor dismayed for the king of Assyria, nor for all the multitude that is with him: with him is an arm of flesh; but with us is Jehovah our God to help us and to fight our battles" (2 Chron. 32:7-8). This is language of lofty faith in a very dark hour. But, for some reason, all this faith oozed out, and Hezekiah succumbed to the "arm of flesh" — we may not know why. If Isa. 22 refers to this period, there was an evident failure of the people to respond to the strong faith and patriotic zeal of the king. With all their preparations for defense, they looked not unto God for help, nor humbled themselves before Him. "In that day did the Lord, the Lord of hosts, call to weeping, and to mourning, and to baldness, and to girding with sackcloth: and, behold, joy and gladness, slaying oxen and killing sheep, eating flesh and drinking wine: let us eat and drink, for tomorrow we shall die" (Isa. 22:12-13). They had no other thought than that the enemy would prevail against them; and in that insanity of recklessness which was but the ripe fruit of their previous and long-continued rebellions against Jehovah, they mocked and jeered, and feasted and danced, in the very face of destruction, bracing each other in their insane revelries with the counsel, "Let us eat and drink, for tomorrow we shall die." No wonder that the prophet, as he looked on this appalling and impious recklessness, said to these mad revelers, "The Lord of hosts revealed himself in mine ears, surely this iniquity shall not be purged from you till ye die." It was an iniquity too revolting and too brazen to be forgiven.

Shebna, chief in authority and the head of the court party, had persuaded those who ought to have been the king's chief supporters into a factious reliance on Egypt for help in the present calamity; so that between the Assyrian party, the Egyptian party, and the profane crowd of reckless revelers, the king and Isaiah were left alone to give vigor to this defense against the besiegers. It is marrow to the bones to listen to the brave prophet in his burning indignation as he hurls the thunderbolts of his patriotic wrath against the infamous Shebna — probably a foreign adventurer who had somehow wormed his way, in these corrupt times, into high position, and with his ring of corrupt courtiers was fattening himself on the spoils of an office which he disgraced (Isa. 22:15-19).

We may, perhaps, judge from these facts why Hezekiah surrendered. It was not that his own faith in Jehovah failed, but that the faithlessness of a corrupt and factious court and population rendered his faith void. He was compelled to yield (2 Ki. 18:14), to the dishonor of Jehovah's name; and in almost heart-breaking anguish the prophet Isaiah exclaimed: "Look away from me; I will weep bitterly; labor not to comfort me, because of the spoiling of the daughter of my people. For it is a day of discomfiture, and of treading down, and of perplexity, from the Lord, the Lord of hosts, in the valley of vision; a breaking down of the walls, and a crying to the mountains" (Isa. 22:4-5). And greatly did Sennacherib exult in this victory. According to the Assyrian inscriptions, as given in Rawlinson's "Ancient Monarchies" (2:435), he made this boast:

And because Hezekiah, King of Judah, would not submit to my yoke, I came up against him, and by force of arms, and by the might of my power, I took forty-six of his strong fenced cities, and of smaller towns which were scattered about, I took and plundered countless number. And from these places I captured and carried off as a spoil 200,150 people, old and young, male and female together, with horses and mares, asses and camels, oxen and sheep, a countless multitude. And Hezekiah himself I shut up in Jerusalem, his capital city, like a bird in a cage, building towers around the city to hem him in, and raising banks of earth against the gates to prevent his escape. . . .

Then upon this Hezekiah there fell the fear of the power of my arms, and he sent out to me the chiefs and the elders of Jerusalem, with thirty talents of gold, and eight hundred talents of silver, and divers treasures, and rich and immense booty... All these things were brought to me at Nineveh, the seat of my government, Hezekiah having sent them by way of tribute, and as a token of his submission to my power.

This self-glorification must doubtless be taken *cum grand salis*,[1] and may even be liberally discounted without injury to truth; but it was a disgraceful defeat to Hezekiah, and a great dishonor to the name of Jehovah. Our only comfort is that it but furnishes the dark background which will soon bring out even more illustriously Jehovah's final victory, and give the greater prominence and significance to Sennacherib's disastrous overthrow.

For some reason, Sennacherib soon violated his new agreement with Hezekiah. If, with Dean Stanley, we adopt an interpretation of Isa. 22 different from that which we have given; if we regard the crime of Shebna to have been that of persuading the king to a present submission to the Assyrians in hope of speedy assistance from Egypt and Ethiopia to break the treaty, and the joy and gladness in the city to have been on occasion of the departure of the Assyrian forces because of this unworthy submission to a proud, idolatrous foe, then we may entertain a probable opinion as to the new demands of Sennacherib. While engaged in the siege of Lachish, the Assyrian learned that a new and tremendous force of Egyptians and Ethiopians were making rapid approaches, and he was led to

---

[1] Latin phrase meaning "with a grain of salt."

regard Hezekiah's submission as a mere trick to gain time until this new army could come to his aid. It is even possible that Hezekiah raised anew the standard of independence, encouraged by promises of assistance from Tirhakah of Ethiopia. Some have so concluded from a comparison of 2 Ki. 19:9, with Isa. 18:1-2. But we see no sufficient evidence of it in these passages. Whether he suspected Hezekiah of this or not, it would not be safe to leave such a power as Judah — necessarily hostile at heart — behind him; it became necessary to subdue Hezekiah utterly, if possible, before this great southern army, under the lead of a skillful Cushite commander, appeared on the field. Accordingly, he sent a military detachment, under the guidance of three of his trusty officers, to Jerusalem, to demand its instant and unconditional surrender. They knew that Jerusalem was torn by factions, that the kingdom was impoverished, and that the terror of Sennacherib's name was overpowering. Their message was haughty, boastful, blasphemous, taunting, insulting; their bearing insolent and provoking to the last degree. Sennacherib himself sent a letter to Hezekiah, repeating the insolences and unrighteous demands already verbally made by his messengers. The distressed king of Judah, in this dire extremity, went up to the house of Jehovah, and spread the blasphemous ravings and imperious demands of Sennacherib before the Lord, and earnestly besought Him to maintain the honor of His own name. It was a prayer arising from an anguished yet trusting heart. He sent also to the prophet Isaiah for counsel. The prophet gave him the most positive assurances that all would be well.

> *Thus saith the Lord concerning the king of Assyria: "He shall not come into this city, nor shoot an arrow there, nor come before it with shield, nor cast a bank against it. By the way that he came, by the same shall he return, and shall not come into this city," saith the Lord. "For I will defend this city, to save it, for mine own sake and for my servant David's sake."*

To the people also did this invincible patriot-prophet address assurances of speedy divine deliverance.

> *The Lord of hosts hath sworn, saying, "Surely, as I have thought, so shall it come to pass; and as I have pur-*

posed, so shall it stand: that I will break the Assyrian in my land, and upon my mountains tread him under foot: then shall his yoke depart from off them, and his burden depart from off their shoulder. This is the purpose that is purposed upon the whole earth, and this is the hand that is stretched out upon all the nations. For the Lord of hosts hath purposed, and who shall disannul it? and his hand is stretched out, and who shall turn it back?" (Isa. 14:24-27)

And the Lord sent an angel, which cut off all the mighty men of valor, and the leaders and captains in the camp of the king of Assyria, and smote in the camp of the Assyrians an hundred fourscore and five thousand men; and when they arose in the morning, behold they were all dead corpses. So Sennacherib king of Assyria departed, and went and returned, and dwelt at Nineveh. And it came to pass as he was worshiping in the house of Nisroch his God, that Adrammelech and Sharezer his sons smote him with the sword: and they escaped into the land of Armenia (2 Chron. 32:21; 2 Ki. 19:35-37).[1]

Thus suddenly and terribly did the might of the boastful Assyrian monarch vanish under the curse of Jehovah. "He was the last of the great Assyrian conquerors," says Stanley. "No Assyrian host ever again crossed the Jordan. Within a few years from that time the Assyrian power suddenly vanished from the earth."

Whether the means of destruction in this case was a pestilence, as Jewish tradition affirms, and as we know to have been true in another instance (2 Sam. 24:15-16), is a question more curious than wise. It is enough to know that the destruction was wrought by a divinely commissioned power; that it was known as Jehovah's work; and that the power of the living God against the idols in which the heathen boasted was thus made manifest before the whole world.

It would hardly do to close without repeating Byron's famous Hebrew melody:

---

[1] The murder of Sennacherib was about eighteen years after this disaster. The silence of the canonical Scriptures, and the unhistorical statement in the Apocrypha (Tobit 1:21) that he was murdered fifty-five days after his return, have led to a false conclusion.]

The Assyrian came down like the wolf on the fold,
And his cohorts were gleaming in purple and gold;
And the sheen on his spears was like stars on the sea,
When the blue wave rolls nightly on deep Galilee.

Like the leaves of the forest when Summer is green,
That host, with their banners, at sunset were seen;
Like the leaves of the forest when Autumn is blown,
That host, on the morrow, lay withered and strown.

For the Angel of Death spread his wings on the blast,
And breathed in the face of the foe as he passed;
And the eyes of the sleepers waxed deadly and chill,
And their hearts but once heaved, and for ever grew still.

And there lay the steed with his nostril all wide,
But through it there rolled not the breath of his pride;
And the foam of his gasping lay white on the turf,
And cold as the spray of the rock-beating surf.

And there lay the rider, distorted and pale,
With the dew on his brow, and the rust on his mail;
And the tents were all silent, the banners alone,
The lances unlifted, the trumpet unblown.

And the widows of Asshur are loud in their wail;
And the idols are broke in the temple of Baal;
And the might of the Gentile, unsmote by the sword,
Hath melted, like snow, in the glance of the Lord!

Who is like unto Thee, O Jehovah, among the gods? Who is like Thee, glorious in holiness, fearful in praises, doing wonders? What a glorious refuge art Thou to Thy people in the day of trouble! Who shall not fear Thee, O Lord, and glorify Thy name! For thou only art holy. Teach us to cast all our care on Thee. O for that faith that will ever endure as seeing Him who is invisible. When the enemy cometh in like a flood, then Thy Spirit lifteth up a standard against him. In the light of such lessons as this, may we learn to do Thy will under all circumstances, and leave the consequences with Thee, assured that Thou wilt never leave nor forsake those who are true to Thee.

Royal Reformers: Hezekiah (Part Three)

Whether the severe and threatening illness of Hezekiah (2 Ki. 20:1-3) was after the flight of Sennacherib, or earlier in his reign, after a deliverance from the threatening presence of Sargon, as many suppose, we shall not here discuss, inasmuch as with all its interest and value as a chronological question it does not touch the objects had in view in these sketches. We strongly incline to the opinion that this dangerous illness preceded the invasion of Sennacherib and his subsequent overthrow; but, at whatever date, such an affliction was sent upon the king. We are apt to covet great gifts, great opportunities, great glory; but it should chasten our ambition when we reflect that, along with these, are sure to come great trials, great afflictions, great burdens of care, anxiety, and grief, These are, as the wise man said, "set over the one against the other" (Eccles. 7:14), to hold things somewhere near the level — to save us from the deformities and monstrosities which either unbroken prosperity or unchecked adversity would produce.

We might have had reason to doubt the truthfulness of the record, so far as internal evidence is concerned, if Hezekiah's splendid career had been altogether free from dark shadings. Such was the glory of his reign and the magnificence of his victories, that the Jews, it would appear from tradition, were fondly disposed to regard him as the promised Messiah, and applied to him such prophecies as those in Isa. 9 and 11. It is quoted as a saying of Hillel, that "there would be no Messiah for Israel in future times, because he had already appeared in Hezekiah." And the traditional testimony is that this king applied to himself, not only the Messianic predictions of Isaiah, but also Psalms 20 and 110. He had even left entirely out of view a successor to his throne, as if he indulged the confidence that no successor would be needed. Sickness and death were remote from his contemplations. It was needful that this idle dream should be spoiled. It was among the greatest of the mercies of his reign that he was "sick unto death." It is doubtful if any man properly appreciates the responsibilities and awful solemnities of life until he is brought face to face with death. Certainly, when a puny mortal is inspired with vast ambitions that mock at death, he will not be apt to "come to himself" until a heavy hand of affliction is laid on him, and he is made to know how frail he is. It was because of the abundance of his visions and revelations that Paul received "a thorn in the flesh, the messenger of Satan to buffet him," "lest," he said, "I should be exalted above measure" (2 Cor. 12:7). And so Hezekiah, and every other highly favored one, must have his "thorn in the flesh," that he be not exalted above measure, lest being lifted up with pride, he fall into the condemnation of the devil. Not only were his delightful visions of perpetual greatness and Messianic immortality and glory dissolved by a disease — perhaps a carbuncle or tumor — that reduced him to a level with other mortals, but the warning came from his inspired and trusted counselor, Isaiah: "Set thine house in order; for thou shalt die, and not live."[1]

What a terrible shattering of the cherished hopes and ambitions of a lifetime! And who is there among the prosperous that does not need to be rescued from exaltation above measure — from the insanities of successful ambition, the intoxications of feverish and victorious achievement — by a counter-irritant of humiliation and disaster? Hezekiah, with all his excellences, was likely to be nothing better than a spoiled child of fortune; and in mercy, a rod of correction was laid upon him with heavy hand. All his glory faded away; midnight darkness encompassed him; he "turned his face to the wall," as one bereft of all earthly consolation, and made tearful, sobbing supplications to Jehovah, his only hope: "I beseech thee, O Jehovah, remember now how I have walked before thee in truth and with a perfect heart, and have done that which is good in thy sight." He may have been tainted with undue ambition, or intoxicated with delusive hopes; but how few among the sons of ambition dare make such a plea of honesty and fidelity before God! That he was subject to an overweening[2] vanity, even after the heavy chastisement he now received, we know; and that he was

---

[1] "In this history, as in that of Jonah (Jon. 3:4-10), and to some extent in that of Ahab (1 Ki. 21:21-29), we see that the prophetic denunciations were often not absolute predictions of what was certainly about to happen, but warnings or menaces, designed previously to prove, or to lead to repentance, those against whom they were uttered, and only obtaining accomplishment if this primary object failed. — *Speaker's Commentary.*

[2] Excessive.

much more subject to it before this chastisement came, is a moral certainty; but it was, after all, but the infirmity of a noble mind. At heart, and in life, he had ever been true to God and to his kingdom; and, whatever his infirmities, God bless the man of truth and honesty. We have to look on Hezekiah as gold, but as yet somewhat mixed with dross that called for the refiner's fire. But he is in the hands of a loving God who afflicts him only for his good. Soon the prophet is sent with another message:

> Thus saith Jehovah, the God of David thy father: "I have heard thy prayer, I have seen thy tears; behold, I will heal thee: on the third day thou shalt go up unto the house of the Lord; and I will add unto thy days fifteen years" (2 Ki. 20:5-6).

O ye afflicted! When the hand of chastening is heavy upon you, yield not to vain and sinful murmurings. Turn your face to the wall, and appeal to God in prayers and tears, that God may say to you, "I have heard thy prayers, I have seen thy tears." These are eloquent pleaders before the merciful God, and you shall not be left unblessed.

It is alike curious and instructive to listen to Hezekiah's confessions in his hymn of thanksgiving after his recovery. Let us hear it.

> I said, "In the noontide of my days I shall go into the gates of Sheol: I am deprived of the residue of my years."
>
> I said, "I shall not see Jehovah, even Jehovah in the land of the living: I shall behold man no more with the inhabitants of the world."
>
> Mine age is removed, and is carried away from me as a shepherd's tent: I have rolled up like a weaver my life; he will cut me off from the loom: From day even to night wilt thou make an end of me.
>
> I quieted myself until morning; as a lion, so he breaketh all my bones: From day even to night wilt thou make an end of me.
>
> Like a swallow or a crane, so did I chatter; I did mourn as a dove; mine eyes fail with looking upward.
>
> O Lord, I am oppressed; be thou my surety.

What shall I say? He hath spoken unto me, and himself hath done it: I shall go softly all my years, because of the bitterness of my soul.

O Lord, by these things men live, and wholly therein is the life of my spirit. Wherefore recover thou me, and make me to live.

Behold, it was for my peace that I had great bitterness: but thou hast in love to my soul delivered it from the pit of corruption; for thou hast cast all my sins behind thy back. For the grave cannot praise thee, death cannot celebrate thee. They that go down into the pit cannot hope for thy truth.

The living, the living, he shall praise thee, as I do this day. The father to the children shall make known thy truth.

The Lord is ready to save me, therefore we will sing my songs to the stringed instruments all the days of our life in the house of the Lord.

In all this there is not the slightest recognition of a life beyond the grave. It is the enthusiasm of joy over fifteen years more of this feverish, anxious life! Beyond, all is darkness and the corruption of the pit. It would not do to say that this enlightened servant of God knew nothing of another life. But he lived under a dispensation of temporal rewards and punishments, in which the sublime realities of a future life were retired into the background — if, indeed, they appeared at all; and, as a king and a reformer, he had been so absorbed in the affairs of the present, so bent on present achievements and present victories, that he had had neither time nor inclination to study into the future. When, therefore, death suddenly stared Hezekiah in the face, he was "without hope." It was to him the end of all things — the blotting out of all blessedness. But, if Hezekiah had but dim perceptions, or no perceptions at all, of a future life, he had that faith in Jehovah, and that devotion to truth for its own sake, which were a constant inspiration to faithfulness, and brought him an ever-present reward. And there are many now whom we are apt to condemn as worldly, and on whom we do not hesitate to pronounce severe condemnations as either not Christians at all, or not more than half-Christians, because they are so little under the influence of the Christian hope, who are, nevertheless crowding their lives with diligent efforts to serve God and their fellowmen, from a high sense of duty, with a sacred devotion to truth and right, because they are truth and right. While they do not furnish the highest type of Christian character, they are greatly the superiors of those whose lives are spent in fruitless speculations over the premillennial or post-millennial coming of Christ, the state of the spirit after death, the number of inhabitants that can be accommodated in the New Jerusalem, etc., etc., speculations which are likely to be about as sensible and valuable as a child's speculations about the moon and the stars. Godliness has promise of "the life that now is," as well as of that which is to come, and the surest preparation for the life to come is a diligent and faithful performance of the functions of the life we now possess. It is not necessary to a genuine piety that we should be continually depreciating the world that God has given us here, and sinning away all its precious opportunities in sentimental whimperings over the short-lived pleasures of earth, leaving the world, at last, none the better for our presence in it. Unquestionably, that is the most desirable path on which streams the radiance of heavenly hope, and that the most enviable life which is supported and sanctified and swayed by a confident anticipation of an endless life. But if we have not yet attained to "the full assurance of hope," or "the full assurance of understanding," let us cling to duty, and be upheld by the consciousness that we are keeping the commandments of God.

There is much precious truth in Wordsworth's ode to Duty:

> *Stern Lawgiver! yet thou dost wear*
> *The Godhead's most benignant grace;*
> *Nor know we anything so fair*
> *As is the smile upon thy face.*
> *Flowers laugh before thee in their beds,*
> *And fragrance in thy footing treads;*
> *Thou dost preserve the stars from wrong,*
> *And the most ancient heavens, through thee, are fresh and strong.*

Yet we opine that honest, earnest souls like Hezekiah, unblessed with the consolations and inspirations of a confident hope of heaven, will be sometime schooled by sore affliction into a sense of their incompleteness, and will learn, through bitter experiences, their need of something better than earth can afford.

And this leads us to remark how paltry were the possessions, the ambitions, the glories of Hezekiah in the presence of death. That patch of land in Palestine — that petty kingdom with its limited revenues, and its feeble splendors — that handful of subjects over whom he held control: what were these, even in comparison with Egypt or Assyria? How utterly contemptible, therefore, as the full measure of a man's ambition, when death was at the door of the monarch, and even these pale glories must be quenched, and these paltry toys of royalty be surrendered? And yet for a very small portion of Hezekiah's diminutive greatness, we are willing to make of our brief life one perpetual toil and struggle, "and call this barren world sufficient bliss!" Multitudes are in worse case than Hezekiah when death comes; for he could look up to God and say truthfully, "I have walked before thee in truth and with a perfect heart," while they have to confess an utter idolatry in the service of vain and worthless idols.

Strange to say, it was *after* this severe chastening that Hezekiah exhibited offensively his great infirmity. He was prospered abundantly (2 Chron. 32:23, 27-30), and "his heart was lifted up." Not always do even the God-fearing learn aright the lessons of affliction. Foolish and wicked devices, suppressed but not destroyed by chastisement, again spring up when the heavy hand of judgment is withdrawn. He became vain-glorious. The wonderful defeat of Sennacherib, and the marvelous phenomenon of the shadow going backward ten degrees or steps on the dial (2 Ki. 20:9-11), had given the king great fame, and the prosperity of his kingdom attracted the attention of other kingdoms, even distant ones. Merodach Baladan, in Babylonia, was striving against Sargon of Assyria with partial success, to release Babylon from subjugation to Assyrian rule, and erect an independent and rival sovereignty. Under pretense of congratulating Hezekiah on his restoration to health, and of inquiring concerning "the wonder done in the land" in the backward movement of the shadow on the dial (2 Chron. 32:31), he sent ambassadors to Jerusalem. The real design was, in all probability, to propose an alliance with the kingdom of Judah, and perhaps with Egypt, against Assyria. Hezekiah was elated that a distant power should thus honor him with an embassy of the princes of Babylon, and with large presents; he felt that he had indeed risen to an exceeding greatness, when his favor was thus courted, and his alliance thus eagerly sought; and to impress his visitors with an idea of his greatness, he made a vain display of the wealth and splendor and power of his throne and his kingdom — "there was nothing in his house, nor in all his kingdom, that he showed them not."

> *Then said Isaiah unto Hezekiah, "Behold, the days come that all that is in thine house, and that which thy fathers have laid up in store until this day, shall be carried to Babylon; nothing shall be left, saith the Lord. And of thy sons that shall issue from thee, which thou shalt beget shall they take away, and they shall be eunuchs in the palace of the king of Babylon" (Isa. 39:5-7).*

This lifting up of the heart in self-exaltation — how natural and how common it is. Take away the privilege of exhibiting their own greatness and glorying in their own importance, from many even of the preachers of the gospel, and you rob them of their chief joy; they will shrivel into nothingness. It is worthwhile to note, therefore, that this sin was exceedingly offensive in the sight of God, and that on account of it there was wrath upon Hezekiah, and upon Judah and Jerusalem (2 Chron. 32:26). There is no more important precept, especially for those in places of trust, than this: "Be clothed with humility." Forever it is true, that "pride goeth before destruction, and a haughty spirit before a fall." Would that we could say of all vain, proud men, what is said of the noble Hezekiah — noble in spite of this infirmity — "Notwithstanding, Hezekiah humbled himself for the pride of his heart, both he and the inhabitants of Jerusalem, so that the wrath of the Lord came not upon them in the days of Hezekiah." If we mourn over his infirmity, we can rejoice in that honesty and manliness which led him to confess his folly and put away his sin.

We ought not to close this sketch without mentioning that this king labored also for the intellectual improvement of his people. From Prov. 25:1 it appears that he appointed a commission to collect the proverbs of Solomon, and according to Jewish tradition, the prophecies of Isaiah were collected by him, and Ecclesiastes and Canticles [Song of Solomon] were preserved. Himself a poet, he sought to preserve whatever was worthy in the literature of his nation, and to cultivate a love of literature during a reign marked by more than ordinary literary activity.

The closing years of his reign were prosperous. Indeed, the entire reign was glorious in its achievements, its victories, and the general prosperity of the people, while its disasters arose mainly out of the complications of previous reigns. While the reformations wrought were largely external, and therefore not permanent, — being the result of royal compulsion rather than of a nation's repentance — they served to show, on one hand, the king's righteous and holy aims, and, on the other, the utter impossibility of attaining to righteousness under the law.

When the fifteen years were expired, Hezekiah died — let us hope with a better view of the future than he was able to take at their beginning — "and they buried him in the chiefest of the sepulchers of the sons of David, and all Judah and the inhabitants of Jerusalem did him honor at his death."

We thank Thee, gracious God, for the lives of true and faithful men, written for our learning, that through patience and through comfort of the Scriptures we may have hope. May we catch inspiration from this noble life. And, while we emulate the virtues of Hezekiah, may we learn from his infirmities how unworthy is even the best service we can render unto Thee. Keep us, O Lord, from pride and vanity. If it pleases Thee to use us to promote the glory of Thy name, may we not exalt ourselves against Thee because of that which may be wrought through us. Save us from the perils of prosperity, as well as from the discouragements of adversity. Teach us to say, after our best achievements, "Not unto us, O Lord, not unto us, but unto Thy name be the glory, for Thy mercy and for Thy truth's sake." And in our extremest adversities, may we be able to say, in sincerity of heart, "Although the fig-tree shall not blossom, neither shall fruit be in the vines; the labor of the olive shall fail, and the fields shall yield no meat; the Rock shall be cut off from the fold, and there shall be no herd in the stalls: yet will I rejoice in the Lord; I will joy in the God of my salvation."

Royal Reformers: Josiah

(Read 2 Kings 22:1 — 23:28; 2 Chron. 34-35)

It is always a sad history — that of a nation's decadence. In the face of a thousand warnings, and in contempt of notable examples of the kingdom's successful navigation of stormy and perilous seas when heedful of the divine chart and compass, — a blind and reckless drifting towards rocks and whirlpools that must surely wreck and swallow up not only the glory but the very life of the nation: it is indeed lamentable. Here and there, in such a history, with its ever-thickening clouds of darkness, surcharged with a wrath which is sure, sooner or later, to burst in appalling destruction upon a doomed people, we may behold, through providential rifts, an occasional outpouring of sunlight; but its splendors are soon succeeded by thicker darkness and increasing portents of national disaster. Such rifts in the clouds were seen in the brief periods of reformation in Judah, under Asa, Jehoshaphat, Hezekiah, and Josiah. They were pious and patriotic efforts to save Judah from an unmistakable trend to apostasy, a stubborn rebelliousness, a blind drifting to inevitable ruin. But they only postponed the final day of consummate apostasy and destruction. The farther on we go, the thicker the darkness, and the smaller and more transient the rifts and the outbursts of sunshine. Thus, the reformatory efforts of Asa and Jehoshaphat were not entirely exhausted of their power for two centuries, while we count but little over half a century — fifty-seven years from the close of the reign of the succeeding royal reformer, Hezekiah, to the next reformation under Josiah; and it was but twenty-two and a half years from the close of Josiah's reign to the destruction of Jerusalem and the overthrow of the nation. Josiah's reformation was therefore the last desperate struggle against falsehood and wrong — the last serious and arduous effort to beat back the swelling floods of corruption.

The noble Hezekiah was succeeded by a son — Manasseh — who proved to be the most infamous of Judah's monarchs; who not only undid all his father's work of reformation, but became the patron of iniquities and abominations more shocking and degrading than had ever been previously known in Judah. And to the multiplication of idolatrous and obscene rites, he added cruel persecu-

210

tion that filled the streets of Jerusalem with the blood of the innocent (2 Ki. 21:1-16). The Jewish tradition is that the venerable
Isaiah, the life-long friend and counselor of Hezekiah, now nearly
ninety years old, was among the victims of Manasseh's blood-
thirstiness, being sawn asunder at his command. And yet this base
idolater and bloody persecutor, the worst among all the kings of
Judah, had a longer reign than any of the best of the kings — being
kept in power more than half a century! True, after Manasseh was
carried in chains to Babylon, he repented, and in view of his repentance, the Lord restored him to his kingdom, and his last years
were spent in efforts to restore that which he had done so much to
destroy; but he found it much easier to do evil than to overcome it
— to inflict wrong than to apply the remedy. It is gratifying to reflect that even under the sternness of that law, and in the case of
such a brazen apostate as Manasseh, the plea of repentance was
sacredly regarded; yet such was the depth of his wickedness, and
the blackness of his crimes, and the extent of the moral ruin
wrought by his authority and example, that while he was personally pardoned, the nation was abandoned to ruin.

> *"Surely at the commandment of the Lord came this
> upon Judah, to remove them out of his sight, for the sins of
> Manasseh, according to all that he did, and also for the
> innocent blood that he shed; for he filled Jerusalem with
> innocent blood: **and the Lord would not pardon**"* (2 Ki.
> 24:3-4).

What an unspeakably dreadful thing sin is! Not even divine
forbearance and forgiveness can wipe it utterly out. It still lives *in
its horrible fruitage*. Though the penitent transgressor finds shelter
under the wing of divine mercy, he may yet be continually humbled and pained in beholding the ruinous consequences of his sins,
which he is powerless to abate. Though the persecuting Saul "obtained mercy," he ceased not to mourn to his dying day, because he
"persecuted the church of God," and to stigmatize himself as "the
chief of sinners." Beware of sin: there is a bitter curse in it, even
after all that divine mercy can do to wash away its stain.

This speedy overthrow of the faith and piety which Hezekiah
thought he had so firmly established suggests an important lesson.
It is evident that the reformation under that king was mainly *exter-*

nal — not with the king himself, but on the part of the people. In their hearts they hankered after the idolatries of the surrounding nations. Only a small minority entered heartily into the king's purposes. The court-party was evidently wedded to a religion of imposing forms, spectacular attractions, and ritualistic pomps, with little or no regard to moral purity and righteousness — such a religion as would leave them free to indulge their passions and place no restraints on their political ambitions and iniquitous practices. And the people at large imagined that they found an easier yoke in such a religion than in the stern requirements of justice, mercy, and truth which the law of Jehovah contained. They conformed, externally, to the royal will, and with their lips drew near to Jehovah, but their hearts were far from Him. Hence, when Hezekiah died, and Manasseh succeeded to the throne, the reaction came — as it came in England when the reign of Puritanism ceased on the accession of Charles II, and, previously, when "Bloody Mary" succeeded to Edward VI. No royal power can *force* a genuine reformation; no voice of a *minority* clothed with power can *compel* a true reformation of the majority of the people. A forced reformation will last just as long as the power lasts which enforces it; and then the terrible reaction comes. And in a country like ours, where there is no royal will but the will of the people — where no law is honored except as it expresses the public sentiment and will — no legislation, however righteous, can enforce a moral reformation, unless it embodies the will of a majority of the people. In a word: true reformation comes *from within,* and is the legitimate fruit of that reign of Christ which is established *within us.* Legislation may be an effective ally of popular sentiment; but it permanently avails only as it is the *result* rather than the cause of reformation.

Amon, the son of Manasseh — named after an Egyptian idol — reigned but two years, when assassination put an end to his wicked career. Then came his son Josiah to the throne, at the early age of eight years. How the son of such a wicked father and the grandson of so infamous an apostate, could be, from his childhood, so noted for piety and uncompromising devotion to the law of Jehovah, we are not able to say. If his mother's name, Jedidah, "the beloved of God," and his grandmother's, Adaiah, "the honored of God," are at all indicative of character, we have a clue to the solution of this problem in their influence over his early years. If the prophet Zephaniah was the great-grandson of the pious king Hezekiah (Zeph. 1:1), we have another clue. At all events, we know that Zephaniah flourished during the reign of Josiah; and Jeremiah came into public life during his reign; and, as the persecutions of the former reign ceased — perhaps through the influence of the queen-mother — the faithful, who had been driven into obscurity, were free to come forth, and would zealously promote the pious education and teaching of one destined to wield, in a few years, the royal scepter.

Of Josiah's zeal and fidelity in the service of Jehovah there can be no question. Indeed it is said that "like unto him there was no king before him, that turned to the Lord with all his heart, and with all his soul, and with all his might, according to all the law of Moses: neither after him arose there any like him" (2 Ki. 23:25). His work of reformation ranges itself under three heads: (1) The restoration of the temple service and the keeping of the Passover festival. (2) The purgation of the temple, the holy city, and the land, of idolatrous abominations. (3) The re-proclamation of the law of Jehovah.

Let the reader turn to 2 Kings, and read chapter 23:4-20, and he may learn to measure the zeal and fidelity of Josiah by the magnitude of the corruptions and abominations that prevailed, and the thoroughness of the destructive work he performed. Not only in Jerusalem, but throughout Judaea, "from Geba to Beer-sheba;" not only in Judea, but also in the country of the ten tribes, "in the cities of Manasseh, and Ephraim, and Simeon, even unto Naphtali," was the destructive sweep of his power felt. The slackness of Assyrian authority in the Samaritan territory enabled him to extend his iconoclastic zeal thus far outside of his own dominion, and the poisonous influence of the idolatries of Israel over Judah doubtless led him to seek to protect his own kingdom by desolating the shrines which had been fountains of mischief to his own people. But two things are especially worthy of note in these proceedings: (1) They were the result simply of royal authority, and not of repentance on the part of the people. (2) There is a fierceness of zeal, and a persecuting spirit, manifest, which detract much from the merit of the performances. The slaying of the priests found at idolatrous altars, and the violation of the sanctity of sepulchers by disinterring the bones of dead priests and prophets (2 Ki. 23:16, 20), look as if a spirit of persecution and vengeful retaliation was mixed with the king's zeal for Jehovah. Rather, it looks as if the case had become thoroughly desperate, and nothing but violence could avail. Manasseh had set the example of persecution, and every memory of the innocent victims of his rage pleaded for vengeance on the idolatrous usurpers and persecutors. Moreover, the people were no longer subject to reason. The day for argument and entreaty had passed. There remained only the strong arm of power to bring lying priests and prophets, corrupt judges, and an apostate nation into submission; and Josiah employed the only available remedy. But it is a sad day for truth and righteousness when they are utterly dependent on the sword for protection. It surely presages[1] the nation's downfall — and this it is which lends so melancholy an interest to Josiah's attempt at reformation. It has no vitality except in the king's own heart and in the hearts of a small circle of prophets and holy men that gather around him — the forlorn hope of a holy cause which is destined to defeat.

The observance of the Passover, while it is said that there was not kept such a Passover from the days of the judges that judged Israel, nor in all the days of the kings of Israel, nor of the kings of Judah" (2 Ki. 23:22), was remarkable only as an *external* observance. As Nature puts on her most gorgeous robes in autumn, and makes a flaring funeral procession to a wintry grave; so this people, on the eve of destruction, sought to hide their doom under cover of a festival of exceeding pomp and magnificence. But it was, after all, a formal, heartless affair. It was, at best, but the hectic flush on the cheeks of a victim doomed to speedy death. The king doubtless sought to honor Jehovah by the revival of this great national festival, and hoped to rekindle the patriotic and pious enthusiasm of the nation; but the patriotism of the nation was already turned to ashes, nor were there enough lingering sparks to be fanned into even a feeble flame. It was a great Passover only because the authority of the king compelled it into greatness. The people were dead to its import; the conscience of the nation was utterly debauched: the priests, the prophets, the courtiers, and the great mass of the sin-hardened people were saturated with idola-

---

[1] Indicates as a warning.

trous superstitions, and drunken with the wine of heathenish fanaticism. The hollowness of the observance is not to be concealed under the showy solemnities and spectacular pomps of an imposing ritual.

The discovery of "the book of the law" by Hilkiah (2 Chron. 34:14) — probably the original copy which had been deposited in the temple — while it does not imply that all other copies had been destroyed, yet indicates that the Jewish scriptures were scarce, and no longer fresh in the memories of the people. Doubtless, during the reign of Manasseh, in the fierce persecution that raged against the servants of Jehovah, every copy of the law that could be found was doomed to destruction. A corrupt priesthood no longer taught it to the people, and even the king was largely ignorant of its contents, as is evident from his surprise and grief when it was read to him. For more than half a century idolatry had been the State-religion, and Jehovah's revelations had been almost utterly forgotten. But Josiah's course on recovering this long-neglected and forgotten law indicates the nobleness of his spirit.

> *Then the king sent and gathered together all the elders of Judah and Jerusalem. And the king went up to the house of the Lord, and all the men of Judah and the inhabitants of Jerusalem, and the priests, and the Levites, and all the people, both great and small: and he read in their ears all the words of the book of the covenant that was found in the house of the Lord. And the king stood in his place, and made a covenant before the Lord, to walk after the Lord, and to keep his commandments, and his testimonies, and his statutes, with all his heart and with all his soul, to perform the words of the covenant that were written in this book. And he caused all that were found in Jerusalem and in Benjamin to stand to it. And the inhabitants of Jerusalem did according to the covenant of God, the God of their fathers.*

Noble monarch! Could he but have infused his own spirit into his subjects, all would have been well. But it was *too late*. Apostasy had proceeded until "there was no remedy." He had nobly struggled to perform an impossible task. His royal presence and his royal mandate compel an external show of submission to Jehovah's law; but the words fall on hard and barren rock. The people are joined to their idols. Their hearts have waxed gross, and their ears are dull of hearing, and their eyes they have closed, lest they should see with their eyes, and hear with their ears, and understand with their heart, and turn, and God should heal them. Have you ever seen a tree standing out alone in a clearing, naked and dead, blasted by the lightning, or fatally "girdled" — such a tree bathed in God's sunshine, watered with dews and rains, saluted by myriads of Nature's living voices, and invited by heaven and earth to live and flourish, yet drinking in the sunlight in vain, and making no response to the light of heaven, or the music of the earth, or the throbbing heart of Nature? Such a tree was the Jewish nation at this time — dead to the roots; not even the voice of God's holy law, nor the voice of living prophets, had for it any quickening power.

Let anyone, after reading these accounts of the apparent success of Josiah's reign, turn to Jeremiah and Zephaniah — prophets who flourished during this reign — and listen to their stern rebukes of the corruptions of this period. They evidently saw beneath the surface; and, though sympathizing with the king in his noble efforts, still saw that while, externally, there seemed to be a desirable work of reformation accomplished, there was no such turning of hearts to the Lord as to bid them rejoice in the assurance of a genuine and permanent reformation of the nation, or lead them, in their prophecies, to make even the barest allusion to it as a hopeful sign of genuine repentance.

The four succeeding kings — Jehoahaz, Jehoiakim, Jehoiachin, and Zedekiah, whose combined reigns amount to only twenty-two and a half years — were all wicked men and unprincipled rulers. Egypt and Babylon were both provoked to wrath against a faithless nation, and by successive spoliations this God-forsaken people were humiliated and subjugated until, at last, as had been foretold by God's faithful prophets, Jerusalem was laid in ruins, her walls broken, her holy and beautiful house burned with fire, and her king, her nobles and her people slain, or carried captive into a strange land, where they sat down by the rivers of Babylon, hanging their harps on the willows, and weeping at every remembrance of the Zion they had forfeited by their stubborn rebelliousness.

Of Josiah himself, it remains but to speak of his untimely end. The king of Egypt was on his way northward on an expedition against the king of Assyria. For some reason not explained, Josiah felt bound to oppose him. The fact that he could muster a respectable force for such a purpose indicates that his reign had been prosperous, and that he had succeeded in restoring to his shattered kingdom something of its former power. Against the protest of the Egyptian king, he insisted on giving battle, and on the famous plain of Esdraelon, near Megiddo, he carried out his purpose, but was fatally wounded, and died before he could reach Jerusalem. His death was the quenching of the last lingering hope of saving Judah from destruction. Not only was his death untimely and universally lamented by his people, and especially by those who were faithful to Jehovah — Jeremiah composing a lamentation over the loss of his beloved monarch — but, says the writer of the Chronicles, "all the singing men and singing women speak of Josiah in their lamentations to this day [after the captivity], and made them an ordinance in Israel." The anniversary of his death was long observed with peculiar solemnity, and during and after the captivity the memory of his loyalty to Jehovah was strongly influential in forming and cherishing that hate of idolatry by which the Jews were ever after distinguished.

Thus, though his reformation was a failure, his life was not a failure, as, indeed, no true life ever was or ever can be a failure. Bravely to do one's duty, against all odds, is the highest attainment of man; and he who does so, though he may seem to fight against fate, is sure to succeed, if not in the full accomplishment of his immediate aims, yet in the immortal power of a true life — a power made the more illustrious in this case by the greatness of the odds against which Josiah contended, and the unbending integrity of soul that forbade all faltering, even with all the outside world and a majority of his own subjects against him.

O God of Truth and Righteousness! Not only in the sunlight of prosperity, when it is pleasant to serve Thee, would we be found faithful to Thee; but equally in the darkest days, when even the most faithful service seems a failure. We would cling to Thee, *because thou art God;* and to Thy service, because truth is truth and right is right forever. We cherish the memory of those who were true to Thee when all others were false, and dared, in their profound convictions of duty, to risk everything for the honor of Thy name. Thus faithful among the faithless may we ever be found.

The Captivity

Throughout these studies in the Old Testament we have sought to keep before the reader the thought of one great purpose, called in Scripture, God's "eternal purpose" or "the purpose of the ages" (Eph. 3:11), stretching like a golden thread over all the centuries. This purpose was the coming of the Messiah, and the redemption of the fallen race of man through Him. Old Testament history and prophecy are interpretable only in the light of this purpose. To the New Testament reader, the facts and predictions of the Old Testament are valuable just to the extent of their contributions to this great "purpose of the ages." To this great consummation everything tends; in the light of this consummation everything is to be understood.[1] The Jews were God's elect people, not that they might be eternally saved, while the great mass of mankind were left to perish; but that through them the way might be prepared for the salvation of all peoples. And to the furtherance of this purpose their adversities, quite as much as their prosperities, were made to contribute. With this thought before us, let us consider the captivity of Judah.

Those who have paid close attention to preceding chapters will have been convinced, in view of the failure of all attempts at national reformation, that nothing more was to be gained in fulfilling this purpose by maintaining the throne of David. Indeed, from the time of Josiah, Judah could hardly be called a kingdom. Not only were the kings the mere puppets of Egypt or of Babylon, but they were the slaves of corrupt princes, who were really oligarchs.[2] Read Jer. 38:14-27, and see how Zedekiah was himself a helpless victim of the policy of these oligarchs — bound hand and foot to their will, so that, although he recognizes the message of Jeremiah as divine, he dare not stir in his own behalf, or in behalf of his

---

[1] We have pleasure in referring to a work no longer widely read — "A History of the Work of Redemption," by Jonathan Edwards, D. D., in which we are gratified to find a train of thought and reasoning and Scripture exposition entirely in harmony with the capital thought that runs through all these Studies. It is worthy the attention of every Bible student. It was published in a volume separately from Dr. Edwards' complete works, by Leavitt, Trow & Co., New York, 1845.

[2] A small group of people who govern a nation, often for their own purposes.

people, even to save the nation from destruction.

The forced reformation under Josiah ended with his death. The treasonable idolatries of the leaders of the people were at once resumed with fanatical devotion. Read Ezek. 8. It would be tedious even to mention the numerous passages in Jeremiah and Ezekiel corroborative of this. Divine protestations, rebukes, and warnings were continued to the very last. The brave Jeremiah, imprisoned, or sunken in mire, or kept on slender rations in the court of the prison, never ceased to warn the king, the princes, the false prophets, the elders, and the people, of the impending doom, nor to point out to them the only possible means of saving the city and the throne; but all in vain. The captivity became a necessity—to preserve the line of David from utter extinction, and the people of Judah from irredeemable apostasy.

1. The Jews, having proved themselves no longer capable of maintaining a nation loyal to Jehovah, became the dependents of other governments, that as the subjects of other powers, removed from the ever-increasing corruptness of throne and court, and under a hand of rigid discipline, they might be redeemed from their idolatrous tendencies, and be reestablished in their monotheistic faith. Accordingly, we find that in their changed condition in Babylon, and under the chastening hand which afterward continued to hold them in subjection to other nations, they renounced idolatry, and ever afterward were true to the faith of one living and true God. For nearly six hundred years they were subject to other nations, with the exception of about ninety years, when, under the dominion of the Maccabees and their posterity, they maintained a sort of military independence. That this was in furtherance of Jehovah's grand purpose is evident from Ezek. 21:26-27. The language refers to Zedekiah, the last of the Jewish kings: "And thou, O deadly wounded, wicked one, prince of Israel, whose day is come, in the time of the iniquity of the end, thus saith the Lord God, Remove the mitre, and take off the crown; this shall be no more the same: exalt that which is low, and abase that which is high. I will overturn, overturn, overturn it; and it shall be no more, until he come whose right it is; and I will give it him." Observe: Nebuchadnezzar, the Babylonian monarch, took off the crown from the head of Zedekiah, and held supreme power over the Jewish people. Then this supreme power was turned over to the Medes

and Persians; after that to the Grecians or Macedonians, under Alexander; and finally to the Romans. It was to be *thrice* overturned, and then he was to come to whom the crown of Israel belonged, and it was to be given to him. Jesus came after the crown had been thrice overturned, and he was placed on the throne of his father David, that he might rule over the house of Jacob forever. Clearly, then, do we see the *divine purpose* in putting an end to the kingdom of Judah, and in guarding the crown of David through all succeeding revolutions of the empires to which Judah was subject, with a view to the grand consummation — the enthronement of Jesus for the redemption of the race.

2. "Blessings brighten as they take their flight." Captives in a strange land, the Jews looked back to their own country with reverence for a law which they had so recklessly and persistently violated; with ardent love for the city of God that now lay in ruins; with an almost fanatical devotion to the dismantled and ruined temple which they had so often defiled, and whose divinely-ordained services they had so frequently and shamefully perverted. "A people banished and demoralized," says Blaikie, "have always a strong inclination to cherish and cling to their national institutions and distinguishing glories. That sense of superiority which refused to humble itself even under a Babylonian captivity, would entrench itself amid the venerable institutions of Moses."[1] How strong and intense was the revolution of sentiment and feeling, appears in Psalm 137:

> *By the rivers of Babylon,*
> *There we sat down; yea, we wept*
> *When we remembered Zion.*
> *Upon the willows in the midst thereof*
> *We hanged up our harps.*
> *For there they that led us captive required of us songs,*
> *And they that wasted us required of us mirth, saying,*
> *Sing us one of the songs of Zion.*
> *How shall we sing Jehovah's song*
> *In a strange land?*
> *If I forget thee, O Jerusalem,*

---

[1] *Manual of Bible History*, page 357.

Let my right hand forget her cunning:
Let my tongue cleave to the roof of my mouth,
If I remember thee not;
If I prefer not Jerusalem
Above my chief joy.
(See also Lam. 1:7.)

Thus their exile intensified their patriotism, and reawakened that sentiment of loyalty to Jehovah which has ever since characterized them. This was especially true after the last deportation, when all dreams of recovering their nationality were dissipated; when they were compelled to face the terrible fact of the hopeless ruin of their throne, their temple, and their holy city; and when the voice of the prophet was heard declaring, "This captivity is long: build ye houses, and dwell in them; and plant gardens, and eat the fruit of them" (Jer. 29:5, 28).

3. The Jews were compelled into a more spiritual worship. Their religion had been stripped of the sensuous attractions of its splendid symbolism and its imposing ritualistic pomps. Not only had the diadem of the house of David been removed, and the temple despoiled, and the city laid in ruins, but the tables of the law were lost, with the other precious memorials laid up in the ark of the covenant; the daily sacrifice had ceased; no golden candelabrum, no altar of incense, no table of shew-bread, no mitred priest, gave dignity and splendor to their worship; the Shekinah no longer dwelt between the cherubim; the high priest, with Urim and Thummim, no longer gave forth answers from Jehovah; even the sacred fire — the heaven-descended flame, which had for ages been vigilantly kept alive at the altar, was quenched. No longer able to rest in external attractions, they were under a necessity of meeting in small groups for a simpler worship, and to listen with keener relish to the reading of the law or the counsels of some prophet (Ezek. 14:1. See also Mal. 3:16, which, while it refers to a later date, is still indicative of the habit of the pious Jews formed in these times of exile and of adversity). And hence, probably, arose that synagogue worship which is so prominent in their later history. There was less sight, and more faith, in their religious culture; the contrite heart and the humble spirit became the temple of Jehovah (Isa. 57:15, 66:1-2).

The reader will find all this embodied in one of the apocryphal books, "The Song of the Hebrew Children," and admirably expressed in the prayer of Azarias, verses 14-19:

> *For we, O Lord, are become less than any nation, and be kept under this day in all the world, because of our sins. Neither is there at this time prince, or prophet, or leader, or burnt-offering, or sacrifice, or oblation, or incense, or place to sacrifice before thee, and to find mercy. Nevertheless, in a contrite heart and a humble spirit, let us be accepted. Like as in the burnt-offering of rams and bullocks, and like as in ten thousand of fat lambs, so let our sacrifice be in thy sight this day, and grant that we may go wholly after thee: for they shall not be confounded that put their trust in thee. And now we follow thee with all our heart, we fear thee and seek thy face. Put us not to shame: but deal with us after thy loving kindness, and according to the multitude of thy mercies.*

And this leads us to say that the prophets themselves rose to a new plane of inspiration, as the result of all these disasters to the Jewish people. Wearied with the repeated and ever more provoking rebellions of God's elect people, both Isaiah (2:1-6), and Micah (4:1-4), had turned to the contemplation of a broader philanthropy, a more comprehensive scheme of mercy, in which "all nations" should share equally with the Jews. Joel (2:28-32) found comfort in anticipating a day when the Spirit should be poured out on "all flesh." Jeremiah (31:31-34) dries his tears and ceases his lamentations as he beholds in vision the ratification of a "new covenant," written in the heart and established in the mind, rich in all spiritual treasures of wisdom and grace. Ezekiel (47), turning as if in disgust from the lamentable failure of a once glorious priesthood, and a once powerful monarchy, cheers his exile with prophetic views of a new order of things — tracing the insignificant drippings of the water of life from the temple, until they grow into a stream that rises as it flows on, to the ankles, the knees, the loins, and finally becomes a great river, lined on either bank with trees of strength and beauty, whose fruit is for meat, and whose leaves are for medicine, emptying into the Dead Sea, and bearing freshness and life into its sullen bosom; and everything lives wherever the river flows. The latter portion of Isaiah's prophecies so abound in cheering views of the new and spiritual reign of Messiah — so far in advance of previous Jewish conceptions that he has been styled "the evangelical prophet" — visions which came in the night of despair, when the hopes that had been centered in fleshly Israel had been crushed, and men were disposed to seek in spiritual aspirations that comfort and security they had failed to find in national pride and fleshly ambitions. It should be noticed, too, what stress came to be laid on the circumcision of the heart (Jer. 4:4); on a new heart and a new spirit (Ezek. 36:26); and on right conduct, as opposed to mere ritualism (Isa. 1:10-20; Micah 6:6-8). There can be no question that the dismal failure of Judaism, and the severe chastenings of the captivity, led to better apprehensions of spiritual life, to a stronger faith in the invisible Jehovah, and to somewhat more worthy conceptions of the approaching spiritual reign of the Messiah. Isaiah's prediction of a *suffering* Messiah would have had no meaning at an earlier date; and it grew in significance as the Jews were led into disciplinary experiences in and after their subsequent captivity.

4. The captivity served as a missionary scheme to spread the knowledge of God over the world. Daniel and his associates at the court of Babylon (Dan. 1); the three Hebrew youths in the fiery furnace (Dan. 3); Daniel's interpretations of dreams and visions (Dan. 2, 4, 5), with all that grew out of them in the dissemination of the knowledge of the true God (Dan. 3:28-29, 4:1-3, 34-37); Daniel in the lion's den (Dan. 6:25-28); the decree of Cyrus for the return of the captives (Ezra 1); the decree of Darius (Ezra 6), and of Artaxerxes (Neh. 2); Mordecai and Esther in their relations to king Ahasuerus, and the knowledge of Jehovah disseminated thereby through the hundred and twenty-seven provinces of the empire — are but illustrations of the mighty results of the captivity in spreading the knowledge of God throughout the earth. But more, perhaps, was accomplished, though in a quieter way, by the captives at large, in their intercourse with the people, and by such prophets as Jeremiah, Ezekiel, and Daniel in the performance of their functions as the messengers of Jehovah. The captives were, as a rule, the cream of the Jewish population. These, themselves purified by affliction, would zealously propagate their faith. They were scattered in different portions of the empire. The language of Bab-

ylonia was not so remotely related to the Hebrew as to make it difficult of acquirement, and soon they were able to communicate the wonderful history of God's dealings with their nation, and of the laws and ordinances of Israel. The larger part of these, and their descendants, never returned to Judaea. By the great changes that happened in the world, many of them were dispersed into adjacent countries. In the time of Esther, they were dispersed throughout all parts of the vast Persian Empire (Est. 3:8). Antiochus the Great, about 200 B.C., on one occasion transplanted two thousand families of the Jews from the country about Babylon into Lesser Asia,[1] and they and their posterity, many of them, settled in Pontus, Galatia, Phrygia, Pamphylia, and in Ephesus; and from thence settled in Athens, and Corinth, and Rome — whence came many of those synagogues in which Paul afterwards preached the gospel of Christ.

We have, somewhere in these Studies, called attention to the fact that God, through his chosen people, moved on the great centers of power, such as the capitals of Egypt, Assyria, Chaldea, etc., and struck at idolatry in its very heart. We may now add that the Jews were inclined, in their scattered condition, to concentrate in the large cities, especially the great centers of traffic; so that the faith they taught was sure to sound out over all the known world. It was thus that, through their exile from their own land, they became Jehovah's medium of communication with all nations. The law and the prophets which, in Babylonia, became to them more than their temple and the throne of David had ever been, as instructors in divine truth, and which were guarded with great care as all that was left to them of the memorials of their religion, were communicated verbally or in writing to the peoples among whom they settled, thus spreading a general knowledge of their hope of a coming Messiah, and creating a general expectation of the advent of a Redeemer and Guide for the sinful and bewildered race.

5. Among the far-reaching results of the captivity was the translation of the Jewish Scriptures into Greek by Jews at Alexandria, some two or three centuries B.C. The Greek language was then, in a large sense, the universal language, and the influence of this translation, known as the Septuagint, in circulating a

---

[1] Asia Minor.

knowledge of Jehovah and his laws, cannot be estimated.

That curiously learned and brilliant essayist, Thomas DeQuincey, in his paper on "The Supposed Scriptural Expression for Eternity," has some observations on the Septuagint translation, which we take leave to present to the reader:

> *It was, as the event has shown in very many instances, an advantage of a rank rising to the providential, that such a cosmopolitan version of the Hebrew sacred writings should have been made at a moment in when a rare concurrence of circumstances happened to make it possible; such as, for example, a king both learned in his tastes and liberal in his principles of religious toleration; a language — viz., the Greek, which had already become, what for many centuries it continued to be, a common language of communication for the learned of the whole* **oikoumene** *(i.e., in effect of the civilized world — Greece, the shores of the Euxine, the whole of Asia Minor, Syria, Egypt, Carthage, and all the dependencies of Carthage, and above all, Rome, then beginning to look upon the western horizon), together with all the dependencies of Rome, and, briefly, every state and city that adorned the imperial islands of the Mediterranean, or that glittered like gems in that vast belt of land, roundly speaking, one thousand miles in average breadth, and in circuit running up to five thousand miles. One thousand multiplied into five times one thousand, or, otherwise expressed, a thousand thousand five times repeated, or, otherwise, a million five times repeated, briefly a territory measuring five millions of square miles, or forty-five times the surface of our two British islands — such was the boundless domain which this extraordinary act of Ptolemy suddenly threw open to the literature and spiritual revelation of a little obscure race, nestling in a little angle of Asia, scarcely visible as a fraction of Syria, buried in the broad shadows thrown out on one side by the great and ancient settlements on the Nile, and on the other by the vast empire that for thousands of years occupied the Tigris and the Euphrates. In the twinkling of an eye, at a sudden summons, as it were*

from the sounding of a trumpet, or the oriental call by a clapping of hands, gates are thrown open, which have an effect corresponding in grandeur to the effect that would arise from the opening of a ship-canal across the Isthmus of Darien, viz.: the introduction to each other — face to face — of two separate infinities. Such a canal would suddenly lay open to each other the two great oceans of our planet, the Atlantic and the Pacific; whilst the act of translating into Greek and from Hebrew — that is, transferring out of a mysterious cipher as little accessible as Sanscrit, and which never would be more accessible through any worldly attractions of alliance with power and civic grandeur of commerce — out of this darkness into the golden light of a language the most beautiful, the most honored amongst men, and the most widely diffused through a thousand years to come, had the immeasurable effect of throwing into the great crucible of human speculation, even then beginning to ferment, to boil, to overflow — that mightiest of all elements for exalting the chemistry of philosophy — grand and, for the first time, adequate conceptions of the Deity.[1]

It is thus seen that the dire calamity which befell the Jewish nation was overruled — perhaps we should rather say, appointed — for the furtherance of the great "purpose of the ages." Not less in their exile than in their national existence in their own land, did the Jewish people fulfill the object of their election, since by them the name of Jehovah was made great in all the earth.

It only remains to say that after the Jews were delivered into the hands of their enemies, an unsleeping Providence watched over the movements of all the nations into whose hands the crown and the people of David were given. A careful study of Daniel's prophecies is sufficient to convince anyone of this. The succeeding empires of Chaldea, Medo-Persia, Greece, and Rome are all prophetically sketched, and their prominent movements, *especially as related to Israel*, noted; and everything tends forward to the days of "Messiah the Prince," and His redeeming work. With this corre-

---

[1] *Theological Essays*, Ticknor and Fields' edition, Vol. 1, pages 146-147.

sponds much that was spoken by Isaiah, Jeremiah, and Ezekiel. However absorbed they may appear to be for a time with the affairs of the present or the near future, they ever and anon rise above all this to grasp "the eternal purpose" to the accomplishment of which everything is tending, and their highest and noblest strains celebrate the consummation of that purpose in the coming of Him who "shall be called Wonderful, Counselor, The Mighty God, The everlasting Father, the Prince of Peace, of the increase of whose government and peace there shall be no end, upon the throne of David, and upon his kingdom, to order it and to establish it with judgment and with justice, from henceforth, even for ever" (Isa. 9:6-7).[1]

> *O the depth of the riches both of the wisdom and the knowledge of God! How unsearchable are His judgments, and His ways past tracing out! For who hath known the mind of the Lord? Or who hath been His counselor? Or who hath first given to Him, and it shall be recompensed*

---

[1] It may be an advantage to the reader to have grouped ti us eye the order and the dates of the several captivities of Israel and Judah, thus:

ASSYRIAN CAPTIVITIES

Year	Assyrian Kings	Kings of Israel	People carried off	Kings of Judah	Years before destruction of Jerusalem
771	Pul	Menahem	Rueben, Gad, etc.	Uzziah	183
749	Tigleth-Pilesar	Pekah	Gilead, Galilee	Ahaz	152
721	Shal-manezer	Hoshea	All Israel	Hezeki-ah	133

BABYLONIAN CAPTIVITIES

Year	Kings of Judah	The Conqueror	People carried off
607	Jehoiakim	Nebuchadnezzar (acting for his father)	Daniel and other princes
599	Jehoiachin	Nebuchadnezzar	10,000 chief people
588	Zedekiah	Nebuchadnezzar	Nearly all the people

unto him again? For of Him, and through Him, and unto Him, are all things. To Him be the glory forever. Amen.

The Restoration

If the overthrow of the Jewish nation might, from one point of view, be regarded as a triumph of heathenism, tending to strengthen the faith of the heathen nations in their idols, this was met by a tremendous counteraction (1) in the previous destruction of Nineveh and the overthrow of the Assyrian empire; (2) in the subsequent overthrow of Babylon and the Chaldaean empire. These, as having been the persecutors of the Jews, were involved in hopeless destruction, and idolatry met with a tremendous rebuke in the dire ruin of the idolatrous powers that had captured and despoiled the elect people of Jehovah. (See Isa. 47; Jer. 1:17-20; and kindred passages.) And, while the wrath of God has not yet spent itself on those lands of idols — the very sites of their once proud capitals being still cursed with desolation, the gazing world was made to see the exiled Jews, after a captivity of seventy years,[1] returning under imperial protection to their own land, reoccupying their ancient territory, and rebuilding the City and the Temple of Jehovah. Viewing this history as an age of controversy between Monotheism and Polytheism — between Jehovah and his people on one hand, and the idolatrous nations of Assyria and Chaldaea on the other — the result is not less significant than in the previous controversy between Jehovah and Baal, as represented in Elijah and Ahab; only the results were mostly *local* in the contest between Elijah and Ahab, while in the other instance the *world* was looking on, and the power and glory of Jehovah were declared throughout all the earth.

The return of the Jews from Babylon may be placed under three dates, as follows — although many more may have returned at other dates and in less notable numbers.

1. The first leader was Zerubbabel, the "Prince of Judah," and in connection with him, Jeshua, or Joshua the high priest, who left

---

[1] See Jer. 25:11-12, 29:19. It may be that seventy is only a round number, not intended to be literally exact. Dating the seventy years from the fourth year of Jehoiakim (Jer. 25:1, 12, comp. Dan. 1:1). which was B.C. 605, the taking of Babylon by Cyrus was B.C. 538. Others, however, place the latter event B. C. 535.

Babylon when Cyrus came to the throne, and who, after the lapse of about twenty years, completed the rebuilding of the temple in the reign of Darius Hystaspes.

2. Next comes Ezra, who went from Babylon about eighty years after Zerubbabel (B.C. 468), in the seventh year of Artaxerxes Longimanus. His labor was chiefly to instruct the people in the law, and reestablish the institutions of Moses.

3. Then comes Nehemiah, who, in the twentieth year of Artaxerxes Longimanus (B.C. 445), upon hearing reports of the low condition of the returned captives, persuaded the king to allow him to go to their assistance. He rebuilt the walls and set up the gates of Jerusalem, and promoted many practical reformations.

There is little need of direct exposition of the books of Ezra and Nehemiah, as tributary to our main purpose in these Studies. We prefer to give to the present study a different cast, which, we hope, will be found not less instructive and profitable, in the course of which we shall be able to note the most important features of the Restoration, and the main facts relating thereto. In doing this we hope to guard against the seductions of mere fancy.

The Old Testament is not only a book of facts, laws, and prophecies, but also a book of *types.* The Epistle to the Hebrews clearly shows this. There is a constant *foreshadowing* of the coming dispensation of grace, or, as the writer of the epistle to the Hebrews expresses it, the law was "a shadow of good things to come" (Heb. 10:1). In other words, "the eternal purpose" of God, underlying the laws, the worship, and the history of the chosen people, crops out all along that history, and furnishes significant intimations of "the powers of the age to come" (Heb. 6:5). In these types or adumbrations,[1] we find not only *persons*, like Melchizedek, Moses, and Aaron; *ordinances,* like the Sabbath, the year of jubilee, the tabernacle, in which everything was arranged according to a "pattern shown in the mount" (Heb. 9:1-12, 23-28); but also *events* — sometimes a long succession of events, divinely ordered as types of things future. Thus, the redemption of Israel from Egyptian bondage and their forty years' sojourn in the wilderness are declared to have been ordered as types, and "written for our ad-

---

[1] Something which gives a sketchy outline of something else, often in foreshadowing.

monition, upon whom the ends of the ages are come" (1 Cor. 10:1-11). Whether we regard these as *divinely appointed types,* or as *suggestive lessons* drawn by the inspired writers of the New Testament, in harmony with Paul's declaration in Rom. 15:4, the result to us is the same. Under such guidance as the Spirit in the New Testament affords, it is our privilege and our duty to study the Old Testament with a constant eye to its foreshadowings of the Kingdom of Christ, in its spirit, character, aims, achievements, and fortunes.

That we should thus study the features and events of this remarkable Restoration is apparent from the fact that the very name of the ancient captor and oppressor of God's people is transferred, in the New Testament, to an oppressive spiritual power, carrying spiritual Israel into captivity (Rev. 14:6-8, 16:19-21. chaps. 17-18 *in extenso[1]*). We may expect, therefore, very suggestive facts in the history of the Restoration of Judah, which to us, as attempting a return from Babylon to Jerusalem, should be highly instructive. If we do no more than point out what seem to us the great moral and spiritual lessons of this captivity and restoration, it may serve to open up a new field of inquiry to many Bible students, and start them in proper paths of investigation.

1. As literal Israel was to be carried into captivity, so was spiritual Israel to be shorn of her glory and subjugated and enslaved by a foreign power. Read carefully 2 Thes. 2. We may not know why this was to be, but certain it is that, as the Lord Jesus Himself, the Head of the Church, was "made perfect through suffering," and reached the crown only by way of the cross, so his Church and Kingdom were to reach final victory and dominion through mighty conflicts, fearful disasters, and terrible sufferings. Please read Rev. 12. Whatever difficulties there may be in the interpretation of many of the symbols in these apocalyptic visions, there need be no mistake as to the general outline of the remarkable prophecies recorded in this book. We see spiritual Israel conducted through a succession of desperate struggles with evil powers sometimes brought so low that the anointed witnesses of God, who had long prophesied in sackcloth, are killed by the beast that ascends out of the bottomless pit, and their dead bodies "lie in the street of the

---

[1] At full length—the whole passage.

great city which spiritually is called Sodom and Egypt" (Rev. 11:7-10) — and coming up out of "the great tribulation" to ultimate victory, when "the kingdoms of this world become the kingdom of our Lord and his Christ," and finally to the immortal blessedness described in the last chapters of the book.

2. The *cause* of the captivity of literal Israel was *persistent departures from the word of God,* and the substitution of *human* for *divine* authority. The proofs of this are so abundant that it is not needful to cite them. Jer. 5 may be taken as a sample of the testimonies that abound in the prophets. They may all be summed up in the language of this prophet (2:13): "My people have committed two evils: they have forsaken me, the fountain of living waters, and hewed them out cisterns, broken cisterns, that can hold no water;" or as Isaiah expresses it (24:5): "They have transgressed the laws, changed the ordinance, broken the everlasting covenant."

And did not this prove true of spiritual Israel? Even in apostolic times this iniquity began to work. There were those who sought to "draw away disciples after them" (Acts 20:30); and in guarding the flock against these "grievous wolves," the apostle says, "I commend you to God, *and to the word of his grace."* This was their only safety. And John, in warning his brethren against the increasing delusions and snares of his time, says (1 John 4:1): "Believe not every spirit, but try the spirits whether they are of God; because many false prophets are gone out into the world." And in teaching them how to "try the spirits," he says — "We [Apostles] are of God; he that knoweth God, heareth us; he that is not of God, heareth us not. Hereby know we the spirit of truth, and the spirit of error." The final appeal is to the word of God — the revelations of the Holy Spirit. Paul, in speaking of the deluding power of the Man of Sin, describes his captives as those "who *received not the love of the truth,* that they might be saved," and as those "who *believed not the truth,* but had pleasure in unrighteousness" (2 Thes. 2:10-12). And in describing the "perilous times" yet in the future when he wrote, he says: "The time will come when they will not endure sound teaching; but, having itching ears, will heap to themselves teachers after their own lusts; and will turn *away their ears from the truth,* and turn aside unto fables" (2 Tim. 4:3-4). There were already painful indications of a purpose to forsake Christ and glory in human leaders (1 Cor. 1:10-17, 3:1-10). And this disposition continued to grow until it prevailed, and the "one body" of Christ was rent into parties and sects under various and conflicting leaderships. Jewish sacerdotalism[1] and Gentile philosophies corrupted the pure faith and worship of the churches; and the concentration of authority first in the hands of parochial bishops, then of diocesan bishops, then of metropolitans, and finally of the bishop of Rome as Primate, never ceased its innovating power until the Pope of Rome was pronounced *infallible,* and *anathema* was pronounced on all who should refuse to accept his *ex cathedra*[2] utterances as the very voice of God! Thus he seeks to "sit in the temple of God, showing himself that he is God."

3. The apostasy of Israel was not sudden, but a *gradual* development. Its history runs through centuries. So, in the spiritual history, the "mystery of iniquity" which was "already working" in Paul's time, gradually developed its power. Even in the first three centuries — the "primitive" period to which many are fond of referring as *authoritatively* exhibiting the doctrine, government, and ordinances that belong to the true *Catholic* Church — this apostasy was extensively corrupting the doctrine and the practice of the churches, so that nothing can be considered authoritative outside of the New Testament. "The Fathers," so often appealed to, while they may be valuable as witnesses to *facts*, are "blind guides" in matters of faith and practice — often half-drunk with heathen philosophy or Jewish traditions, and abounding in the wildest fancies and the most disgusting puerilities.[3]

4. Not *all* Israel was carried captive. There still remained many in the desolate land, lingering amid the ruins of Jerusalem, taking pleasure in her stones and having pity on her dust (Ps. 102:14. See also the Lamentations of Jeremiah).

Even so, through all the wide reign of the fearful apostasy of spiritual Israel, there were faithful souls who clung to Zion even in her desolation. The gates of hell did not *entirely* prevail against the Church. There were always those who were true to the word of

---

[1] The requirement of special priests to intercede on behalf of God's people. This is what the Catholic Church practices.

[2] "From the chair." This describes official pronouncements from the Pope while sitting in his throne chair, which the Catholic Church claims are infallible.

[3] Childish silliness.

God. If the Church was in the wilderness (Rev. 12:14), she still had an existence. We are not anxious to trace out a succession of *churches* through the ages, holding forth the word of God — for the Church, in its large sense, is not a visible *organization,* but is composed of all who love and serve our Lord Jesus Christ, whether in Babylon or out of it. The Lord had a people *in Babylon* (Rev. 18:4), and many more who never went to Babylon. He never left himself without witness among men. If he had his Ezekiels in Babylon to call back the people to his law, he also had his Savonarolas[1] in spiritual Babylon to bear witness to his truth.

5. The Jews returned from captivity. And so was spiritual Israel to return from spiritual captivity. The passages already quoted concerning spiritual Babylon, all look forward to the ultimate overthrow of this spiritual oppression and the final restoration of the original faith and practice of the Church of God. And Daniel looked far beyond the oppressions of his own time, and the return of his own people to their own land, when he saw the rise and fall of empires, and the rise of the "little horn that made war with the saints and prevailed against them" (Dan. 7:8, 20-21). But it was not a total nor a final prevailing; it prevailed against them "until the Ancient of days came, and judgment was given to the saints of the Most High, and the time came that the saints possessed the kingdom." The captive people of God are to come back again. As God directed the rise and fall of empires in the interest of his ancient people, to prepare the way for their restoration, so did he guide the governments of Europe and the progress of human affairs with a view to the return of captive spiritual Israel. Step by step, in the revival of letters and of science and art; in the growth of the doctrine of civil and religious liberty; in the increased facilities for travel and the enlargement of intercourse among the nations, God has made possible the recovery of his people from spiritual bondage.

6. The Restoration was a gradual process. At first, there were but 42,360, including children above twelve years of age (1 Esdra 5:41).[2] To these, indeed, it was a great event, worthy of celebration

---

[1] Girolamo Savonarola was an Italian Dominican friar who pushed for religious reforms in the Catholic Church.

[2] This is an apocryphal book, believed to contain some factual historical in-

in exultant song:

> *When the Lord turned again the captivity of Zion,*
> *We were like unto them that dream.*
> *Then was our mouth filled with laughter,*
> *And our tongue with singing:*
> *Then said they among the nations,*
> *Jehovah hath done great things for them.*
> *Jehovah hath done great things for us,*
> *Whereof we are glad.*
> *Turn again our captivity, O Jehovah,*
> *As the streams in the South.*
> *They that sow in tears shall reap in joy,*
> *Though he goeth on his way weeping, bearing forth the seed,*
> *He shall come again with joy, bringing his sheaves with him.*[1]

Yet it is evident that this intense patriotism was limited to the minority. The larger portion of the people, the generation born and reared in Babylonia, were content to remain in a land that had become their home, among a people no longer strange to them. And those who returned found their old territory largely occupied — on the south by the Edomites, who were not conquered until the time of John Hyrcanus, 130 B.C.; in the center by the descendants of the mixed races settled in it by the Assyrian kings after the destruction of Samaria; in the north by the descendants of the Scythians, whose occupation dates back, according to Herodotus, to an invasion in the reign of Josiah. In the west, their ancient enemies, the Philistines, held sway.

> *The new colony was thus hemmed in on all sides by other races. It held only a small district round Jerusalem and the city itself, and even for that it had to thank the favor of Cyrus. The list of towns named by Ezra and Nehemiah as the first homes of their brethren, includes only Bethlehem on the south, while on the north their territory did not extend beyond the narrow limits of Benjamin (Neh.*

---

formation.
[1] Psalm 123.

7:25-30; Ezra 2:23, 28, 34). Even a generation after-wards, Southern Judah had not been won by the Hebrews (Zech. 7:7). In the time of Nehemiah, however, nearly a hundred years later, they at last got a footing in Hebron, to which its Canaanite population had once more given the old name Kirjath-Arba, and they had pushed their boundaries some distance into the Negeb (Neh. 11:25-35). Beer-sheba, indeed, in the edge of the southern desert, then had again a village around its wells, and the clan of Temple-singers ultimately established themselves in the Jordan valley, having forced the Edomites to give them lands in that district. On the west, however, the Philistines eagerly reasserted their independence, speaking their own language and worshiping Dagon, as of old, in their capital, Ashdod (Neh. 4:7, 13:24; 1 Macc. 10:84)."[1]

It will be seen that the return to their own land was only the beginning of new conflicts to recover their lost territory and reestablish the religion of Jehovah. It was as late as the days of Nehemiah before an attempt was made to rebuild the walls, and the open hostility of the Sanballats, Tobiahs, and Geshems that rose up against them, and the secret plottings of the Noadiahs, and Eliashibs, and many of the nobles, made indeed "troublous times" for the faithful. Sometimes half the forces wrought with their hands while the other half stood armed for the defense; and sometimes the whole force wrought with one hand and held a weapon with the other — ready to work or fight, as the occasion might require. See Nehemiah, chaps. 3-6, 13. New prophets, such as Haggai and Zechariah, and new reformers like Ezra and Nehemiah, had to make their appearance, in successive periods, to carry forward the work of restoration, or all that was gained in the first return would have been forever lost.

Can we not read in this the *successive steps of reformation* by which the return from spiritual Babylon has been distinguished? Beginning with Wycliffe, and following on to Huss, Luther, Zwingli, Calvin, Wesley, Fox, etc., is it not evident that the work of restoring the original Gospel and Church of the New Testament

---

[1] Geikie's *Hours with the Bible*, Vol. 6, pages 413-414.

has been only through partial and successive reformations; and that it is not even yet complete? In this light only can we vindicate the history of Protestantism, and apologize for much that is deplorable in the present condition of Protestant Christendom.

Grant us, O Thou who art the Fountain of all wisdom and knowledge, to gather both knowledge and wisdom from Thy revelations. Open thou our eyes to behold wondrous things out of thy law. May the things written aforetime for our learning, be so apprehended that we, through patience and through comfort of the Scriptures, can have hope that what is there foreshadowed may, in these last days, be fulfilled in the gathering of thy scattered people out of Babylon unto Jerusalem, and in the restoration of Thy Gospel and Thy Church in their primitive integrity and beauty. And may we never cease to labor for this blessed consummation.

The Restoration (Part Two)

7. Let us look at the steps by which it was sought to restore the law and the worship of Jehovah.

(1). The altar of Jehovah was built, and sacrifices were offered thereon according to the law (Ezra 3:1-6). Every true reformation must begin in a sense of dependence on God, and in a spirit of devotion to Him. If it springs from earthly ambition, or is employed as a measure of policy, there will surely be a blight upon it. It was especially fit that a people who had been so addicted to idolatry, and so terribly punished for it, should begin the work of restoration by the solemn worship of Jehovah, even before the foundations of the temple were laid, and when they were exposed to enemies on every side.

(2). They began to rebuild the temple of the Lord (Ezra 3:8-13). And the returned captives from spiritual Babylon have endeavored to reconstruct the Church of God — the real spiritual temple. In both cases it has been found a work of great difficulty. The men of Judah soon found opposition to their undertaking (Ezra 4-6), and in course of time became themselves indifferent to the enterprise, being much more interested in providing homes and making fortunes for themselves than in rebuilding the temple of God (Haggai 1:4). And even when they were aroused to complete the task, the new temple was so inferior to the old that Haggai speaks of it as "nothing in comparison." Even amid the exultation accompanying the laying of the foundations, we are told that the ancient men that had seen the first house, "wept with a loud voice" over what they discerned of the inferiority of the second temple (Ezra 3:12). And has it not been true that in the efforts to reestablish the spiritual temple, the oppositions of wicked men, the interference of earthly governments, and the growth of worldliness among the people, have interfered with and marred the work? And, after all that has been done to rebuild the Church, viewing it in the most favorable light, is it not so manifestly inferior to the original temple as fashioned under God's own direction, that such as are familiar with the divine glories of the original structure as splayed in the New Testament can but "weep with a loud voice" over the failure of the best efforts at reconstruction?

(3). They renounced all other lordships for that of Jehovah, and restored his law as their rule of faith and practice. Whatever may have clung to them of the apostasies of their fathers before the captivity, and whatever of error and wrong may have accumulated during their seventy years of exile among idolaters, was searched out by the light of God's own law, and abjured; and whatever laws and ordinances had been neglected or violated, were reinstated and religiously observed.

It was a strange and spirit-stirring scene when "the people gathered themselves as one man into the street that was before the water-gate, and spoke unto Ezra the scribe to bring the book of the law of Moses which Jehovah had commanded unto Israel" (Neh. 8:1). It is no longer Josiah calling an unwilling people to listen to God's law, and by royal authority binding it on them for observance; it is the people crying out for the law, that they may know it and walk in its light. "Blessed are they who hunger and thirst after righteousness: for they shall be filled." Ezra — glorious man! — to whose pious and persevering labors even we now are indebted for the restoration of the law, and for many of the precious treasures of knowledge and wisdom stored up in the Jewish canon — brought out before the people the book of the law. Standing on a "pulpit of wood" made for the purpose, in a position where he could be seen and heard by the eager throngs, and surrounded by the chief men of the nation, he "opened the book in the sight of all the people; and when he opened it, the people stood up. And Ezra blessed Jehovah, the great God; and all the people answered Amen, Amen, with lifting up of their hands: and they bowed their heads, and worshiped Jehovah with their faces to the ground." After the hollow mockeries we were called to contemplate in previous chapters in the history of Judah's apostasy, it is refreshing to look on a scene of genuine devotion like this. Blessed be the captivity that works out such a conversion.

On that day of the Feast of Trumpets began the word of God to sound out anew in the ears of the people. From early morn to midday the reading proceeded. "They read in the book, in the law of God, distinctly, and gave the sense, so that they understood the reading." And "all the people wept when they heard the words of the law;" — wept for joy, doubtless, that they had found "the pearl of great price;" wept in grief, that they and their fathers had strayed so far from God. Then, when their grief was hushed by the counsel of their leaders, "all the people went their way to eat and to drink, and to send portions, and to make great mirth, *because they had understood the words that were declared unto them.*" Here is a genuine revival — the fountain of a true reformation. The most prominent mark of a genuine religious reformation is *a renewed interest in the word of God.* There can be no complete restoration of Christianity until *the people* are thus brought to hunger and thirst for God's own word.

Not only on that day, and the following, but in the seven days' festival which succeeded, was this public reading and exposition of the law continued. "Day by day, from the first day unto the last day, he read in the book of the law of God. And they kept the feast seven days." This festival closed on the twenty-first day of the month. The next day there was a solemn convocation. Then, after a day of rest, "in the twenty and fourth day of this month, the children of Israel were assembled with fasting, and with sackcloth and earth upon them. And they stood up in their place, and read in the book of the law of Jehovah their God one-fourth part of the day, and another fourth part they confessed, and worshiped Jehovah their God" (Neh. 9:1-3).

We have been particular in noting these facts, because we are profoundly convinced that all genuine religious reformation must have its origin in reverence for and delight in the Holy Scriptures, from the presence of which all human traditions, all sectarian pride, all hallowed usages, will retire as vain and worthless. Once possessed of this devotion to God's own word, we will, with Paul, "count *all things*" — even our most cherished sectarian idols — "but loss, for the excellency of the knowledge of Christ Jesus our Lord." It is a long way yet, we fear, for the numerous sects of Protestant Christendom, to that repentance which must surely come before there can be a complete restoration of the purity, simplicity, unity, and catholicity of apostolic times; ere they will, like these Jews, assemble with fasting, and with sackcloth and earth upon them, to read the word of God, and weep over their departures from it, and confess their sins, and turn back from their wanderings.

Let us see what results were wrought out by this reverential and eager study of the word of God.

a. They restored neglected ordinances. They found written in the law that the Israelites should dwell in booths in the feast of the seventh month. Away they hied[1] after olive-branches, and pine-branches, and myrtle branches, and palm-branches, and branches of thick trees, to make booths; and they kept the feast "*as it is written,*" "and there was very great gladness" (Neh. 8:13-18). There was no objection raised that, in so doing, they would condemn the generations of their fathers who had failed of this observance, and cast doubt on their own past orthodoxy; no question asked, 'What about my father and mother, who never kept this feast of tabernacles?' no attempt to hide themselves behind learned authorities, contending that this observance was a "non-essential" that could be safely dispensed with. *There it is, written in the law.* That settles all doubts, hushes all objections. *"It is written,"* was a finality with our blessed Lord (Matt. 4:4, 7, 10). It should be a finality with us.

And are there not ordinances of the gospel which, during the great apostasy, were neglected or perverted, that have not yet been restored? Has not baptism in its very symbolism (buried with him in baptism, Rom. 6:4; Col. 2:12); in its subjects, (He that believeth and is baptized, Mark 16:16); in its design (Repent and be baptized every one of you in the name of Jesus Christ for the remission of sins, Acts 2:38); in the terms of admission to it (If thou believest with all thy heart, thou mayest, Acts 8:36-38; Rom. 10:8-13), — has not this "one baptism" been so perverted that the sprinkling of unbelieving babes on one hand, and the rejection, on the other hand, of believers who, though trusting in Christ, cannot conscientiously utter the theological shibboleths of sects, and the substitution of other and unauthorized evidences of pardon, have completely "changed the ordinance and broken the everlasting covenant"? And do not these perversions stand today directly in the way of the union of believers? And that other beautiful ordinance, the Lord's Supper, which was a weekly observance in the apostolic churches (Acts 20:7) — a prominent part of the worship (1 Cor. 11:20-26) — has it not lost its primitive simplicity as a refreshing feast of holy memories, and been transformed into an awful sacrament, a pompous ceremonial, to be observed only at long intervals, and to be approached with superstitious awe? A thorough refor-

---

[1] To go quickly.

mation will restore these divine ordinances to their proper places, and in their restoration, as in the restoration of the feast of booths, there will be "very great gladness."

The Sabbath, too, was shamefully perverted (Neh. 13), and worldly interests came into conflict with divine authority. But with uncompromising fidelity Nehemiah insisted on *what is written*, and redeemed Jerusalem from the curse attendant on a fearful desecration of God's holy day.

b. *They abandoned all unlawful alliances.* — They found written in the law that "the Ammonite and the Moabite should not come into the congregation of God for ever;" and at once, when they heard the law, they separated from Israel all the mixed multitude" (Neh. 13:1-3). But they were brought to a severer test than this. They had intermarried with the surrounding peoples. The princes and rulers were chief in this trespass (Ezra 9:1-2). The sin pervaded all classes of the people. They had married wives of Ashdod, of Ammon, and of Moab; "and their children spake half in the speech of Ashdod, and could not speak in the Jews' language, but according to the language of each people" — a mixed dialect, half-Philistine, half-Hebrew (Neh. 13:23-24). For wise reasons, the law had forbidden such matrimonial alliances (Deut. 7:1-4; Josh. 23:12-13). Here, then, was an extensive and tremendous guilt. To insist on a return to the law of God would involve the disruption of families, the sacrifice of cherished affections, and would, in many cases, tear the very heart-strings. But the principle of implicit submission to divine authority required the sacrifice. The integrity of Israel as the elect people of God required it. There could be no genuine loyalty to Jehovah as long as such unsanctified marriages exposed every family to the corrupting influence of heathenism. And the longer reformation was delayed, the greater would be the difficulty of reforming — for this, like all other sins, would increase and extend its power as long as forbearance was exercised towards it. The people, therefore, although they "wept sore" over it, came up to the stern demand of the law, and broke up all their unlawful marriage connections.

And has not the cause of reformation been grievously damaged, and the work of the Lord retarded, by the unhallowed alliances of spiritual Israel? Look at the union of Church and State, with its prolific brood of mischiefs; the unlawful wedding of Faith and Philosophy, with its progeny of ungodly and perplexing strifes, alienations, and schisms; the unholy marriage of the Bible and Human Creeds, with its mongrel offspring of sects; the invasions of worldliness that have transformed the churches into temples of fashion and resorts for intellectual entertainment, artistic display, and rhetorical pyrotechnics; listen to the impure mixtures of the speech of Ashdod with the language of inspiration — a corruption so wide-spread and so influential, that to speak, today, in the "pure speech" of the Bible, and to eschew the popular but corrupt speech of even orthodox parties, is to expose one at once to the suspicion of damnable heresy! We must get back to "a pure language" (Zeph. 3:9); and in order to do this, we must free ourselves from all these entangling and corrupting alliances, and come back to the word of God alone as our Light and our Guide in all spiritual things. God calls us away from all this Babylonish confusion and corruption. "Come out of her, my people, that ye be not partakers of her sins, and that ye receive not of her plagues" (Rev. 18:4).

As illustrative of the tenacity with which we adhere to unauthorized alliances, and of the impossibility of achieving a thorough restoration of the Gospel and the Church while such alliances remain unbroken, we may be allowed to refer to the recent action of one of the leading orthodox ecclesiastical bodies of this country. One of the questions now forcing itself to the front in this country is that of Christian Union. It is certain that, while professed Christians are divided into various sects, wearing various names, possessed of differing creeds, and held apart by differences of name, of doctrine, of church government, and of worship, we are not yet out of the smoke and confusion of Babylon. The unity and catholicity of the churches in the apostolic age are not now witnessed. The weakness and barrenness growing out of sectarianism are beginning to be generally felt and deplored, and earnest voices are heard on every hand pleading for an abandonment of sectism, and a restoration of the oneness in faith, in spirit, and in practice, that was the glory of the Church of God in the apostolic age, and resulted in matchless spiritual conquests. The Protestant Episcopal Church is one of the most conservative of religious and ecclesiastical organizations. When such a question enters into her counsels, and her Bishops deem it their duty to make a deliverance on it, it is beyond doubt that Christian Union is growing into prominence as a leading issue of the present age. At the last meeting of the Convention of this church, in Chicago, in the autumn of 1886, this subject not only came up, but the Bishops, in response to pressing applications, gave forth a thoughtful address, frankly acknowledging the importance of the question, and suggesting certain considerations as bearing on its practical solution. Such suggestions, from such a source, under such circumstances, are entitled to grave consideration. The following extract embodies their view of what should be insisted on as "essential" to the union of all Christians:

> *"But, furthermore, we do hereby affirm that the Christian unity now so earnestly desired by the memorialists, can be restored only by the return of all Christian communions to the principles of unity exemplified by the undivided Catholic Church during the first ages of its existence; which principles we believe to be the substantial deposit of Christian faith and order committed by His apostles to the Church unto the end of the world, and therefore incapable of compromise or surrender by those who have been ordained to be its stewards and trustees for the common and equal benefit of all men.*
>
> *"As inherent parts of this sacred deposit, and, therefore, as essential to the restoration of unity among the divided branches of Christendom, we account the following, to-wit:*
>
> *"1. The Holy Scriptures of the Old and New Testaments as the revealed word of God.*
>
> *"2. The Nicene Creed as the sufficient statement of the Christian faith.*
>
> *"3. The two sacraments — Baptism, and the Supper of be Lord, ministered with unfailing use of Christ's words of institution, and of the elements ordained by Him.*
>
> *"4. The Historic Episcopate locally adapted in the methods of its administration to the varying needs of the nations and peoples called of God into the unity of His Church."*

It is not within our province, here, to enter into a discussion of this basis of union. We quote it for the purpose of showing that the historical development of the first three centuries is placed on a level, *in point of divine authority,* with the teaching of the word of God; and that, from a period thronging with departures from apostolic authority, is drawn forth a system of church government which is made as "essential" to fellowship as the "one Lord, one faith, and one baptism" which the pen of inspiration records as essential to the unity of the followers of Christ (Eph. 4:1-6). Evidently, human and divine authority have yet to be divorced. The *historical development* of the first three centuries is not the same thing as the word of God. To the authority of Christ Jesus as Lord, we may and must all bow, and find our oneness in submission to Him; but to demand that the enlightened conscience of the whole Christian world shall bow to the Church of the first three centuries, and receive its historical development as the voice of Christ, is to impose a condition of Christian fellowship that cannot be accepted. We must put away all "strange wives," and be wedded to *divine authority only.* The "historical development" of the first three centuries was a development of that "man of sin" described in 2 Thes. 2 — that "mystery of iniquity" which had even then germinated, and only awaited the removal of hindering causes to spring into fullness of life.

c. They returned from unrighteous ways. — They had enslaved their poor brethren, and refused to release them in the sabbatical year, or to return their houses and lands, according to the law — thus extorting the gains of oppression (Neh. 5); and they were required to restore to those whom they had wronged, their lands, their vineyards, their olive-yards, and their houses, and a hundredth part of the money, and the corn, and the wine, and the oil that they had exacted of them.

They had turned the Sabbath into a day of traffic, when the men of Tyre came with their wares within the gates of the holy city and sold them. Wine pressing, harvest-gathering, and all kinds of business for gain, went forward as on other days. Nehemiah closed the gates, and put an end to these profanations (Neh. 13:15-22).

In the same spirit of avarice, the lawful dues of the priests and Levites were withheld, and these servants of the temple were driven to the fields to earn their bread. All the men of Judah were required to bring the tithe of the com, and the new wine, and the oil, unto the treasuries (Neh. 13:10-12).

No religious reformation is worthy of the name that does not result in the overthrow of injustice and a return to the way of right-eousness. Every religious movement is to be judged by its fruits. The greatest of all dishonors done to God and man in the great apostasy is found in the inhumanities, the oppressions, the injustic-es, the flagrant crimes it engendered or tolerated. A history red with innocent blood, black with appalling crimes of injustice and oppression, cannot be justified or excused by reference to its better features — its records of actual good accomplished, or positive benefits conferred. And the Church will never be "the light of the world" in the higher sense until her fearless teaching and her incor-rupt practice shall rebuke all wrong, and vindicate the loftiest righteousness and the widest philanthropy. Then will she shine forth "fair as the moon, bright as the sun, and terrible as an army with banners."

We do not assume that we have pointed out all that is sugges-tive in the history of the restoration of God's ancient people to their own land. But if we have opened up fields of inquiry which others may explore, and started the reader in paths of investigation which he may pursue with interest and profit, our object is accom-plished. It is not our purpose to do the thinking for our readers, but to wake them up to think and study for themselves.

We believe that, as surely as literal Israel was restored from Babylon to Jerusalem, will spiritual Israel be restored to spiritual Jerusalem. It is slow work; so was that which we have been con-templating. But much has already been accomplished. The history of Protestantism, with all its blots and blurs, is a glorious history — glorious in its achievements in behalf of civil and religious lib-erty, glorious in its fruitage of literature, science, art, and human progress; glorious in its humane and philanthropical accomplish-ments, its educational and governmental advances, its moral and spiritual victories. Its past successes are a prophecy of its continual progress until its mission shall be finally fulfilled in the complete restoration, in letter and in spirit, in principle and in practice, of New Testament teaching. "For the vision is yet for the appointed time, and it hasteth toward the end, and shall not lie; though it tar-ry, wait for it; because it will surely come, it will not delay" (Hab. 2:3).

O God of Israel, who wrought so wondrously for Thine ancient covenant people, grant also Thy mercy to Israel after the spirit, and recover Thy captive and scattered people from all the provinces of Babylon and guide them back to Jerusalem. Heal their backslidings. Recover them fully out of apostasy. Break every chain of enslavement to human authority and ecclesiastic domination, and unite them in the love of Thine own word, that walking in the light as Thou art in the light, they may have fellowship one with another, while the blood of Jesus Christ shall cleanse them from all sin. Hasten the day when sects shall cease, and Thy children, being of one mind and heart, shall strive together for the faith of the gospel.

Special Providences[1]

(Read the Book of Esther.)

It is now generally agreed that the Ahasuerus of the Book of Esther is the Xerxes of profane history.[2] Indeed, Ahasuerus, in one of its Greek forms, is Xerxes. The Hebrew Ahashuerus, or Akhashverosh, is said to be the exact correspondent of the Persian *Khshayarsha,* which the Greeks and Romans rendered by Xerxes. The date of the Return from Babylon is B.C. 536. The date of the accession of Xerxes to the Persian throne is B.C. 485. The Book of Esther, then, relates to events that occurred half a century and more after the Return, and is valuable as giving us some insight into the condition of the Jews who remained in the land of their exile, and of God's dealings with them at that date.

In the third year of the reign of this Ahasuerus, he made a feast at Susa unto all his princes and his servants, the power of Persia and Media, the nobles and princes of the provinces [a hundred and twenty-seven provinces, reaching from India unto Ethiopia] being before him. "This was the year, according to Herodotus, when Xerxes assembled the governors of the provinces at Susa, for consultation concerning his contemplated expedition against Greece. We thus learn the occasion of this remarkable gathering. This course of feasting lasted one hundred and eighty days altogether, as the nobles and princes of all these provinces could not all attend at the same time, and it is not likely that any of them could be spared from their duties for so long a period. This protracted season of festivity rounded out with "a feast unto all the people that were present in Shushan the palace, both unto great and small, seven days, in the court of the garden of the king's palace." On the last day of this feast, "when the heart of the king was merry with wine," and when, we may safely conclude, his guests were far gone in drunkenness, he commanded that Vashti, the queen, should

---

[1] One of the most delightful and profitable treatises on the Book of Esther is that of Alexander Carson. It has suggested the title of this study.

[2] The arguments in favor of Artaxerxes Longimanus will be found well stated in Prideaux's Connexion, at the close of Book 4.

be brought in, that this maudlin[1] crowd might gaze on her beauty.

Anyone who is disposed to reject this as too absurd to be believed, should reflect (1) that nothing can be too absurd or too outrageous for a drunken monarch to propose, or for a crowd of wine-soaked courtiers to approve; (2) that even if there had been no madness of intoxication in this case, those who have read of Xerxes' mad efforts to scourge the sea; of his murder of the engineers of his bridge because their work was injured by a storm; and of all that folly and caprice by which his immense army in that famous Grecian expedition was destroyed, will have no difficulty in giving credit to this narrative. They will say, "It is just like him." It would be of no service to appeal from Xerxes drunk to Xerxes sober, for Xerxes, drunk or sober, was a tyrant and a fool. The Queen indignantly repelled this outrageous demand, so at war with the immemorial usage of Persia, and nobly preferred to be dis-crowned and cast out or even to die, rather than sacrifice her womanly and queenly dignity by consenting to expose herself to the rude gaze of a leering crew of drunken men

This brought up the question of Woman's Rights — an old question, it will be seen; and the conclusion reached was worthy of revelers who had not yet half recovered from their drunken debauch. They said, "This deed of the queen shall come abroad unto all women, so that they shall despise their husbands in their eyes, when it shall be reported. The king Ahasuerus commanded Vashti the queen to be brought in before him, but she came not. . . . Thus shall there arise too much contempt and wrath." That is: Because a modest and virtuous woman refuses to sacrifice her personal dignity in obedience to the mad tyranny of a drunken husband, *therefore,* disgrace her and cast her out from her place, that all women may learn that they are but slaves to do the bidding of tyrants — that neither virtue nor modesty has any claims to respect in a woman, against the tyrannous demands of her husband. Therefore, Vashti was dis-crowned, and a royal decree went forth unto all the provinces, translated into all the languages spoken therein, that "every man should bear rule in his own house" — that is, that every woman should be the helpless, absolute slave of her husband. One delights to read, after this, of the stupendous failure of the

---

[1] Extremely drunk and red-eyed.

Grecian expedition of Xerxes. Had there been no other reason for the failure, the calamity was not one whit too terrible if regarded simply as the punishment of this despot for his outrageous sin against Vashti, and against all the women of his wide realm.

We need not have given so much space to this; but we have styled this a chapter of Special Providences — and it is important to note that, while there is nothing out of the range of human events in what we have recorded — no miracle, no angelic visitation, not even anything extraordinary, if we understand the genius of Oriental despotisms and the habits of ancient Persia — yet if Vashti had not been cast off, the succeeding events recorded in the Book of Esther could not have occurred. Esther could never have been queen, and the deliverance of the Jews from destruction could not have been accomplished.

It was after the return of Xerxes from his disastrous expedition into Greece, that the subsequent events recorded in the sacred narrative occurred.

Among the captives first carried away by Nebuchadnezzar from Judaea was one Kish, a Benjamite.[1] Hadassah (myrtle), or as the Persians called her, Esther (star), was an orphan girl, who, after the death of her parents, was adopted by Mordecai, a descendant of Kish, and a blood relative of Esther, and brought up as his own daughter. Mordecai was in some way employed in the king's service. Whether he was merely a porter, as some infer from chap. 3:2, or in some higher position,[2] we can not determine. On the return of Xerxes, it was determined that another queen should be chosen in place of Vashti, and the beauties of the empire were

---

[1] Although the "who," in Est. 2:6 may refer to either Kish or Mordecai, the facts compel us to refer it to Kish. The captivity referred to, in Jechoniah's reign, was B.C. 598, which was 113 years before Xerxes obtained the throne. If Mordecai was among the captives, he must have been more than 120 years old at this time, in the seventh year of the reign of Xerxes. And if Esther, as many suppose, was carried captive from Judaea at that time, she could not have been, at 120, a blooming maiden such as would captivate the heart of Xerxes! Evidently it was Kish who was carried captive — and Mordecai, and Esther, the daughter of Kish's brother, were both natives of the land of captivity. In Persia, maidens were ripe for marriage at twelve, and began to fade at twenty.

[2] The fact of his sitting in the king's gate does not necessarily imply that he was merely a porter; for all state officers were required to wait in the outer courts until summoned to the royal presence.

gathered in large numbers, that the king might make choice among them. Among them was Esther, who won the king's heart, and was elevated to queenly dignity — her race, however, and her relation to Mordecai, being concealed.

Here, again, note a special providence, although everything proceeds, on the human side, according to the laws which govern human nature and society, and there appears not to be the slightest infringement of the king's freedom of choice. Xerxes was not only a despot, but an unusually capricious despot. There were evidently numerous candidates for this high position. The chances were all against the success of this lowly Jewish maiden. If there were any subtle influences employed to control the choice of the king — and it is not unreasonable to suppose that very powerful influences would be brought to bear on a decision of such momentous interest — such influences did not, because they could not, come from Mordecai in behalf of Esther. They would come from powerful families in behalf of their favorites. But "the king loved Esther above all the women, and she obtained grace and favor in his sight more than all the virgins; so that he set the royal crown upon her head, and made her queen instead of Vashti." Had his caprice taken another turn, the Book of Esther would never have been written.

Haman the Agagite was promoted to be Grand Vizier, or Prime Minister — the highest in authority next to the king. He was evidently a man of ability and energy, but vain, ambitious, revengeful, and unscrupulous. All his inferiors were required to prostrate themselves before him, in a sort of semi-adoration.[1] As he advanced to the royal palace, all the king's servants waiting in the courts bowed in the dust at his approach — all but Mordecai: he "bowed not, nor did him reverence." Whether this was because of the undying enmity between the Jews and Amalekites (See 1 Sam. 15); or from a religious scruple about rendering worship to any but the invisible Jehovah, — a scruple which, after the Jews were cured of their idolatrous proclivities in the land of their captivity, was urged to the last extreme; or, as some conjecture, because of Mordecai's knowledge of Haman's complicity with the assassins who sought to murder the king (referred to in chap. 6:2); or, whether all these considerations combined to determine Mordecai

---

[1] Such, at least, is the idea conveyed in the Septuagint.

to refuse this honor to Haman, we can only conjecture. It is not best to attach much importance to conjectures. But, from some cause, Mordecai the Jew stubbornly refused to bow before Haman the Agagite. It is evident that Jewish faith and Jewish prejudice still lived in the hearts of the exiles. When Haman learned of the indignity thus persistently cast upon him, he determined on revenge, and revenge on a large scale. He would not stoop to notice this insignificant Jew; he would strike at the whole race — an indication that the quarrel had its origin in an intense race prejudice. He represented to the king that the Jews, though scattered through all the provinces of the empire, were a distinct people, with laws of their own, who paid no respect to the king's laws — a dangerous people, therefore, a standing menace to the peace and safety of the empire. True, they were of much advantage to the public revenue; but, rather than have the order and security of the government thus seriously and perpetually endangered, he would agree to pay out of his own purse ten thousand talents of silver,[1] if the king would issue orders for the total destruction of this people. The king, with characteristic impulsiveness and recklessness, accepted the infamous proposal.

Lots were cast to determine the luckiest time for the proposed slaughter. The lots were cast in the first month (Nisan), and the decision was in favor of the thirteenth day of the twelfth month (Adar). Accordingly, the royal decree went forth into all the provinces, "to destroy, to kill, and to cause to perish, all Jews, both old and young, little children and women, in one day, even upon the thirteenth day of the twelfth month, which is the month Adar, and to take the spoil of them for a prey." Although, even by the splendid system of posts established by Cyrus and improved by his successors, it would require some time to send these dispatches throughout all the one hundred and twenty-seven provinces, the lot had decided on so late a day that there was still time for adverse influences to be set at work, and for new and unexpected events to

---

[1] About $12,500,000. "With respect to the ability of Persian subjects to make presents to this amount, it is enough to quote the offer of Pythius (Herod. 7:28) to present this same monarch with four millions of gold darics [$22,500,000], and the farther statement of the same writer that a certain satrap of Babylon had a revenue of nearly two bushels of silver daily (Herod. 1:192)." — Speaker's Com. See also Dr. Adam Clarke's interesting note on Est. 3:9.

checkmate Haman's diabolical purpose. The promulgation[1] of the decree necessarily struck terror to the hearts of the Jews. "In every province, whithersoever the king's commandment and his decree came, there was great mourning among me Jews, and fasting, and weeping, and wailing; and many lay in sackcloth and ashes." Mordecai, when he learned of it, "rent his clothes, and put on sackcloth with ashes, and went out into the midst of the city, and cried with a loud and bitter cry, and came even before the king's gate." But, overwhelmed with grief as he was, he would not bow down to Haman, or seek in any way to propitiate[2] him. He had taken a stand that he was convinced was right, and no consideration of consequences could drive him from it.

Esther, hearing of his distress, sent to learn the cause of it — for as yet she knew nothing of Haman's cruel purpose. Mordecai informed her, through a confidential messenger, of the fatal decree, and charged her to go to the king and make supplication to him for her people. Esther would be thunderstruck at the tidings, but what could she do? As she reminded her cousin and foster-father, if any ventured uncalled into the presence of the despot, they were doomed to instant death, unless he held out the royal scepter to them; and, she added, "I have not been called to come in unto the king these thirty days." What would it avail to her doomed people if she were thus to perish in an uncertain attempt to save them? We have always admired Mordecai's reply to this: 1. Your life is doomed, as well as ours; you may as well yield it now, if need be, as a few months later. 2. If you refuse to act, God will raise up deliverance from some other quarter; but divine vengeance will light on you and your father's house for your unfaithfulness. 3. "Who knoweth whether thou art come to the kingdom for such a time as this?" If this is what Jehovah purposed in raising you to your queenly dignity, be careful lest you miss a splendid opportunity to work out His will.

These arguments prevailed with the queen. She sent back word to Mordecai: "Go, gather together all the Jews that are at present in Shushan, and fast ye for me, and neither eat nor drink three days, night or day: I also and my maidens will fast likewise; and so will I

---

[1] Purposeful spreading of information.
[2] Appease.

go in unto the king, which is not according to the law: *and if I perish, I perish.*" Noble heart! weak and despairing though it be; for it is just because of this weakness and despair that this resolve takes on the highest stamp of nobility. It involves all the dignity and beauty and glory of self-sacrifice for the sake of duty. This poor, fluttering heart resting in faith on the unseen presence of Jehovah, and nerving itself for a martyr's fate for duty's sake, is a touching and inspiring picture. Not all the strength and courage of woman died out with Vashti's disgrace. It still lives, and is destined to triumph, even in the royal palace.

Esther "put on her royal apparel." She arrayed herself in all possible beauty and dignity, that she might appear lovely in the king's eyes, and then, so far as the record goes, she went *alone* into the court, in sight of the king, and modestly and tremblingly awaited his command — for life or death. Here is another instance in which everything seems to hang on the caprice of this most capricious[1] despot. The chances are that in the first flash of indignation at this daring intrusion — this bold defiance of the royal will as taught to all the women in the land by the fate of her predecessor, Vashti — he will doom her to instant death. But no! "The king held out to Esther the golden scepter that was in his hand. So Esther drew near and touched the top of the scepter." She was safe. His mind was swayed toward her, and not away from her. Had he withheld the golden scepter, much that is now permanent history would never have occurred.

The king was sure that only extreme urgency could have emboldened his submissive queen to such a venture, and he anxiously inquired, "What ails thee, Queen Esther? And what is thy request? It shall be even given thee to the half of the kingdom." But she was too wise to prefer her request then and there. She would merely smooth the way for its utterance. "If it seem good unto the king," she replied, "let the king and Haman come this day unto the banquet that I have prepared for him." She thus appeared as thinking kindly and fondly of the king, and as desirous of ministering to his pleasure. Moreover, she flattered him in bestowing so unusual an honor on his Grand Vizier. The king clearly perceived that some more serious wish than this lay concealed in her heart, for, at the

---

[1] Impulsive.

banquet he again urged her to make known her request. And he must have felt that it related to weighty matters when again she evaded its utterance, but promised that if the king and his prime minister would favor her with their presence at another banquet on the morrow, she would then make *full* answer to the king's gracious inquiries.

"Then went Haman forth that day *joyful* and with a glad heart; but when Haman saw Mordecai in the king's gate, that he stood not up, nor moved for him, he was full of indignation against Mordecai." Poor fool! How easily his *joy* is made and unmade. A token of apparent respect from the queen — although it cannot be believed that she lavished special attentions on him — exalts him to the seventh heaven of bliss; and the sight of the unceremonious and uncompromising Mordecai tumbles him in a moment into a hell of furious passion. Little did the proud and wicked wretch dream that wise, omnipotent fingers were quietly weaving a net of circumstances about him that would encompass him with disgrace and shut him up to speedy ruin. Suppressing his wrath against Mordecai, he went home with gay step, and called together his friends, and Zeresh his wife, to listen to his story of self-glorification. He "told them of the glory of his riches, and the multitude of his children, and all the things wherein the king had promoted him, and how he had advanced him above the princes and servants of the king." And, as men unaccustomed to great heights grow dizzy at unusual elevations, this vain, vulgar fellow began to reel as he dwelt upon his exaltations. "Yea," he blurted out in his intoxication of pride and vanity, "Esther the queen did let no man come in with the king unto the banquet that she had prepared, but myself; and tomorrow am I invited unto her also with the king." But even here, in this delirium of joy, the demon of revenge possesses him and racks him with torment. "Yet all this availeth me nothing so long as I see Mordecai the Jew sitting at the king's gate." The manly independence of a humble Jew startles his basest passions into exercise, and drops poison into the golden cup of his happiness, until his highest felicities turn to deadly bitterness.

His silly wife and the circle of flatterers gathered about him, propose a speedy removal of this trouble. "Let a gallows be made of fifty cubits high, and tomorrow speak thou unto the king, that Mordecai may be hanged thereon: then go thou in merrily with the king unto the banquet. And the thing pleased Haman, and he caused the gallows to be made." One cannot but feel pity for this deluded man, bad as he is, to see him blindly working out his own destruction; yet, to those who love righteousness, there arises a feeling of exquisite satisfaction when they see the wicked taken in their own snare.

That night of Haman's feverish exultation was a sleepless night for the king. He could not tell why, but all attempts to lull him into slumber were vain. The hours wore away heavily, and he tossed upon his luxurious couch in impatient restlessness. At last, he ordered the chronicles of the kingdom to be read before him, that he might be read to sleep; or, if this could not be, that he might refresh his memory of the great events of the kingdom, and thus while away the weary hours of darkness. "And it was found written that Mordecai had told of Bigthana and Teresh, two of the king's chamberlains, the keepers of the door, who sought to lay hand on the king's life." Mordecai had actually saved the king from assassination. When it was, we are not told, nor are we authorized to indulge the conjecture that Haman was concerned in this attempted crime, and that this was the secret of Mordecai's hatred towards him. We can only say, from subsequent development, that this pretentious Agagite was not too good to engage in so monstrous a deed. But Mordecai's faithfulness, like too many noble deeds, was soon forgotten in succeeding excitements, and went unrewarded. The sleepless monarch soon became interested in his long-neglected benefactor, and determined that some suitable testimonial of his gratitude should be made.

It was now early dawn. Haman was early astir to carry out his revengeful purpose against Mordecai. He had already made his way to the royal palace, to request the life of the hated Jew. He was admitted just at the critical moment when the mind of the king was seeking to decide what should be done for the man to whom he owed his life, "What shall be done," asked the king of Haman, "unto the man whom the king delighteth to honor?" And the conceited wretch said to himself, "To whom would the king delight to do honor more than to me?" So, without seeming to violate the strictest modesty and humility — speaking apparently for another, — he made the most extravagant suggestions concerning the honors that should be conferred on such a one — suggestions that would never have been made if he had not expected them to contribute to his own glory.

> *Let the royal apparel be brought which the king useth to wear, and the horse that the king rideth upon, and the crown royal which is set upon his head: and let this apparel and horse be delivered to the hand of one of the king's most noble princes, that they may array the man with whom the king delighteth to honor, and bring him on horseback through the street of the city, and proclaim before him, Thus shall it be done to the man whom the king delighteth to honor.*

And the king replied: "Make haste, and take the apparel and the horse, as thou hast said, and do even so to Mordecai the Jew, that sitteth at the king's gate: let nothing fail of all that thou hast spoken." Whether the king was cognizant of Haman's bitter hate of Mordecai, and meant to humiliate him; or, whether he had detected the growing pride and haughtiness of his prime minister, and meant to administer a severe rebuke, we can only imagine. Certain it is that if either was his intention, he could not have succeeded more completely. It is difficult even to imagine, much more to express, the disappointment, humiliation, and bitterness of anguish worse than death, with which Haman heard these words. But he did not dare to refuse, or to betray the least unwillingness. He smothered his rage. Mordecai was arrayed in the king's robe and decked in all the splendors of royalty, and placed upon the king's own charger, and Haman came from erecting the gallows or tree on which Mordecai was to be impaled, to act as his slave — leading the horse through the streets of the city, and proclaiming in behalf of his most despised and hated enemy, "Thus shall it be done unto the man whom the king delighteth to honor!"

How Mordecai must have enjoyed it! Yet there are no indications of an undue exultation of spirit, or of gratified vanity or hate. He was humbly passive and imperturbable in the whole affair, and, as soon as it was over, quietly returned to his old subordinate position at the king's gate. But Haman, with covered head, and mourning bitterly, hastens home to hide his shame. Again he assembles his friends, with his wife Zeresh, to tell a story as dismal and humiliating as that of the previous day had been bright and self-glorifying. And his friends and his wife chime in with his own dark forebodings of impending destruction, telling him that as he had begun to fall before this despised Jew, he must read in this a prophecy of utter defeat in his hostility to the Jews. But in the midst of these sorrowful vaticinations,[1] messengers came to conduct him to the queen's banquet. After all, he might be yielding too readily to his fears. The queen was still his friend. So he plucked up courage and hurried himself to the banqueting room, where he hoped to drown his sorrows in revelry and chase away his fears in the bright smiles of the queen's favor. The king's anxiety over the queen's concealed trouble is evidently weighing heavily on him, for he is prompt to remind her that she has not yet made her request known. We cannot but admire her reply, so natural, so honest, so straightforward, and withal so skillful. "If I have found favor in thy sight, O king, and if it please the king, let *my life* be given me at my petition, and *my people* at my request." Since Mordecai the Jew was now known to have been the king's savior, and had just been so remarkably honored, it was no longer perilous to reveal her nationality, and her relation to Mordecai. *"For we are sold,* I and my people"' — referring to the large amount of money offered by Haman to purchase the power to annihilate them — "to be destroyed, to be slain, and to perish. But if we had been sold for bondmen and bondwomen, I had held my tongue, although the enemy could not [by such a sum] countervail the king's damage" [in the loss of an industrious, enterprising, thrifty, orderly class of subjects]; but to be sold *to death,* to indiscriminate slaughter, to gratify the bad passions of one man — it was too much, and she must needs cry out to the king against this enormous wrong.

The king is confounded. It is a vastly greater grief than he had been able to anticipate. What? His queen sold — doomed to death! "Who is he, and where is he that durst presume in his heart to do so?" "The adversary and enemy is this wicked Haman," the queen replied. Haman's guilty and frightened countenance betrayed him. The king arose in his wrath, and went into the palace garden — both his rising and his leaving the room being, according to Persian custom, indications of Haman's doom. Haman, with all his other meannesses, was a coward. He lacked the courage and the firmness

---

[1] Predictions.

to meet the consequences of his own deeds. He prostrated himself at the feet of the queen, on the couch where she reclined, to beseech her to importune the king for his pardon. The king returned to find him in this position, and, putting the worst possible construction on it, ordered him away to execution. Harbonah, one of the king's chamberlains, suggested that the doomed man had just erected a gallows or a tree fifty cubits high, whereon to impale or crucify Mordecai. "Hang him thereon," said the enraged king. "So they hanged Haman on the gallows that he had prepared for Mordecai!" In a world of fearful inequalities — where the wicked so often and so long prosper, and the innocent and just so frequently fall without remedy, that we are tempted to ask, sometimes, whether there is a righteous God that judgeth in the earth — it is positively refreshing and exhilarating to meet, now and then, with such direct and prompt retributions as this, to prove to us that justice is not dead, and to be to us a pledge and a prophecy of a final righteous adjudication of human affairs.

We ask the reader to note that this righteous consummation hinged on *the king's sleeplessness* on a certain night. And here is detected the quiet working of another special providence. There was no miracle — no visible interposition of an almighty hand. Simply the king was sleepless. In his sleeplessness he called for the reading of the chronicles of the kingdom. This reading brings to mind a forgotten fact — that Mordecai had saved the king from assassination. This sets the king to thinking on his neglect of Mordecai. At this juncture Haman appears. Had the king slept soundly that night, Haman's request for the death of Mordecai would, in all probability, have been granted, and all the Jews in the empire would soon have been slaughtered. There is no restraint laid on anyone's action; yet, by a combination of events and influences all tending to a certain result, Haman expiates his crimes on the gallows, and Mordecai is exalted to the highest honors. This is what we call a special *Providence* — a divine overruling of the free actions of men, so as to produce a certain result.

The rest is soon told. The investment of Mordecai with the dignity and authority of Grand Vizier; the issuance of a new decree, granting to the Jews in all the provinces of the empire authority to defend themselves against attack and to destroy all who assail them; the slaughter of seventy-five thousand of their enemies in the provinces, and eight hundred in Shushan, including the ten sons of Haman; the institution of the feast of Purim; and the greatness of Mordecai — "next unto king Ahasuerus, great among the Jews, accepted of the multitude of his brethren, seeking the wealth of his people, and speaking peace to all the seed:" these form the glorious culmination of what had well-nigh been a fearful tragedy. A few things need to be briefly noted in conclusion.

1. We notice that some writers are disposed to judge Esther severely because, after the first day's slaughter in Shushan, she requested that another day be granted for a like purpose. It is condemned as contrary to the Christian spirit. But Esther was not a Christian — she was a Jewess. Moreover, she was not acting for herself, but for her whole people, and not under the impulse of personal vengeance, but with a wise regard to national security. It was necessary for the welfare of the nation that all who sympathized with this most iniquitous purpose should be rooted out; it was needful to the safety of the Jews that all who had sought to spoil them should be spoiled; and it was a wholesome terror to all evil doers that Haman's sons, who had sympathized with their father in his cruel schemes, should be publicly impaled or crucified on that tree which had been erected for the execution of Mordecai. Esther stood between the throne and the people, for their protection. We cannot condemn her because she performed her duty thoroughly, regardful alike of the welfare of the throne and of her own persecuted race.

2. We gain much insight into the condition of the Jews in exile. They were dispersed through all the provinces of the empire, from the Indus to Ethiopia (chap. 3:8); they maintained a separate existence, and observed their own laws, as far as it was possible to do so; they were thrifty, and contributed so largely to the maintenance of the empire, that a sum expressed by $12,500,000 was offered in lieu of it (chap. 3:9); they were so numerous as to be able, in Susa, to slay eight hundred of their enemies in two days, and throughout the whole empire seventy-five thousand (chap. 9:6, 15-16); they had many enemies; while they were unable to observe many of the requirements of the law in a foreign land, they were firm in their opposition to idolatry, and in their reliance on the invisible God, seeking unto Him in fasting and prayer (chap. 4:1-3, 16); and while this book does not once mention the name of Jehovah, it exhibits a

strong faith in His special care of those who trust in Him, and is throughout an impressive record of His providential superintendence of human affairs,

3. It should not pass unnoticed that, as the result of God's dealings with his exiled people, "many people of the land became Jews, because the fear of the Jews fell upon them" (chap. 8:17). We may learn from this that in the land of exile, as well as in their own land, this people, under divine guidance, were spreading the knowledge of Jehovah, and turning the heathen "from darkness to light, and from the power of Satan unto God." The favor shown by his successor to Ezra and Nehemiah probably resulted from the impressions made on Xerxes by these wonderful events, and from the supreme influence of Esther and Mordecai.

4. We are sometimes doubtful as to special providences, and in our faithlessness we put God far away from us. This wonderful little book, in its unfoldings of God's workings *through ordinary channels,* leaving men to act freely, and yet so presiding over human affairs as to bring about His own purposes, ought to be of great value to us. The selection of Esther for queenly dignities; the disposition of the lot, so as to put off the execution of the murderous decree against the Jews to the twelfth month; the disposing of the king's heart favorably to Esther when she appeared uninvited before him; the sleeplessness of the king, leading to such important results: all these, quietly used so as to bring about the deliverance of the Jews from a fearful doom, and to lead the Persians to a knowledge of the one living and true God, should teach us that God is above all, and through all, and in all, and that He is a very present help in time of trouble.

O God, though we see Thee not, yet art Thou ever present, working all things according to Thine own will. O the depths of the riches of the wisdom and knowledge of God! How unsearchable are His judgments, and His ways past finding out! May we learn to trust in Thee as a God nigh at hand and not afar off. May we fully believe that Thou encompass all our paths, and knowest our down-sitting and our uprising, and that there is not a thought of our hearts that is not known to Thee. May we be so impressed with this truth that we may always, even in the most trying times, believe that Thou art, and that Thou art the rewarder of them that diligently seek Thee. In this blessed assurance, may we ever cling to the right, and leave the results in Thy hands. May we commit our souls unto Thee in well-doing, as unto a faithful Creator, casting all our care on Thee, knowing that Thou carest for us, and that Thou wilt never leave us nor forsake us; so that we may boldly say, "The Lord is my Helper, and I will not fear what man can do unto me."

The Mysteries of Providence: The Problem Of Human Suffering

The great variety of opinion among critics as to the date, character, and design of the Book of Job, has made us doubtful as to its proper place in these Studies, and it has thus been crowded out from place to place, until it is found last, though certainly not least, in the series. Whether it was written before the time of Moses, or by Moses himself, or in Solomon's time, or after the Captivity; and whether it is historical, or a fictitious dramatic composition — written by one author, or growing into its present form by the contributions of different writers at various times: these are questions respecting which there is no general agreement. As these Studies are not intended to be critical disquisitions, we do not enter into a discussion of these questions here. We take leave, however, to say that after a careful investigation of the various theories of critics and theologians, we strongly incline to the opinion that the book was written at an early period — as early as the time of Moses; and that it is a veritable history, dramatic, indeed, in form, and, in dealing with the high problems of fate and human will, resorting to highly poetical imagery, yet presenting a literal narrative of events in the life of a real person.

As to the date of these occurrences — whenever and by whomsoever the book was written — the internal evidence certainly points to the patriarchal age. We have patriarchal manners, customs, and allusions, but no reference to the captivity in Egypt, the Exodus, the giving of the law, or any of the later events in the history of the Jewish nation, which would have so forcibly illustrated the doctrine of Providence taught in the book; and this, to us, is decisive, as to the rightful place of the book in the patriarchal age, at a time when the knowledge of the true God was prevalent, and when the traditions of antediluvian and post-diluvian times were held sacred; and yet a time when the earliest form of idolatry — the worship of the heavenly bodies — was not unknown (31:26-27). It was a time when there was no special order of priesthood, but the head of each family was its priest (1:5); when burnt-offerings were sin-offerings, and the nicer distinctions of the Levitical sacrifices were unknown; and when there was no written law to appeal to as the end of controversy. It is to us incredible, if this book belongs to Solomon's time, or to the later period of the Captivity, that there should be this utter silence touching the law from Sinai, the ordinances of the sanctuary, the voice of the prophets, and the grand events of Jewish history which would have illustrated so felicitously[1] much of the teaching of the book concerning prosperity and adversity. And if Job was a fictitious character, we cannot understand why the Lord, speaking through Ezekiel, should place him in association with Noah and Daniel, who are acknowledged to be real characters (Ezek. 14:14, 20; see also Jer. 15:1), nor why a New Testament writer should refer to him as an example, along with others, of patience under suffering (Jas. 5:10-11).

But, so far as our purpose is concerned, it matters little when the book was written, or whether it is a book of fact or of fiction — a history, a poem, or a drama — since, if it is inspired fiction, worthy to rank in the canon of Scripture, it must accord with truth, recording what might truly have occurred.

The book falls naturally into five parts: 1. The introduction. 2. The controversy between Job and his three friends. 3. The speech of Elihu. 4. The settlement of the controversy by God himself, and job's acquiescence in the decision. 5. The *finale* of the history.

Job is introduced as a patriarchal chieftain or sheik of great wealth and eminent rank — "the greatest of all the children of the east." His own description of his rank and affluence in chapter 29 presents him as one of the most favored of mortals. And in character he was as eminent as in wealth. The divine testimony is: "There is none like him in the earth, a perfect and an upright man, one that feareth God and escheweth evil" (1:8. See also chapter 31). Not only in righteousness was he eminent, but in beneficence also. Not in any vain conceit, but for his vindication against cruel accusations, he says of himself (29:11-17):

> *For when the ear heard me, then it blessed me;*
> *And when the eye saw me, it gave witness unto me:*
> *Because I delivered the poor that cried,*
> *The fatherless also, that had none to help him.*

---

[1] Suitably.

The blessing of him that was ready to perish came upon me.
And I caused the widow's heart to sing for joy.
I put on righteousness and it clothed me:
My justice was as a robe and a diadem.
I was eyes to the blind,
And feet was I to the lame.
I was a father to the needy:
And the cause of him that I knew not I searched out.
And I broke the jaws of the unrighteous,
And plucked the prey out of his teeth.

He had a wife, and seven sons, and three daughters, with abundant means to provide for them. It is scarcely possible to draw a picture of human excellence and happiness more complete — of a life more desirable in all the elements of personal worth, domestic comfort, honorable position, pleasant relations to the public, general usefulness, and excellent reputation.

Yet this man — so good, so prosperous, so honored, so happy, is plunged in miseries and calamities until he becomes abjectly poor, wretched, dishonored, and despised — calamity following calamity until life itself is a burden unbearable, and the grave is sighed for as the only refuge from suffering and despair. His prosperity is pictured in the brightest colors, and his adversity in the darkest — thus making it inclusive of all other cases in which life is a mixture of good and evil.

The introduction lets in light on the strange history that follows by lifting the veil and permitting us to look beyond the ordinary range of mortal vision to the source of the good and evil which on earth are so perplexingly intermingled. We are taught that there is an evil power in the universe, here denominated Satan, which is actively engaged in working ill to our race; that this power is not omnipotent, but subject to divine control; that God allows it scope only so far as the evil it inflicts may be made to minister to wise and gracious ends; and that good men, even the best of men, may be assaulted by this evil power, but only that their integrity may be tried, and their faith and patience made the more illustrious. The question of Satan, "Does Job serve God for naught?" lets us into the secret of the afflictions heaped upon this eminent saint, and teaches us (1) that genuine integrity can only be known when tested; (2) that however severe and protracted the test, God will not forsake his tempted children, nor suffer them to be tempted above what they are able to bear. The question here is *Job's integrity.* It is to be tried to the last extreme, but is to be gloriously maintained. Necessarily, this involves two questions: 1. Whether human nature is capable, under any circumstances, of unimpeachable integrity and fidelity to truth and duty. 2. The divine intention of permitting the infliction of suffering on the righteous, and the high lessons taught to the moral universe by the patient endurance of the suffering.

Not alone in the book of Job is this perplexing problem of suffering and of the inequalities of human life dealt with. The book of Ecclesiastes is devoted to it; and it springs up ever and anon in Proverbs and in the Psalms, as, for instance, in Ps. 37 and 72. It may be true, as Bacon says, that "prosperity is the blessing of the Old Testament, and adversity the blessing of the New;" that is, the Old Testament taught *present* and *earthly* rewards of obedience, while the more spiritual new covenant teaches us not to look for rewards to earthly prosperity, but to look beyond to eternal life, that we may suffer here and reign hereafter. Yet it is true, as the same eminent author further observes, that "even in the Old Testament, if you listen to David's harp, you shall hear as many hearse-like airs as carols; and the pencil of the Holy Ghost hath labored more in describing the afflictions of Job than the felicities[1] of Solomon." Nor is the effort to solve this puzzling problem confined to Jewish and Christian sages. In all lands and ages, among all classes, from the savage to the philosopher, we find the human race confronted with this mysterious problem, and engaging in anxious and ever unsatisfying efforts to "harmonize the actual course of human events with the postulates of the doctrine of retribution." But its treatment in the book of Job is peculiar. It is not a philosophical treatise, dealing with the questions of suffering and retribution abstractly, and attempting to "vindicate the ways of God to man," but rather a concrete exhibition, in the history of a human life, in the world of fact, of the extremes of happiness and misery, with light poured in from heaven concerning the agencies at work in this world of ours, and the sleepless watch-care of Jeho-

---

[1] Joys.

vah over his suffering saints. And this human life is made to embrace the farthest extremes of good and evil, so that all other human histories are included in its range of actual experiences, that the good of all ages may take courage when they suffer, and learn to exercise faith and patience; while the other characters introduced serve to present various views of the philosophy of suffering, and to set forth the errors that spring from religious bigotry or from narrow and one-sided views of things.

Let us look now at the calamities in which Job was plunged.

1. *The loss of Property.* Cattle, sheep, camels, servants — and in these the wealth of the patriarchs largely consisted — were preyed upon by marauders, or blasted by lightning, or consumed by fire, until he was suddenly reduced to poverty. This would be a sufficient test in many cases. We have known not a few who were regarded as quite saintly until they lost their property, whose piety was lost along with the property, leaving them as anemic in soul as in fortune. Satan's sneering question, "Does Job serve God for naught?" meets, in such instances, with a speedy answer, such as the adversary may exult in. A faith that burns to ashes in the first blaze is poor stuff. It is a good work that the fire of calamity accomplishes when it consumes such dross. But it failed to detect any weakness in the faith of job, as we shall soon see.

2. *The loss of children.* The last messenger with evil tidings of the loss of property had scarcely fulfilled his errand, when the fourth courier arrived with news of greater calamity: while job's children were gathered at a festival, a hurricane or cyclone struck the building and they were all killed. This was a much severer test. We have known those who bravely bore the loss of property, who succumbed when their children were taken. The murmurings and repinings of some of these, which seemed to us closely akin to blasphemy, echo in our ears today. The frantic arraignment of God as unjust and cruel — as if all the high purposes of infinite wisdom in the government of the universe were as nothing in comparison with the undisturbed happiness of *their* homes — and this from lips long accustomed to praise or adoration, is appalling. Yet there are many whose piety perishes at this touch of calamity. Let us not speak lightly of such an affliction. It is terrible — this yielding up of beloved ones to death, especially to sudden death. The breaking of our home circles, the quenching of the lights that give to life its

brightness, the closing of bright eyes and sweet lips that shall answer us no more with looks of love or merry prattle, and the consignment of fair forms to darkness and silence — the vacant chair, the silent hall, that echoes no more to the familiar footfall, the desolate hearts that yearn in vain

> *for the touch of a vanished hand*
> *And the sound of a voice that is still:*

Oh, it is terrible, and we would deal tenderly with the sacred grief. But Job lost not only one child, but *all* his children. He lost them suddenly. There was no opportunity even for a fond farewell. The light of his eyes, the pride of his heart, the joy of his life — the sons and daughters in whom centered the highest hopes and noblest ambitions of his soul — all these were lost in a moment, and thick darkness settled on his bright and happy home. He was not only reduced to poverty, but left utterly childless. And what did he say of his lost property and his lost children? He was not insensible to the greatness of the calamity. He did not affect indifference. He keenly felt the weight of this accumulation of griefs, and staggered under the terrible burden. He "arose, and rent his mantle, and shaved his head, and fell down upon the ground." He would have been much less or more than human if he had not been overwhelmed with grief. But what response did he make to all this? "The Lord gave, and the Lord hath taken away; blessed be the name of the Lord" The pure gold of his faith and reverence stood the fierce flame, and suffered no harm. "In all this Job sinned not, nor *charged God with foolishness.*" "Doth Job serve God for naught?" inquired Satan. Well, thus far he shows that there was something more precious than wealth, and stronger and holier than even the love of children, to bind him to his God. He did not murmur because God had taken what He gave; but in a grateful recognition of that love which had blessed him so abundantly all his life long, and which he was sure was still present even in these overwhelming calamities, he was able to say, with an enlightened faith and a submissive heart, "Blessed be the name of Jehovah."

3. Loathsome and distressing disease. Touch his bone and his flesh," said Satan, "and he will renounce thee to thy face." He was given liberty to test him in this also, only he must not take his life. Job was therefore smitten with a disgusting and tormenting disease

— probably the black leprosy, or elephantiasis — incurable by human skill, and throwing black despair over all the future of life. And just at this point, when he most needed sympathy and tender care,

4. *His wife turned against him.* Many a man heroic in *active* life loses all courage and patience when he is called to passively endure pain and weakness. Yet if a faithful and loving wife remains as an angel of mercy at his side, to soothe his pains and cheer his spirit, he may learn to bear his suffering with some degree of courage and cheerfulness. But what can such a man do when his wife turns against him? There are a great many men whom the world esteems brave and noble, who owe their greatness more to the inspirations of wifely affection and sympathy than to any inborn excellence. And many a noble life is wrecked through the incompatibilities, or the cold indifference of an ill-matched wife. The real history of failures and successes is largely unwritten, and even unsuspected. In that great day when the secrets of all hearts and lives shall be revealed, it will doubtless appear, in thousands of instances, that the ruin of men and women is traceable to the absence of true companionship in wedded life; and in thousands more that success was owing to holy and congenial companionship. The man who can be true to God, to his family, to himself, and to society, in spite of uncongenial marriage relations, is a genuine hero; and the woman who triumphs over the heart-pangs. arising from the indifference or antagonism of an unworthy husband, and silently and cheerfully performs her duties with this serpent perpetually gnawing at her heart and poisoning the very fountains of life, is a genuine heroine — and many such uncrowned and unsung heroines there are, with their names nowhere written but in God's Book of Life.

Not the least of job's calamities was an unsympathizing, irreligious wife. She was unworthy of her husband. She may have been, in many respects, a good sort of woman, but she was a utilitarian in morals and religion. The utilitarian school must have been popular at that time, if we may judge from the doctrine of Job's three comforters. It was "the greatest happiness principle" that inspired all their reasonings. They believed in a cash business in morality and piety — the pay down when the service is rendered, and no credit. If the pay ceased, even for a day, it was because the worker was a rascal, or the employer was bankrupt. And so with job's wife. As long as Job was prosperous and the children healthy, and the family honored, she was disposed to be decorously religious, just as any fair-weather Christian is now. But when her religion did not *pay*, she would have none of it. When she saw that their prosperity was all gone, and their children all dead, and their consequence in society greatly diminished, and her husband stricken with leprosy, she saw no *utility* in the morals and religion to which Job clung so tenaciously, and she said to him, "Dost thou still hold fast thine integrity? — Renounce God and die." As much as to say. "Don't you see that your religion doesn't *pay*? Where are your cattle, and sheep, and camels? Where are your children? Where is your health — You have been scrupulously true to Jehovah, and this is what you get for it. What is such a religion worth?" A precious comforter to her husband in his distress! Such a wife is enough to drive a man to the devil, if everything else is favorable to sainthood. But Job — blessed be his memory — could not be disturbed even by a termagant[1] wife. "Thou speakest as one of the impious women speaketh. What! Shall we receive good at the hand of God, and shall we not receive evil?" Are we privileged characters, that we dare refuse to drink of the same mixed cup of life that is pressed to the lips of others? Shall we ungratefully forget the innumerable blessings and bounties that have long crowned our lives, and think only of the evils of the present? Must we lose faith in God because He chastens us, and renounce Him because things do not go to please us? Must we deny Him because he has taken back what He gave, and forfeit that lovingkindness which is better than life — and which we need now more than ever — by our faithlessness and ingratitude?

In replying to his accusers, Job made a statement of his condition at this time, which may aid us in forming a conception of his extreme wretchedness and desolation, poetical in form, but true in fact:

> *Know now that God hath subverted me in my cause,*
> *And hath compassed me with his net.*
> *Behold, I cry out of wrong, but I am not heard:*

---

[1] A propensity for arguing, criticizing, and quarreling.

I cry for help, but there is no judgment.
He hath fenced up my way that I cannot pass,
And hath set darkness in my paths.
He hath stripped me of my glory,
And taken the crown from my head.
He hath broken me down on every side, and I am gone:
And mine hope hath he plucked up like a tree.
He hath also kindled his wrath against me,
And he counteth me unto him as one of his adversaries.
His troops come on together, and cast up their way against
*   me,*
And encamp round about my tent.
He hath put my brethren far from me,
And my acquaintances are wholly estranged from me.
My kinsfolk have failed,
And my familiar friends have forgotten me.
They that dwell in my house, and my maids, take me for a
*   stranger:*
I am an alien in their sight.
I call unto my servant, and he giveth me no answer,
Though I entreat him with my mouth.
My breath is strange to my wife,
And my supplication to the children of my mother's womb.
Even young children despise me;
If I arise, they speak against me.
All my inward friends abhor me,
And they whom I loved are turned against me.
My bone cleaveth to my skin and to my flesh,
And I am escaped with the skin of my teeth.
Have pity upon me, have pity upon me, O ye my friends;
For the hand of God hath touched me.
    (Job 19:6-21)

Yet "in all this did not Job sin with his lips."

5. *Harsh judgment and unrighteous condemnation.* It was probably a considerable time after Job was smitten with disease that his three friends, Eliphaz, Bildad and Zophar, "made an appointment together to come to mourn with him and to comfort him." The disease had had full time to develop itself in all its

loathsomeness, and the change in his circumstances as well as the disgusting and terrifying character of his ailment had driven away all his summer friends and alienated even the members of his own household, until not only had his wife forsaken him, and those whom he loved turned against him, but even his slaves despised him and mocked at his authority, and little children, with whom he had evidently been a favorite, fled from his presence.

These three friends were either patriarchal chieftains, somewhat equal to Job in rank, as Eliphaz and Bildad, or men held in high repute for wisdom and sanctity, though younger in years, as Zophar. They were fair representatives of the best wisdom of that time, and of its purest religious faith. They were sincere and warm-hearted friends, coming in good faith to comfort one whom they loved.

> *And when they lifted up their eyes afar off, and knew him not, they lifted up their voice and wept, and they rent every one his mantle, and sprinkled dust upon their heads toward heaven. So they sat down with him upon the ground seven days and seven nights, and none spoke a word unto him: for they saw that his grief was very great.*

Whether it was in pure sympathy that they thus kept silence, or because their religious prejudices were shocked, and their convictions, if uttered, must have distressed him, we may not positively say; but we take the latter supposition to be the more probable, — for, when the wretched sufferer broke the silence by a very natural lamentation over his calamities, they gave vent to their cruel suspicions with a plainness and positiveness which, however honest, was exceedingly cruel. They had a moral philosophy and a religious creed which, to them, were more sacred than human sympathies or the ties of friendship. They believed in God — in His ever-present power, and his righteous providences: that He uniformly rewards the just and punishes the unjust. Their inevitable logical conclusion was that Job must have been guilty of great crimes, or these calamities would not have overtaken him — that while he had affected great sanctity and was universally held in saintly odor, he had been all the while acting the hypocrite, and God was now exposing his odious hypocrisy to the light. They therefore called on him to confess his crimes and repent, as the only means of deliverance from his wretchedness.

It is interesting to note the variety of mental characteristics developed by the different speakers in advocating and defending the same creed. Eliphaz was not only superior in age, but was the fairest exponent of this creed. He utters many truths concerning God and His providential dealings with men; but he reasons on the surface, and his views are bounded by a limited horizon. He has no conception of those invisible powers, good and evil, which, in the first chapter, are represented as busy in human affairs, nor of the far-reaching designs of God in permitting evil to befall his children. His utterances are therefore only half-truths, and all the more mischievous for the amount of truth that is in them. While, at first, he insinuates rather gently his convictions of Job's secret transgressions, and seeks with some tenderness to win him to an acknowledgment of his sins, when Job indignantly spurns the suggestion and vehemently asserts his innocence, and the discussion increases in heat as the outraged sufferer proceeds to explode the theory of his accuser, Eliphaz is provoked to describe him as an undoubted hypocrite and a bold blasphemer, hiding his crimes, railing against God, and doomed to destruction. He may be regarded as an able and skillful exponent of a theory which not only then, but in all ages, has been largely accepted as the best vindication of the ways of God to man.

Eliphaz is the oracle. Bildad and Zophar but repeat what he has said. They serve to represent large classes of men, and to unfold the secret of their religious opinions — many, like Bildad, being content to receive almost passively their ideas of the great mysteries of Providence, and to repeat, parrot-like, what they have been taught; and many more, like Zophar, clinging to a theory in sheer bigotry, and knowing much better how to denounce those who differ from them, than to support their own opinions by sober reasoning. Poor Job had to receive the poisoned shafts of all these archers, and we imagine he was much less disturbed by the careful reasoning of Eliphaz, than by the provoking echoes of Bildad, and the bigoted assertions of Zophar.

It may not be said that, in this discussion, Job "sinned not with his lips." In the heat of argument he sometimes went too far, and in his just indignation at the assaults on his integrity, in asseverating[1] his own integrity he is impelled to speak with an air of self-righteousness that cannot be commended. In attempting to account for the calamities that had befallen him, the whole matter was involved in such mystery that he seems to complain against God as having afflicted him without cause. Yet, on the whole, he was remarkably patient, and held fast to his integrity. He admits the truth of much that Eliphaz says, yet shows that he spoke only half-truths. He clearly and unanswerably proves that in multitudes of cases, in this life, wickedness triumphs and righteousness goes unrewarded, and therefore that his calamities are no proof that he has been guilty of great sins. He finds no solution of this perplexing problem, except in the fact of a future adjudication of human affairs, and, however dim this truth may have been to him, he clings to it as the only source of rest to his troubled spirit (19:23-27). If, in vindicating his own integrity, he sometimes uses language such as a becoming humility would not approve, we must remember that he was, personally, exceptionally free from fault, and that God himself had described him as "a perfect and an upright man," — that in this respect "there was none like him in the earth." It is not genuine humility, but disgusting affectation and hypocritical cant,[2] when one assumes an unworthiness that he knows does not belong to him — especially when his character is unjustly assailed. If he was driven, sometimes, under the pressure of his sufferings, and the false accusations made against him, to complain of God's dealings with him, and almost to arraign the wisdom and justice of the divine proceedings in his case, it was only when, for the moment, in the overwhelming griefs of the hour, he forgot to look above and beyond the present. But he soon recovered out of this despair, and was able to say, with triumph,

> *Though he slay me, yet will I wait for him:*
> *Nevertheless, I will maintain my ways before him;*
> *This also shall be my salvation.*

If, under a tempest-force of calamity, he was sometimes swayed to the outmost verge of faith, and momentarily even be-

---

[1] Stating something earnestly.
[2] Insincerities.

yond it, he yet was not swept away, but invariably returned from the unfamiliar and uninviting realm of doubt and distrust, and still maintained his integrity.

6. But we have not measured Job's afflictions to the full. He was denied even such refreshment and recuperation as come to the weary through sleep.

> *When I say, "My bed shall comfort me,*
> *My couch shall ease my complaint;"*
> *Then thou scarest me with dreams,*
> *And terrifiest me through visions;*
> *So that my soul chooseth strangling,*
> *And death rather than these my bones.*

There are many who know the terrors of insomnia, but it does not half express the horrors of Job's condition. It was not mere sleeplessness; it was, even when sleep came, a succession of nightmares, or of horrible dreams and visions that allowed of no peaceful slumber. His nights were hideous with terrifying dreams and apparitions that drained his diseased nerves of all strength and left him prostrate when the next day's battle with pain came on.

7. Worse than all, *he felt himself abandoned by God.* "I cry unto thee, and thou dost not hear me: I stand up, and thou regardest me not" (30:20). The only anguish that ever wrung a complaining cry from the suffering Jesus, was that occasioned by the withdrawal of the divine presence: "My God! My God! Why hast Thou forsaken me?" Every ill and wrong and pain may be borne with some degree of patience and submissiveness, if only the light of God's presence is with us. We may then pass all the way through the valley of death-shade, and fear no evil. But when that presence is withdrawn, all lights go out, and the soul is immersed in more than Egyptian darkness. It must be remembered that Job was given up to Satan to try his integrity in every possible way — only his life must not be taken. This severest of all temptations was therefore allowed to come. The heavens were shut against him. Not only earthly friends, but his heavenly Friend forsook him, that Satan might toss his desolate soul on the billows of despair, where, amid the thick darkness of a starless night, the sweep of the fierce winds, and the wildest rage of the waves, he should cry in vain to the heavens for help. Will he still hold fast his integrity? If so, it will

be a triumphant answer to the Satanic sneer, "Doth Job serve God for naught?" It is not surprising that, under such a pressure, there should be extorted from the sufferer cries of bitter complaint, expressions of distrust and despair, which, comfortably seated at the fireside, we may coldly criticize as unbecoming in a "perfect man" but let us not forget that he was *purposely* given up to be tempted to the last extreme, and that these anguished cries are but so many evidences of the appalling severity of the trial. Satan desired to sift him as wheat, and he was allowed to do so; but his faith failed not. He was bewildered, confounded, terrified; but he still held fast his integrity.

We have enumerated seven distinct and terrible trials. They touch this question of suffering at every point. There is no form of suffering to which man is subjected that is not involved in this history of a suffering saint, except that of the anguish of a guilty, impenitent soul. And these trials are in their greatest fullness as well as, in their severest forms. If the human soul can maintain its integrity in all these, and God can overrule them all to the promotion of gracious ends, then this perplexing problem has come as near to a final solution as we are likely to reach in this life.

The youthful Elihu is well introduced, after the discussion between Job and his three friends has closed, to express, if a younger, certainly a broader and better faith than had yet found utterance.

> *"The three aged friends,"* says Dean Stanley, *"are the 'liars for God,' the dogged defenders of the traditional popular belief. Elihu is the new wisdom of the rising world, that, with the sanction of the Almighty, sets at naught the subtle prejudices of the older generation."*

Elihu reviews the discussion. He sees very clearly that the three advocates of the traditional creed have failed to answer job. He sees, too, that Job has been tempted into an extreme of self-justification, and has failed to justify God as he might and should have done; that he has failed to recognize the important truth that when we cannot explore the mysteries of God's ways, our faith in His infinite wisdom and goodness should lead us to keep silence before Him, and to trust and adore where we cannot comprehend. His wise conclusion is:

Touching the Almighty, we cannot find him out; he is excellent in power; And in judgment and plenteous justice he will not afflict.
Men do therefore fear him,
He regardeth not any that are wise of heart.

This is a balancing of accounts from a human standpoint — the best that the pious and enlightened heart was then capable of. But it is not to end here, with merely human efforts to solve this difficult problem. God himself is introduced to set forth the divine side of the question, and, in language of solemn grandeur befitting the theme, to rebuke the pride and presumption of man. The utter folly of man, with his narrow vision, in attempting to pronounce on the ways of infinite wisdom, profoundly ignorant as he is and must be of many things — of all things, indeed, except on the surface of the phenomenal universe — is most impressively set forth, and Job, as well as his friends, is taught that he should not meddle with things too high for him. It is impossible to read this wonderful address without feeling deeply that it is not only folly, but wicked presumptuousness for mortal man, with his very limited range of observation, to arraign the All-Wise, and pronounce judgment on His ways. The overwhelming majesty of His presence, too, is startling, and in the awful light of that Presence, all human goodness, as well as human wisdom, pales into nothingness; and Job, who, measuring himself by human standards, had so stoutly contended for his own righteousness, humbly and contritely confesses,

Behold, I am vile: what shall I answer thee? I will lay mine hand upon my mouth. Once have I spoken, but I will not answer: Yea, twice; but I will proceed no farther... I have uttered that [which] I understood not; things too wonderful for me, that I knew not... Wherefore, I abhor myself, and repent in dust and ashes.

Yes, we may be bold and strong in self-justification, when we compare ourselves with others, in the light of human standards of character; but, when we come face to face with God, and are made to stand out in the pure white light of His throne, who is there among mortals — even if he have a matchless reputation for righteousness — that will not be constrained to say, "Behold, I am vile!"

But, if Job failed of approval for utterances forced from him under the pressure of accumulated woes, there is a direct and positive condemnation of his friends for their narrow and harsh judgments, their false views of the divine government, and their grievous presumption in their interpretations of divine providence. Their shallowness, narrowness, harshness, and bigotry were alike unjust to Job and dishonoring to God; and according to the simplicity of the worship of patriarchal times, when there was no priestly hierarchy, Job acts as priest in their behalf, in presenting their burnt-offerings and confessions of sin, and in interceding for their pardon, that they might thus be purged of their guilt and be accepted before God.

We gather, from this Study, the following conclusions.

(1). There are, in this life, such rewards of righteousness and punishments of iniquity as to assure us that a righteous God reigns over the affairs of men.

(2). There are, nevertheless, such manifest and numerous exceptions to this — such inequalities in the distribution of rewards and punishments — that prosperity cannot be regarded as a decisive testimony of acceptance with God, nor can adversity be regarded as necessarily a token of divine displeasure. A future judgment is necessary to vindicate the ways of God to man.

(3). Suffering is not always and necessarily penal.[1] It is allowed and controlled, in many instances, with a view to the discipline of the good. Men also may innocently suffer, because, through their suffering, while it may be made a means of higher development to themselves, worthy ends may be wrought out in behalf of others. Human lives are sometimes vicarious.

(4). There are powers of evil, under the leadership of Satan, that delight to inflict suffering on the human race, and especially on the righteous. This they are allowed by God, for His own wise and gracious purposes, to do; but they have no absolute power; they can only go as far as God permits.

(5). God's plans are so far-reaching, and so inscrutable to us, that no adequate interpretation of His providences, in many instances, is possible to us. Our horizon is too limited, our powers

---

[1] A punishment.

too feeble, to allow us to comprehend the ways of Him who wor-keth all things according to His infinitely wise will. While, there-fore, there are general providences that we may understand and rejoice in; and special providences that we may so far safely inter-pret as to find in them occasions of thanksgiving and lessons of trust; there are also mysterious providences which confound our wisdom, and which therefore it is presumptuous to attempt to in-terpret. It is the part of true faith and piety to be silent before God when these appear — to adore where we cannot comprehend — to submit, in holy trust that "the judge of all the earth will do right."

The pleasant rounding out of this remarkable narrative with the restoration of Job to health and prosperity, must not be taken to teach that, in all cases, the righteous will be vindicated and re-warded *in this life*; but rather that when "the end of the Lord" is reached, whether in this life or the life to come, it will be seen that "He is very pitiful and of tender mercy," even in the darkest dis-pensations of His providence. In many cases, this *end* reaches over into the life to come. In job's case, to complete the demonstration, it was necessary that the final vindication should be made within the limits of the present life.

It is, perhaps, well that this history of Job should close our Old Testament Studies. Not only is it true that this problem of suffer-ing, in thousands of individual cases, taxes severely the faith of obedient souls, but in the larger view, as it relates to all righteous enterprises, the workers in the cause of humanity are confounded by the adversities and apparent failures attendant on their best ef-forts to serve God and their fellow-men. The triumphs of falsehood and wickedness; the failure and disaster that befall the noblest ef-forts of the righteous; the cry that comes from souls under the altar, "How long, O Lord, how long?" the cruel opposition to even the noblest characters by the Eliphazes, Bildads and Zophars who can see no good in a suffering life, and esteem it "smitten of God and afflicted:" all these are discouragements that are too apt to shatter our faith in the ultimate triumph of the right, and paralyze our ef-forts to do good, so that we grow weary in well doing. The history of our race is a history of heroic struggle of right against wrong, with the victory generally on the side of wrong. Chains, dungeons, martyr-fires, scaffolds, guillotines, are the rewards of the faithful. We grow weary in longings and waitings for the triumph of the right. Ages pass by, and still the wicked are in power, and the saints and heroes of faith and righteousness look in vain for the dawn of the day of deliverance. Even the righteous are tempted to say, "What is the Almighty that we should serve him? And what profit shall we have if we pray unto Him?" In all the Old Testament History which we have been studying, in the perpetual conflicts between good and evil, truth and falsehood, right and wrong, how often has the battle gone the wrong way, and what defeats and failures have marked the history of God's elect people. Yet we see, as we take a large view of this history, and look over the ages of the conflict, that truth has snatched victory from defeat, and, in the long run, even the failures and disasters over which we mourned, become prolific in good results. God's purpose never fails. "The end of the Lord" is sure to be accomplished.

It will be a cheerful faith with which to lay down this volume, that through all changes God lives and reigns; that His purposes never fail; that no true life can fail; that in the trials and disappointments of life, we may learn "to suffer and be strong;" that in our bitterest afflictions God does not forsake us; that even in our darkest hours, and under the heaviest pressure of temptation, when all things seem against us, and God seems to hide his face from us, it is always safe to do right; that there is no honor and no safety for us but in clinging to God and duty, saying, "Though he slay me, yet will I trust in Him." The ultimate triumph of truth is inevitable. The ultimate triumph of righteousness is sure. If we grow weary by the way, if our faith ever falters, let us return to the history of this noble patriarch, and renew our failing strength.

> *Take, brethren, for an example of suffering and of patience, the prophets who spoke in the name of the Lord. Behold, we call them blessed which endured. Ye have heard of the patience of Job, and have seen the end of the Lord, how that the Lord is full of pity, and merciful.*

And now, Lord, as we lay down this volume, in which we have traced many of Thy wonderful ways, may we be enabled to love Thee more, and serve Thee better. May we acquaint ourselves with Thee, and be at peace. Especially when we are subjected to trials, may we be enabled to endure as seeing Him who is invisible. May faith triumph over sense, and may the examples of Thy suffering but faithful saints instruct and encourage us to be submissive to Thy will. Teach us to rejoice in tribulation, assured that it is appointed for our good; and when we come up out of the tribulations of earth, may we be numbered with those who have washed their robes and made them white in the blood of the Lamb, who shall hunger no more, neither thirst any more, neither shall the sun smite them, nor any heat — but the Lamb that is in the midst of the throne shall feed them, and lead them unto living fountains of water, and Thou shalt wipe away all tears from their eyes. Graciously hear us, we beseech Thee, in the name of Jesus our Savior. Amen.

Made in the USA
Columbia, SC
01 July 2022

62641456R00153